ROMAN LONDON

Peter Marsden

ROMAN LONDON

with 160 illustrations

Thames and Hudson

© 1980 Thames and Hudson Ltd, London

First published in paperback in the USA in 1986 by
Thames and Hudson, Inc., 500 Fifth Avenue,
New York, New York 10110

Library of Congress Catalog Card Number 80–51908

Printed and bound in the German Democratic Republic

Contents

To Fran
with grateful thanks for her help

Introduction

There is little to show the modern visitor to the City of London that, beneath its streets and the towering concrete and glass office blocks, there lie several superimposed ancient cities, each built on the rubbish and ruins of the earlier. Londinium lies at the bottom of these, and it may seem that the modern square mile, the home of international finance, can have little in common with Roman, Saxon and medieval London. Yet each of these cities occupied the same site, and each was a very important trading centre in its own day.

London has always had one overriding problem: disposing of its rubbish. In the past it usually proved preferable to dump the rubbish underfoot or in pits, rather than to cart it out of town. For nearly two thousand years therefore, the people of London have lived on top of an increasing mound of rubbish and building debris, so that today the streets of the City commonly lie at least 6 m above the natural land surface. In some areas, particularly around the Bank of England and the Mansion House, the rubbish is even thicker, and one would have to dig down more than 9 m to reach the natural surface. It is curious that this rubbish is the most precious and uniquely historic document that now exists concerning Londinium, for there are no ancient maps or pictures of the city of that time and few references to it in Roman literature.

When we speak of London in more recent times, it is so easy to forget that only the City encompasses the historic London. Westminster was, and still is, a separate city, and for hundreds of square miles around lies the modern sprawl of Greater London, which has swallowed many old villages, hamlets and even towns that nowadays exist as little more than shopping centres with ancient parish churches.

Within the City there is a long history of archaeological research, though the methods used in exploring the past have been improved considerably since the earliest known archaeological excavation took place in March 1385.[1] This was on a site adjacent to the church of St Michael Bassishaw, at the rear of Guildhall. The mayor and aldermen had organized a gang of masons and carpenters to uncover the foundations of an old house believed to have stood there in earlier times. Their purpose was to settle a right-of-way dispute, for William, the church parson, had dug a ditch across a path leading to the house of Sir Adam Fr'unceys; but Sir Adam claimed that as the path used to lead to an older house it was clearly a right-of-way that had existed 'from time out of mind'. But the men found nothing of consequence, for the old house was probably built of wood which had completely rotted away; this did not, however, effect the outcome of the case, and the parson had to fill in the ditch!

Nowadays there are few past disturbances to the subsoil of London that cannot be detected by careful excavation, for the study of minute soil changes is routine work making it possible to map extensive traces of even the most decayed timber buildings.

Since the Second World War there has been an enormous increase in knowledge about the Roman city, though many of the excavations still remain to be published. Excellent summaries were published more than ten years ago, particularly by Ralph Merrifield of the former Guildhall Museum, and by Professor W. F. Grimes who directed excavations for the Roman and Medieval London Excavation Council for nearly two decades immediately after the war.[2] Since 1972, however, the staff of sixty people in the Department of Urban Archaeology of the Museum of London have been carrying out a major excavation and publication programme, and it is as part of this that the earlier work of the Guildhall Museum is to be published.[3]

Apart from Professor Grimes's work, for the decade before the war and about twenty-five years afterwards, City archaeology was in the hands of a succession of individuals employed by the Society of Antiquaries and by the Guildhall Museum. Although interim reports have already appeared in print,[4] it has been clear for some time that a summary should be published, particularly incorporating not only the most recent discoveries, but also an account of those sites that were investigated by Guildhall Museum and which have not yet appeared in print. This is desirable because it will be some years before the backlog of research reports is published, and also because finds from the excavations have now been identified and provisionally dated for the first time by specialists. Hence the associated Roman strata and structures have also been dated. On a more personal level, I consider that an account of the researches is also necessary as a mark of gratitude to the many individuals who have assisted, particularly during the 1960s.

Because there is a continuing programme of excavation, there can be no final word on the subject of Roman London, and the conclusions proposed here can only be considered as an interim statement. Nevertheless, it is becoming increasingly clear that one of the most important factors to be taken into

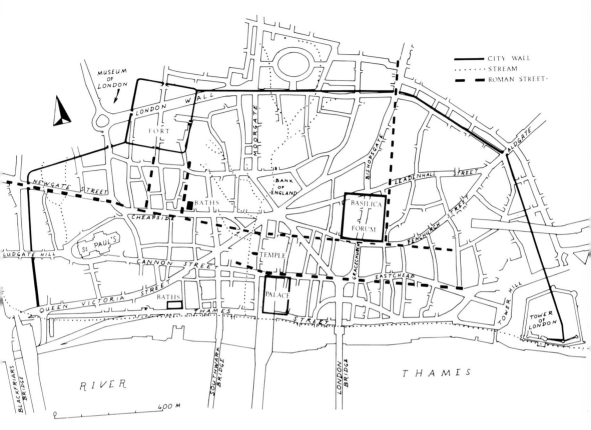

The location of the main features of Roman London superimposed on a map of the modern city of London.

account is that the town had several distinct phases, each with its own historical pattern; and so the true story of Roman London must resemble several superimposed and variant jigsaw puzzles. Therefore, if one were now to assemble a scatter of pieces from each of these to make a single jigsaw representing a multi-period city, this would be overcrowded with seemingly conflicting details, and convey a false impression. It is of particular importance, then, that the archaeology of London should be placed in an historical framework, even though the picture of each phase is far from clear.

In essence, my basic historical thesis is that the City of London did not have a military beginning as a camp built during the Roman invasion of A D 43, but was founded about A D 50 as a carefully planned civil trading settlement of Roman merchants. Almost from the beginning it was to be the main port for the province, supplying both the army and more particularly the new towns, and it soon became the administrative centre for the province. But during the second century London declined as the main port, perhaps because other towns had grown more successful in trade and industry, and were increasingly able to supply their own needs. In the late second and

9

third centuries there was probably a major effort to revitalize the city. This failed to restore the old level of trade and the density of population, though London remained an important provincial administrative centre. Like other towns in Britain, it suffered from and defended itself against barbarian attacks in the late fourth century, but after the collapse of Roman rule in the first decade of the following century, Roman London gradually declined until finally it ceased to exist in any organized urban sense.

However much of this may prove to be true, it is clear that the history of Roman London is much more complex than we shall ever know, and so the main purpose of this book is not to replace any excavation reports or thematic studies, but to propose a possible reconstruction of that history. Since the evidence in most cases is capable of alternative selection, interpretation and stress, I do not expect these proposals to receive full agreement from other specialists. Indeed it would be wrong if this was the case, for debate is the most satisfactory path to follow in the search for the truth. Nevertheless, it is important to stand back from the excavations from time to time to consider what the information, recovered at considerable cost, might mean in a broad historical view. If the reconstruction expressed here, therefore, stimulates discussion and helps to define research priorities, then this study will have been worthwhile.

Finally it gives me pleasure to thank the various people who have helped, and in particular I am especially grateful to John Wacher and Hugh Chapman who read the text which has been improved by their suggestions. Naturally, responsibility for the views expressed is mine, and because it is not always possible to argue in detail the reasons for each conclusion, footnotes and selected references to primary sources are also included. Thanks are also due to Ann Phillips for so carefully and rapidly typing the various manuscripts, and to my colleagues at the Museum of London, especially to the Director, Max Hebditch, and in the Department of Urban Archaeology to John Bailey, Trevor Hurst, John Maloney, Sara Parfitt, Dominic Perrin, Steve Roskams, John Schofield, Chris Unwin and Tony Wilmott. Acknowledgment to others is included in the text. Thanks for permission to reproduce various illustrations are due to the Museum of London, the Society of Antiquaries, the Southwark Archaeological Excavation Committee and to the British Museum.

I
The Roman invasion camp

There is one certain fact about the origin of London: it was founded by the Romans sometime between AD 43, when they initiated their invasion, and AD 60, when the earliest written record of the town tells us that it was destroyed in a British uprising against Roman tyranny. No trace of any earlier occupation has ever been found on the site that can be considered in any way a predecessor of the Roman town; had there been any, the extensive excavations would have revealed it by now. In any case, the few prehistoric finds are from scattered sites, and date from as early as the Bronze Age, long before the Roman invasion.[1]

The question of exactly how and when the town was created during those seventeen years has been the source of much speculation, and until recently there have been almost no clues. The Roman army swept across the English and Welsh countrysides during that time from their landing site in south-east England, and by AD 60 they had reached Anglesey. The origin of London is clearly linked with the early events of the Roman invasion, and until recently the most popular assumption was that it began as a Roman military fort and supply base guarding the river crossing, and that it was around this that the town subsequently grew.[2] The latest discoveries, however, do not support this hypothesis and it has been found necessary to re-examine the early stages of the invasion to find out how the new clues from London most easily fit into our knowledge of the Roman occupation of Britain.

In the spring of AD 43 the Roman invasion fleet landed, in part at least, at the site of the former coastal promontory at Richborough near Sandwich, where excavations in 1927 disclosed a broad Roman beachhead of the mid first century, defended by a double ditch and rampart clearly representing the presence of a considerable military force. Initially the commanding general, Aulus Plautius met no opposition, but soon he found himself confronted by a force led by the brothers Caratacus and Togodumnus, rulers of the Catuvellauni whose capital was Camulodunum near modern Colchester. The Britons were routed in initial skirmishes and retreated to assemble at the river Medway. A major battle lasting two days took place here, perhaps in the Rochester area where there was already a native town and no doubt a river crossing. A hard-won Roman success, in which German auxiliary soldiers distinguished themselves, forced Caratacus to flee westwards towards a place where he could cross the Thames. And so it was that the pursuing Roman army first arrived near the site probably to be occupied by London.

Assuming that this is the correct site, here they found the broad meandering river Thames, clear and fast-flowing to judge from the sands and gravels deposited in the river bed at that period.[3] The tide had probably not yet reached the area as the sea level was about 3 or 4 m lower than at present. The contemporary land surface around the south bank of the Thames has been identified in various excavations and geological borings, and it was clearly very different from that of recent times. Flat semi-marshland existed in a broad strip up to half a mile wide alongside the river, and in it various meandering streams and creeks flowed down to the low river bank.[4] The north bank to which the enemy was retreating was different, for there lay what appeared to be several low flat-topped hills up to 12 m high which descended steeply to the river. In fact these were the remains of an ancient terrace of river gravels and clays which had been eroded by streams and small rivers, like the Fleet and the Walbrook, flowing into the Thames.

Cassius Dio, writing about a century and a half after the invasion but no doubt using official documents, described how

the Britons retired to the river Thames at a point near where it empties into the ocean and at flood-tide forms a lake. This they easily crossed because they knew where the firm ground and the easy passages in this region were to be found; but the Romans in attempting to follow them were not so successful. However, the Germans swam across again and some others got over by a bridge a little way upstream, after which they assailed the barbarians from several sides at once and cut down many of them. In pursuing the remainder incautiously, they got into swamps from which it was difficult to make their way out, and so lost a number of men.[5]

The Roman soldiers, especially the German auxiliaries who had been trained to swim in full equipment, had probably crossed the Thames in various places, most of which were presumably fords. One of these may have been at Fulham where the particularly fine sword of a Roman army officer was found in the river, still in its sheath decorated with a scene depicting Romulus and Remus. Another find, possibly from the river but from an unknown London site, is a bronze legionary's helmet now preserved in the British Museum.[6]

Aulus Plautius halted his army to await the arrival of Claudius so that the Emperor himself could take possession of Camulodunum. This pause lasted some weeks as Claudius and his retinue travelled from Rome. During that time Plautius

Opposite, Roman sword and sheath. *Below*, decoration on the sheath, showing the figures of Romulus and Remus. From the Thames at Fulham.

Bronze helmet of a legionary soldier found in London, probably in the Thames.

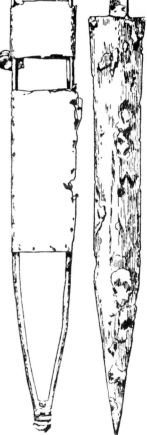

consolidated his position on the banks of the Thames, and must have built a major fort there for the safety of his troops and equipment. It has been suggested that he built a bridge too, partly to occupy his troops, as this would explain the reference by Dio to a bridge apparently crossing the river. Since it is extremely unlikely that the Britons could have built such a major structure, it is possible that Dio, writing much later, may have confused the subsequent Roman London Bridge for a native one.[7]

There is no reason to suppose that Plautius' camp lay actually at the future site of the Roman town of Londinium; it is far more likely that it was built close to an established Iron Age ford such as at Brentford, Fulham, Battersea or Westminster where concentrations of antiquities in the river bed show that fords probably existed.[8] An absence of prehistoric finds in the river around London Bridge, however, suggests that there was no ford there, so building the camp in a position like that away from an established ford, and therefore away from the land routes leading to it, would have removed the advantage of their being able to police British movements during this critical phase of the invasion. Indeed, the suggestion that the camp lay elsewhere is supported by the study of the earliest stratified coins and imported samian ware from Gaul found in Southwark, which indicates that Londinium was not established until about AD 50.[9]

Until recently it was no more than guesswork to locate Plautius' camp, but new evidence from Southwark tentatively

13

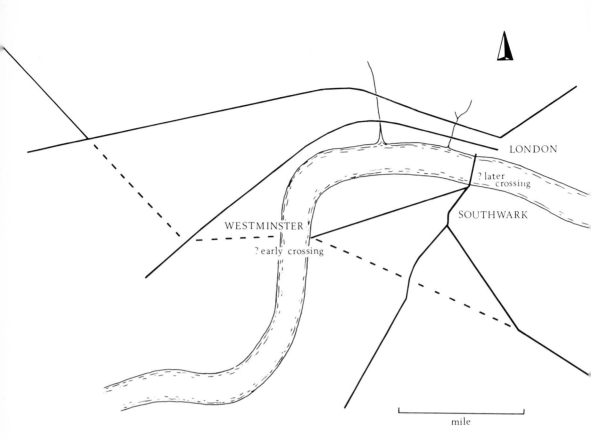

LONDON

? later
crossing

WESTMINSTER

SOUTHWARK

? early crossing

mile

Early Roman roads suggest
that a ford may have been
used at Westminster during
the invasion of AD 43, and
that about AD 50 a bridge
was built across the Thames
at London Bridge to lead into
the new planned city of
London.

points to the Westminster region as a distinct possibility. It has
long been recognized that the line of one of the earliest Roman
roads, Watling Street, which led from the invasion base at
Richborough in Kent to the Thames, surprisingly by-passed
Roman London heading for a possible crossing at Westminster,
where it was met on the north bank of the river by the line of a
road leading north to Verulamium, a native town. It therefore
seemed likely that these roads and the possible crossing at
Westminster had been established before that of London
Bridge. Until now the Westminster crossing was mere conjec-
ture, but as at last its existence is indicated by the discovery at
the south end of London Bridge of a Roman road, of mid-first-
century date, heading directly towards the same place, it seems
likely that there was a ford there and that the traces of Roman
occupation found on the naturally defended site of Thorney
Island at Westminster long ago, particularly under the Abbey,
formed part of a small later riverside settlement at the ford.[10]

The presumably slightly later Roman roads leading to
London from the south coast and from the north and west all
seem to cut across the early line of Watling Street, and lead to a
second and presumably later river crossing at London Bridge

where the new Roman town was to be built. It has been suggested that traces of buildings found close to London Bridge in the areas of Cannon Street station and in Gracechurch Street might have been early Roman military ones; but this is unlikely on the present evidence, not enough of the plans of the Roman buildings having been found to enable their purpose to be identified. They could equally well have been houses, shops or commercial warehouses in a civilian town.[11]

A more valid clue is the undoubted trace of the formal planning of streets and buildings on the plateau overlooking the site of London Bridge, planning that occurred right at the beginning of Roman occupation in the area. In particular there is the major east-west street that now lies beneath Lombard Street and the western end of Fenchurch Street.[12] This degree of formal planning at the beginning of the Roman occupation of Britain must reflect the activity of Roman military officials, and so it is possible that this was the main street of Plautius' camp, retained when the civil town moved on to the site. It is equally possible, and in view of subsequent events perhaps more likely, that the street was built for the new town that was named Londinium.

With the arrival of Claudius in the high summer of AD 43, accompanied by a troop of elephants to overawe the Britons, the initial phase of the conquest was brought to a satisfactory conclusion with a triumphal entry into Camulodunum. A fort for the XX Legion was erected near by while the main invasion force pushed northwards and westwards. Claudius stayed in Britain for only sixteen days, and after receiving the surrender of various tribes at Camulodunum, he returned to Rome in triumph.

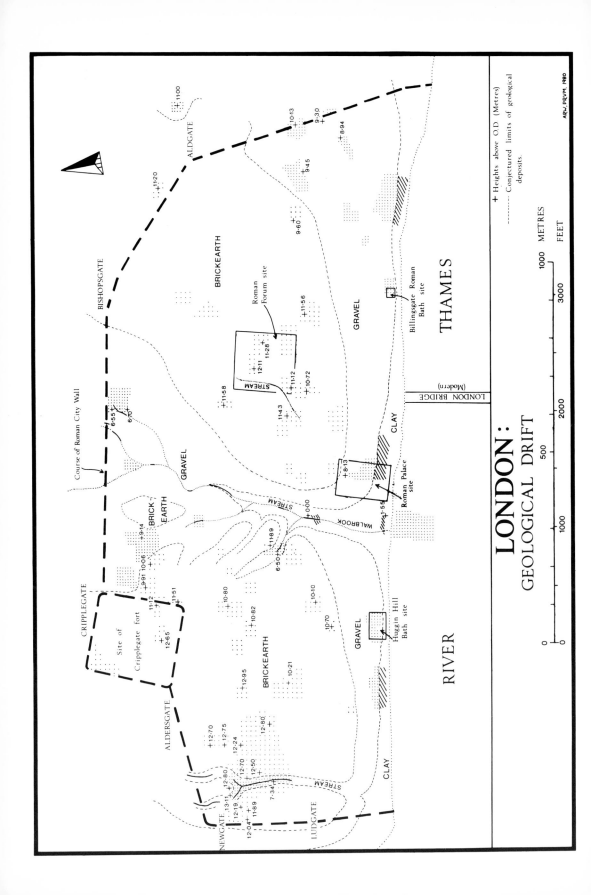

LONDON:
GEOLOGICAL DRIFT

ALDGATE

+ 11·00

+ 11·20

BISHOPSGATE

BRICKEARTH

Roman
Forum site

+ 10·13
+ 9·30
+ 8·94

+ 9·45

+ 9·60

+ 11·56

+ 11·58

+ 12·11   + 11·28

+ 11·12
+ 10·72

+ 11·43

STREAM

GRAVEL

Billingsgate Roman
Bath site

THAMES

LONDON BRIDGE
(Modern)

CLAY

+ 8·13

Roman Palace
site

+ 1·55

+ 0·00

WALBROOK   STREAM

+ 11·89

+ 6·50

GRAVEL

Course of Roman City Wall

+ 6·55
+ 6·70

GRAVEL

BRICK
EARTH

+ 9·14

+ 9·91 10·06

CRIPPLEGATE

Site of
Cripplegate fort

+ 11·12
+ 11·51

+ 12·65

+ 10·80

+ 10·82

BRICKEARTH

+ 12·95

+ 10·21

+ 10·80

+ 10·10

+ 10·70

Huggin Hill
Bath site

GRAVEL

CLAY

RIVER

ALDERSGATE

+ 12·70
+ 12·75

+ 12·24

+ 12·80

+ 12·80
+ 12·70
+ 12·50

+ 13·11
+ 12·19
+ 11·89

+ 7·34

STREAM

+ 12·04

NEWGATE

LUDGATE

CLAY

+ Heights above O.D. (Metres)

------- Conjectured limits of geological
        deposits.

METRES
FEET

0   500   1000

0   1000   2000   3000

ARJ, PRVM, 1980

The origin of Londinium

Lines of rotted wooden posts, shallow gullies and spreads of hard rammed gravel overlying the yellow-brown natural clay surface, are all that one normally sees of the beginnings of London. These first layers of occupation lie about 6 m below the streets of the modern City on the plateau overlooking London Bridge, where they are dated by a scatter of pottery fragments, coins and other debris. A rainy day can cause havoc as one excavates the clay, for it sticks like glue to boots and tools alike; and it is clear that this same sticky clay had caused similar problems for those first Londoners who, nearly two thousand years ago, soon left a dirty grey trampled surface littered with their rubbish and discoloured by the ash from their many hearths. It is not surprising, therefore, to find that drainage ditches, gravelled roads and buildings of timber and clay are among the earliest traces of Londinium. It has taken many years to map the pattern of usually indistinct features, and although the details are few it does seem that the first Roman settlement was carefully planned, with an organized layout of streets and buildings.

There are two basic hypotheses about the origin of London: firstly, that it began about AD 43 as a military base around which a civil settlement grew, and that when the military were moved elsewhere the settlement developed into a Roman town; and secondly, that it was planned as a town from the start. It is still far from clear what actually happened, but on balance the evidence favours the latter, and that it may have been founded about AD 50, when the governor, Publius Ostorius Scapula, pushed the Roman frontier westwards beyond the Fosse Way.

The creation of London was perhaps linked with the withdrawal of troops from south-east England, for Ostorius, who was concerned that there would be a vacuum in the Roman authority, set about founding cities there, both as a model of the Roman way of life and to help develop the wealth of the new province. Camulodunum, present-day Colchester, was one of these, and the old legionary barracks within the fort that had existed there were converted into housing occupied by retired veteran soldiers. It was given the status of *colonia*, a colony of Roman veterans, whose Italian style of town constitution was granted by the Emperor to allow the citizens to govern their own affairs through a local council. The town of Verulamium,

Opposite, Roman London was built on a terrace overlooking the Thames. Erosion by the Walbrook stream and the Fleet river had long ago created two hills, and it was on the eastern hill, now called Cornhill, that the Roman city centre was built. Roman baths and a palace tapped water from the spring-line where gravels overlie the London City.

17

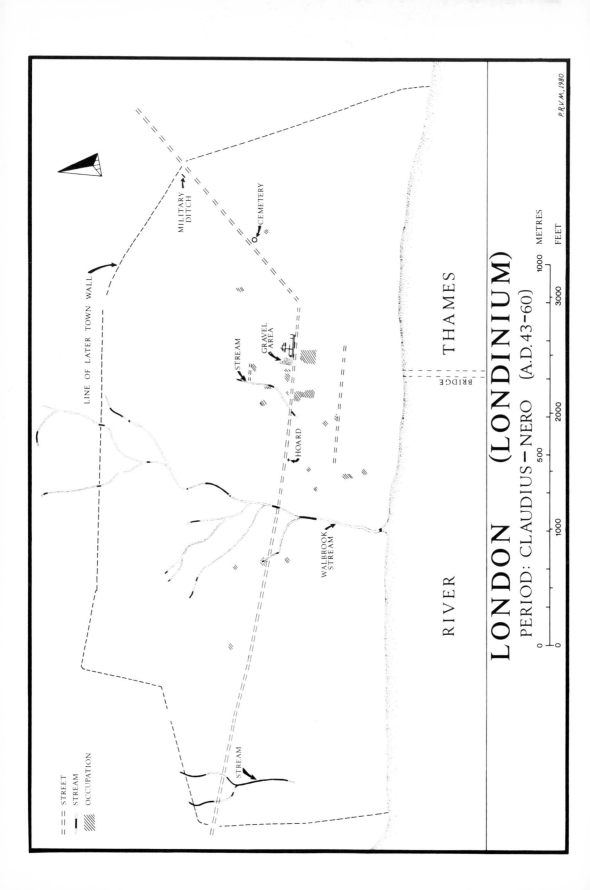

LONDON (LONDINIUM)
PERIOD: CLAUDIUS−NERO (A.D. 43−60)

First-century military ditch
found at Aldgate in 1972.

near St Albans, with an existing population of native Britons, was apparently given the civic status of *municipium* so that its inhabitants, some of whom had been granted Roman citizenship, could also govern its affairs. The town of Londinium, therefore, may have been created by merchants who required a deep-water port that would be a trading centre in the new province.[1]

Had London been a military base, then we should expect a variety of pieces of military equipment, weapons and parts of armour to occur in the earliest layers, as indeed have been found on other sites of known military origin, such as Chichester, Richborough and Colchester. In fact, however, with the exception of an outlying fort or camp at Aldgate, not a single military object has been found in any of the earliest pits, ditches and occupation layers of London. Equally important is the recent study of coins and pottery from those earliest layers in the City and in Southwark at the south bank of London Bridge, for these seem to reflect a date of about AD 50 for the beginning of occupation.

Traces of the ditches initially dug to drain the flat clay-covered river terrace are not easy to find, since they had such a short life. A major ditch 1.5 m wide and 1.8 m deep was discovered dug into the natural clay in Lombard Street, where it drained northwards towards a nearby stream that was found on several sites earlier this century;[2] while another much smaller ditch only 60 cm wide and 40 cm deep has been uncovered in Fenchurch Street.[3] Both ditches had soon been filled in, once

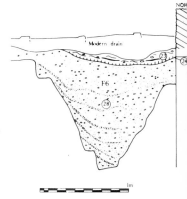

Section across the
first-century military ditch
found at Aldgate.

Opposite, traces of the
carefully planned Roman city
centre built during the first
decade of the existence of
Londinium.

the land was drained; the one in Lombard Street was so rapidly filled with dumps of building debris, domestic refuse and gravel that its almost vertical clay sides had no time to be eroded by the weather.

Assuming that Londinium was a civil foundation, it seems that the concept of the town planners was on a large scale, and soon the main street 9 m wide was being built along the plateau in a straight line parallel with the river. Constructed of hard rammed gravel, and cambered at the sides to allow the rainwater to drain off into side ditches, one of which was 0.7 m wide and 0.45 m deep, this street was to be the axis of the new town beside which the most important buildings were erected. Curiously, the road still exists in a slightly distorted form as parts of Lombard Street and Fenchurch Street. The original road has been found on several sites overlying the trampled natural clay surface, though a small pit half filled with rubbish found beneath it in Lombard Street some years ago does show that it took the builders a little while to get themselves organized: the upper filling of gravel in the pit indicates that it was half open when the road was built over it.[4]

Traces of the very first buildings of London, timber-framed structures, and a minor street leading off the main road, were found in Fenchurch Street; although their planned layout

Plan and section of the main street of Roman London discovered in Lombard Street, 1962. Because the gravel metalling overlies the natural brickearth it is clear that the road was built during the middle of the first century.

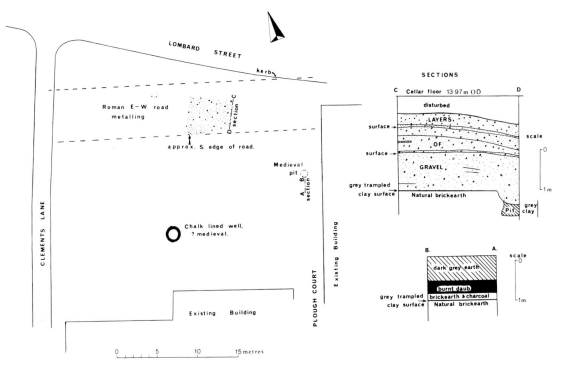

P.R.V.M., 1963.

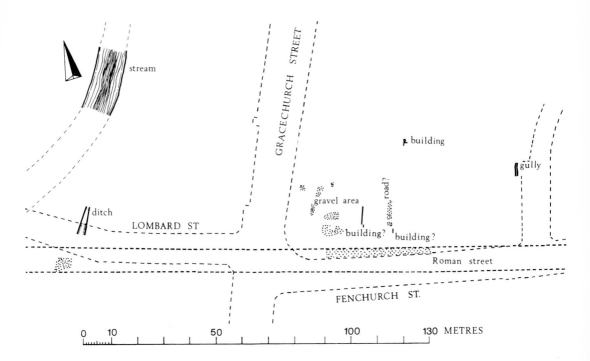

seems military in style, they may well have been civilian buildings erected under military supervision, as was usual in new
planned towns.[5] Under one of those first buildings was found a
small circular pit just 0.28 m wide in which there lay the con-
tracted skeleton of a young sheep or goat, presumably an
offering to the gods to bring good fortune to the house and its
occupants.[6]

Apparently from the beginning of its existence, a large area of
ground in the town centre had been set aside as an open space
with a gravelled surface, the ground having been most carefully
prepared and levelled, with the removal of the topsoil before the
spread of clean gravel was laid down. Discovered only about
ten years ago, this area, which seems to have covered more than
1,120 sq. m, is likely to remain the centre of much discussion for years to come. To those who favour a civil beginning to
London it will be interpreted as a market-place,and to those
who favour a military beginning it may be interpreted as a
parade ground. Not one military object having been found
here, and the fact that in AD 60, when the town centre was
undoubtedly civilian, the gravelled area was still in use, all
suggests that it was a market-place. This interpretation is
strengthened by the fact that only twenty years later the first
forum, the public market-place was to be built on its site.[7]

It is fortunate that London was destroyed in the uprising of
Queen Boudica in AD 60, for the fire layer is easily seen, even on

Traces of timber structures,
the earliest buildings of
Roman London, constructed
beside the main street and a
large gravelled area in the
city centre, about AD 50.

21

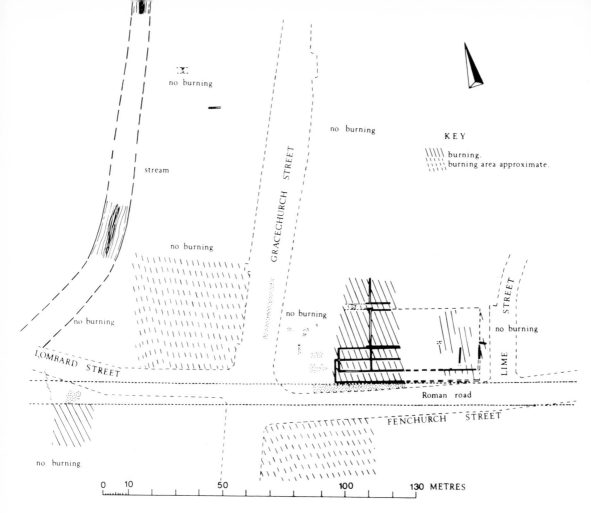

Plan of the Roman city centre in AD 60 showing the main road, the gravelled area under Gracechurch Street which was probably a market-place, and beside it timber-framed buildings, probably including shops.

building sites, and as a result there is a fixed datum point from which to explore the earlier history of the Roman city with the certain knowledge that any remains below the fire layer must date from the preceding seventeen years. For example, it is known that the main street had been resurfaced twice before AD 60, the 'market square' resurfaced once, and a room in a house or shop beside the main street replastered and repainted four times before AD 60, all of which indicates a time span of several years before the fire.[8]

The fire also enables us to assess the character of the buildings. One of them at the east corner of the main street and the 'market square', has been particularly carefully investigated and seems to have been a large building comprising a block, 28.6 m wide, behind a verandah or portico nearly 58 m long fronting the main street. The admittedly incomplete plan of the building has the appearance of a range of shops immediately behind the portico, with behind these various living rooms. Its construction varied somewhat, suggesting that the shops had been separately built; but as the inner portico wall evidently carried the main load of the roof, it had a particularly solid foundation, a large wooden beam about 0.45 m square, laid on timber piles at the bottom of a foundation trench 0.60 m wide and 0.45 m deep. This originally supported the upright timber framework of the building, the gaps between the beams having been filled either with sun-dried clay bricks or with clay daub on a framework of wicker wattling. The eastern end of the load-bearing portico foundation was built of flint and mortar about 1 m deep, a difference in construction which may have been necessary because this end of the building, to judge from the large quantity of grain found there, probably housed the workshop of a miller, baker or grain dealer who presumably required more solid foundations.[9]

This building seems to have had a curiously unified plan, linked by the continuous portico, which compares with another large building of the same date that was found at Verulamium. This too had been burnt in the uprising of AD 60, and it had a long verandah, behind which lay a series of shops and living quarters.[10] The suggestion that these may have belonged to a single wealthy owner, who had rented out individual shops, would possibly apply to the building in London. The idea is supported by the fact that after AD 60 the burnt building at Verulamium was replaced by a new building of similar plan ready to be rented out anew, though no such rebuilding apparently occurred in London. Perhaps wealthy property developers renting out their buildings were, as today, an important factor in the growth of new towns.

Although the walls of this clay and timber-framed building in London were flimsy compared with later Roman buildings of stone, it seems to have been fairly comfortable inside. The absence of roof tiles in the burnt debris suggests that it had a thatched roof; and the absence of window glass indicates that it had shuttered openings that could be closed at night and in bad weather. Floors were of trampled clay perhaps originally supporting wooden floorboards, while wall plaster, found painted mostly white and very occasionally red or green, shows that the wall decoration was probably a simple design, possibly with large rectangular white panels surrounded by the red and green borders which are so typical of Roman wall painting. A wooden pipe made of interconnecting links joined by iron collars or rings ran alongside the front of the building, ensuring a supply of running water to at least some of the tenants, one of whom was no doubt the baker, miller or grain supplier. His shop at the east end of the building had a front room 7 m wide, and it was through the end wall of this room that a wood-lined drain emptied waste water into the area beyond.

Traces of other timber-framed buildings, with wattle-and-daub walls, have often been found, including one on a site in Lombard Street which was revealed as a spread of burnt daub 0.30 m thick and nearly 15 m wide beside the main Roman street. Although nothing is known in detail about its layout, at one point a scorched clay floor was recorded together with fragments of wall plaster painted red and white. Although evidently a building of somewhat similar construction to that found in Fenchurch Street, there was no evidence to show whether it was a house or a range of shops.[11] Behind the building were found traces of clay floors, post and stake holes and rubbish pits that were not burnt in the fire of AD 60: but as they were adjacent to the building and contemporary with it, this had probably been an open 'back yard' area upon which various temporary structures had been erected from time to time.[12]

The size of the town in AD 60 is not known, though judging from the extent of the occupation debris it apparently covered an area of at least thirty acres, and extended for a considerable distance beyond. The only known clue to the size of the settlement is the situation of burials, for according to Roman law these should have lain outside the official limits of the settlement. Several scattered burials of the first century have been found to the west near the Walbrook stream;[13] but more important is the Roman cemetery to the east that was found by Quentin Waddington in 1925 at the corner of Fenchurch Street and Billiter Street. Most of the cremation burials found there were enclosed in cists of thick oak planks, sometimes clamped with iron; one cist was made from a Spanish amphora, and one of the wooden cists even had a cover of thin Purbeck marble. Since some of the objects themselves are lost, the burials cannot be dated with precision within the first century, but their find spot in London is important since they lie well inside the ring of late first-century cemeteries, in the Minories, Bishopgate and St Paul's regions, which presumably indicate the city's enlarged limits by the end of the century.[14] It is perhaps significant that this early Roman cemetery lay close to the main road leading to Camulodunum, and although traces of occupation debris have been found even to the west of the Walbrook stream, it was presumably mainly in the new town centre to the east of the stream that a formal grid of streets was constructed dividing the town into square islands (*insulae*) of land upon which the new buildings were erected. Within this settlement we have few details of other buildings, except an east-west wall foundation 0.35 m wide and 1.45 m deep, built of ragstone and clay, that no doubt carried a load-bearing wall. This was found in Corbet Court, off Gracechurch Street, just south of what seems to have been an east-west road;[15] while in Bush Lane, beside Cannon Street station, a series of slots for timber foundation beams have been found possibly dating from as early as the 50s.[16]

The question of the status of Londinium before AD 60 has been a problem for many years. Here we seem to have a large planned Roman town which in that year, according to the classical writer Tacitus, was 'a place not indeed distinguished by the title of *colonia*, but was crowded with traders and a great centre of commerce',[17] the implication being that at that time Londinium was a town of Roman citizens that had not yet received the right to govern itself. Nevertheless, the degree of town planning shown by the recent archaeological discoveries suggests that there may have been a planning authority. What was that authority, and what was the status of the town in AD 60? As it was evidently not a chartered town, was it a town of non-Roman citizens under military control, or was it something more? We have no positive answers to these questions, but it is difficult to believe that this important town and trading centre mentioned by Tacitus, a town that was soon to become the provincial capital, had no special status. Indeed, its layout of streets, buildings and the large gravelled 'market square' seem to bear witness to the aspirations and need of its inhabitants – traders who require the framework of a fully Roman town for their activities.

Another clue is provided by the traders themselves; where did they come from? They are unlikely to have been Britons, for there was no major native town or political centre nearby from which to draw a population. Indeed the fact that during the decade before the destruction of AD 60, these traders were importing goods from the established Roman world, not merely from Gaul and Germany, but from the other ends of the Empire, shows that some were powerful and wealthy people from the Mediterranean who were settling in Londinium, and that they were keen to enlarge their already established and sophisticated trading empires. A quick examination of the mid-first-century groups of objects from London shows that from Italy the merchants imported fine glass tableware, decorated pottery lamps, and even red-coloured pottery tableware made within sight of Vesuvius and containing volcanic ash. From central and southern Gaul there were fine, colourful tablewares of various types of pottery, most notable the red-glossed samian ware, as well as wine from southern Gaul. From the Seville region of southern Spain great globular amphorae probably filled with olive oil, were brought in merchant ships. From Rhodes in Greece fine wine arrived in narrower amphorae, while Syria supplied beautiful glassware.

The classical world also apparently introduced its social problems into London, for a minority of less scrupulous individuals arrived who were apparently keen to exploit the wealth of the new city by illegal means. One of these was a forger whose buried hoard of worthless coins was found at the corner of St Swithin's Lane and King William Street about 1840. All the 89 coins were silver-plated copper copies of silver denarii; but the remarkable feature about them is that such a considerable number of coins was produced from the same small group of dies or moulds, suggesting that they had been made locally. The forger had not been particular about the age of the coins that he was copying, but merely that they were all of silver. For this reason about half of the hoard were copies of Republican coins, some as early as about 90 BC, and the other half were of the Emperors Augustus, Tiberius and Caligula. The latest was a copy of a coin of Claudius, showing that the hoard had probably been made about AD 50.[18] As all of this occurred within a decade of the founding of Londinium, it seems unlikely that its wealthy, well-established traders could have been anything other than Roman citizens operating in the new province.

And yet by AD 60 London had apparently not been granted a charter to govern itself: how is this possible? Surely this links back to the town planning which implies the existence of a planning authority, and, in particular, to that large gravelled area in the heart of the town, for whatever the possibility of its having had a military origin, it is clear that it was a central feature in the town of AD 60, and can be most satisfactorily interpreted as a market square. To operate this market the London traders probably had to have had the permission of the Emperor or Senate in Rome, and it is unlikely that this would have been granted unless the traders had a suitable status and had been able to devise a satisfactory petition.[19]

It was Professor Haverfield who, as long ago as 1911, suggested a possible solution to the problem.[20] It semed most reasonable to him that many of the traders of London were Roman citizens, whose new town perhaps was not considered sufficiently developed for them to be granted a full self-governing status at the same time as Camulodunum and Verulamium. Nevertheless, as a community of Roman citizens permanently settled abroad, Londinium may have been permitted a degree of limited self-government while still under military control. Their title would have been *cives Romani consistentes Londinii*, and as such they would have been permitted to have a town council to govern local affairs until such time as the town grew beyond a certain size and could receive a full chartered status. Such *cives Romani* corporations were common during the late Republican and early Imperial periods in other Roman provinces, such as Pannonia (modern Hungary and Yugoslavia) in the towns of Aquincum and Brigeto.[21] The creation of such new towns, together with grants of citizenship, soon had a major effect on the development of the new provinces, for it was through them that the Empire was primarily administered. Although in Britain Claudius created only two chartered cities, this was part of a much more general policy of urbanization in the Empire, which led him to create, for example, five *municipia* in the province of Noricum alone.[22] It is against this wider background that the founding of Londinium should be seen as something that Claudius and the Senate in Rome would have encouraged.

So far one vital factor has been omitted from this reconstruction of the founding of London – its bridge. This was in many ways the key factor in choosing the site of London, for communication routes were essential if this trading centre was to succeed. A deep navigable river brought shipping to the port, while a bridge at the lowest crossing-point on the river would focus land routes on the same place. Roman engineers found that the London bridge site was far from ideal, for although

Stane Street, crossing the Southwark marshes to London Bridge, was carefully built upon a raft of logs in particularly wet areas.

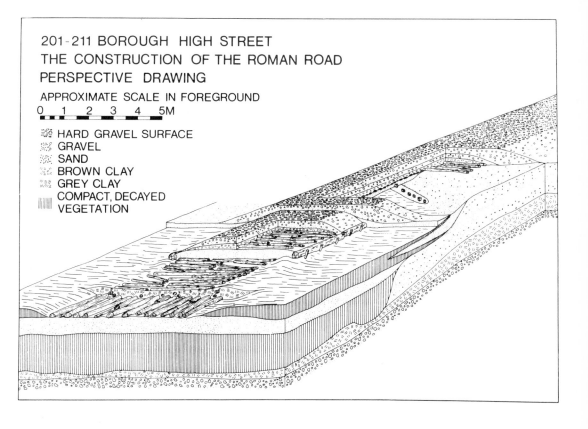

201-211 BOROUGH HIGH STREET
THE CONSTRUCTION OF THE ROMAN ROAD
PERSPECTIVE DRAWING
APPROXIMATE SCALE IN FOREGROUND
0   1   2   3   4   5M

HARD GRAVEL SURFACE
GRAVEL
SAND
BROWN CLAY
GREY CLAY
COMPACT, DECAYED
VEGETATION

high, hard ground lay on the north bank of the river to form a suitable bridgehead approach, the south bank was entirely different and very marshy. Much research has been carried out in Southwark in recent years, not only to understand the technical problems faced by the Roman engineers, but also to find the site of the bridge. The problem that faced Roman engineers was the strip of marshland, 1,000 m wide, on the south bank of the river which was intersected by many natural drainage channels and creeks. Fortunately there were also several low sandbanks rising very slightly above the marsh, and these could be used as a kind of natural causeway on which to build the roads to the edge of the river. Between the sandbanks there was waterlogged marshland, however, and upon this they had to lay logs, as many as three layers deep, to provide a stable foundation for the gravel road.[23]

There are three clues which indicate that the Roman bridge lay approximately on the same site as the medieval bridge, just downstream from the present London Bridge: firstly, the two roads, one leading south towards Chichester and the other south-west towards Westminster, converge on the river bank at about the south end of the medieval bridge site. Secondly, a line across the river of Roman coins and other antiquities, which was revealed by dredging in the 1830s, must have been dropped from the Roman bridge.[24] And finally, there was a major road leading down towards the edge of the river at the medieval bridge site, from the monumental entrance of the second Roman forum on the north bank. It is unfortunate that the river bed around the modern London Bridge contains literally thousands of waterlogged piles from several earlier bridges, for this makes it virtually impossible to tell the age of any timbers found.

It was in Southwark that particularly important dating evidence was recently recovered to indicate the date at which the roads to the bridge, and therefore the bridge itself, were built. It took two forms – coins and red-glossed samian ware. The majority of the coins of the Emperor Claudius (AD 41–54) found in London were unofficial issues of copies which are believed to have been made towards the end of his reign. Their suggested date is supported to some extent by the study of coins from such early Claudian sites as Camulodunum where only 58 per cent are copies, and Richborough where 36 per cent are copies. The main evidence for their date is that the known later Claudian sites, like Sea Mills and Cirencester in Gloucestershire, have very few official issues but instead an extremely high proportion of imitations (90 and 82 per cent respectively). On this basis the fact that 92 per cent of the Claudian coins found in Southwark and 87.5 per cent of those from the City of London are copies, possibly indicates that London was founded some years after AD 43. In fact, a coin found underlying the earliest timber buildings on the site in Fenchurch Street was probably a copy of a Claudian original.[25] The samian ware also reflects this later date, for in Southwark no specifically Claudian forms have been found, though types dating from the next two decades (i.e. about AD 50–70) are abundant.[26]

So, apart from the logical need, at least from our point of view, for the Romans to have defended the important route centre and river crossing with a fort, there is no actual evidence that London had a military beginning. Its function as a town of merchants, importing goods from the Mediterranean world for sale to the Roman army and to the officials and settlers in the new towns of the province is perfectly understandable. But whatever its status, it is clear that just before its destruction in AD 60 London was rapidly becoming a major city, and main port of a Britain intimately connected with the Continent of Europe.

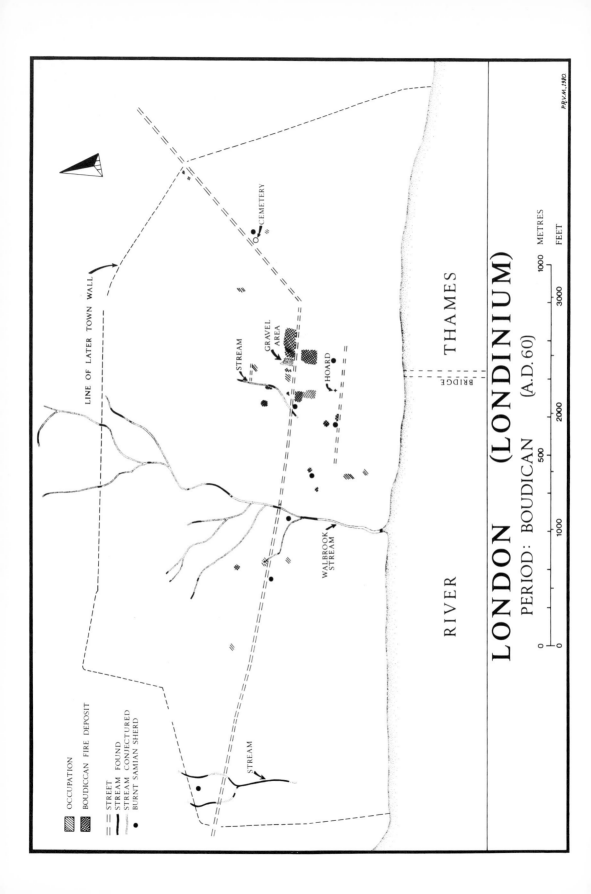

OCCUPATION

BOUDICCAN FIRE DEPOSIT

= = STREET
STREAM FOUND
STREAM CONJECTURED
• BURNT SAMIAN SHERD

LINE OF LATER TOWN WALL

CEMETERY

STREAM

GRAVEL
AREA

HOARD

STREAM

WALBROOK
STREAM

STREAM

RIVER   THAMES   BRIDGE

LONDON (LONDINIUM)
PERIOD: BOUDICAN (A.D. 60)

0   500   1000   METRES
0   1000   2000   3000   FEET

P.R.V.M. 1970

AD 60: *Fire, sword and gibbet*

Whatever the uncertainties that surround the origin of London, the events involving the British uprising in AD 60 are extremely clear. Tacitus describes how the Roman Governor Gaius Suetonius Paullinus managed to arrive in Londinium ahead of the British rebels.

The speed with which he had travelled from north Wales had parted him from most of his troops, and now all that he could do was earnestly to urge the people of London to abandon their homes quickly and to move far from the city before the hordes of Britons reduced it to a smouldering ruin. Tacitus wrote that Paullinus

decided to sacrifice the single town in the interest of the province as a whole. Neither the tears nor the entreaties of the stricken citizens bent him from his purpose. He gave the order for the departure, taking those who would follow as part of his column; and those whom the weakness of sex, frailty of age, or reluctance to leave their homes remained within the town were overwhelmed by the enemy.[1]

Judging from the slight indications found on various archaeological sites, it seems clear that most people left with much of their furniture and other belongings, and that, for a short while in that year, Londinium probably became a town of empty houses, silent streets, and a windswept market-place. Few remained to chance their future.

What happened next is described by Tacitus in just a few words: 'The enemy neither took nor sold prisoners nor indulged in any of the traffic incidental to ordinary warfare, but massacred, hanged, burned and crucified with a headlong fury that was stimulated by the knowledge of forthcoming retribution and by the desire to snatch meanwhile at the vengeance within reach.' Far below the modern streets of the City of London the events of AD 60 are indelibly scorched on the soil as a red layer of burnt debris approximately 0.45 m thick.

The cause of the rebellion is not difficult to discover, since it was led by Queen Boudica, widow of the wealthy King Prasutagus of the Iceni of Norfolk. Seventeen years earlier the Iceni had concluded a treaty with Claudius which had established their status as a 'client kingdom' while under Roman rule. It is unlikely that in AD 60 Boudica and her people had realized that on the death of the king the terms of the treaty

Opposite, the extent of occupation and burnt debris at the time of Boudica's revolt in AD 60. Both suggest a piecemeal burning of the town, especially around the town centre and the probable market-place (gravel area). The eastern limit of the town at this stage probably did not extend as far as the Roman cemetery.

would end. This now became clear to them as his estates and possessions reverted to the Empire. The Queen was stripped of her office and possessions by Roman officials, particularly the staff of the Procurator, Catus Decianus, and gross outrages and excesses took place which the Iceni found intolerable. But it was when their Queen was flogged, and her daughters raped as if they were slaves, that at once the Iceni responded in the only way they knew – by slaughtering the hated Roman officials. The rebellion quickly spread to neighbouring tribes eager to avenge themselves on the Roman veterans at Camulodunum; and, following a siege of the Temple of Claudius, that town was looted and set on fire, and the rebels turned towards London.[2]

Even if there had been no written record of Londinium being destroyed in AD 60, the archaeological evidence alone would have shown that this occurred. The fire layer has so far been found on more than a dozen sites, at a depth of roughly 4 m, mostly north of London Bridge, and in general it shows a surprisingly clear and consistent picture of a deserted town being engulfed in a holocaust. Frank Lambert, of the old Guildhall Museum, was the first to make a proper record of the fire debris which he saw on three building sites in King William Street about 1920.[3] Other traces were recorded by Gerald Dunning and Frank Cottrill during the 1930s, and in 1945 Dunning published the first general study of the traces of the fire, though unfortunately omitting most of Lambert's discoveries.[4] Because very little of the fire had been seen even then, he was forced to use other and less certain evidence as a clue to the extent of the burning. Searching through the Guildhall Museum's collection, he found a few pieces of burnt samian ware dating from about AD 60, which, although casual finds by workmen from building sites, he believed had probably come from unrecorded excavations in the fire layer. In the light of what has since been discovered, this distribution map was proved to be remarkably accurate in showing the extent of the fire and the area of occupation by AD 60. Additional discoveries since then, however, have made this map somewhat unsatisfactory, since it gave no information about the character of the town at that time. With this in mind a new map has been compiled of the distribution not only of the fire layer, but also of traces of mid-first-century occupation where the burning did *not* occur. The result, although far from complete, begins to give a picture of the town in AD 60.[5]

At its height the scene in London must have been slightly reminiscent of the city almost nineteen centuries later in the middle of the Blitz. Towering columns of fire and smoke rose from outlying buildings, in Southwark and at Aldgate for example, while in the city centre, where Lombard Street and

Gracechurch Street now intersect, it was probably like a single raging fire, with the rubble of fallen walls collapsing out onto the streets.[6] Tests to establish at what temperature samian ware turns black and fuses show that the heat in the city centre must have been in excess of 1000 °C.[7] In the outlying building that was recorded at 18–20 Southwark Street, next to the Borough Market, the characteristic red burnt daub was found covering a scorched clay floor upon which there lay a complete cooking pot, fragments of a lamp and other domestic pottery, a bone dice and an iron key;[8] while even in the market-place at the city centre burning ash was deposited as a layer on the gravel surface.

Immediately east of the market-place, the very large building with a portico, fronting the main street of the Roman city, was found in Fenchurch Street in 1969 to have been completely gutted leaving the grain store of the shop at its eastern end a charred mass up to 1 m thick on its clay floor.[9] In the room of a nearby Roman building there was found a mass of smashed household crockery – jugs, bowls, and even a lamp, all lying on the clay floor. The sherds had been burnt red, including one particularly fine jug neck stamped with the potter's name C.ALBVC. The crockery lay together, suggesting that it may have been the contents of a cupboard or shelf that had crashed to the floor in the flames.[10]

Imaginative reconstruction looking west of the main street of Roman London being destroyed in the fire of AD 60. On the right is the timber framed range of shops found in Fenchurch Street, and just beyond is the gravelled market place. Burnt debris of the other buildings shown has been found on the sites of the Midland Bank, Gracechurch Street, and Barclays Bank, Lombard Street.

In another building nearer London Bridge, someone had hidden a small hoard of bronze coins, no doubt hoping that he could recover them later. They were found about 1920 in a burnt condition during the rebuilding of 42 Gracechurch Street, and included two coins of Agrippa, who had died in 12 BC, and fifteen coins of Claudius (AD 41–54).[11] Their condition is somewhat similar to another burnt coin of Claudius that was likewise found by workmen in Clements Lane, off Lombard Street, also presumably from the fire layer.[12]

Farther west, and closer to the Walbrook stream, the burnt debris of yet another wattle-and-daub building was discovered in 1950 on the site of St Swithin's House, Walbrook.[13] Close to the Roman building was found a rubbish pit about 1.8 m deep and 1.2 m wide that had been dug to dispose of the ordinary household refuse not long before the revolt occurred. By the time the house was abandoned, rubbish had filled only the bottom of the pit with broken cooking pots, bowls, pot lids, jars and samian ware cups and dishes. Two coins of Claudius were also found in the pit. On top of the rubbish there lay a complete Spanish amphora and a large jug which may have been thrown away by looters in an attempt to break them. The house had been set on fire at this stage, and as it collapsed the reddened daub, wall plaster and burnt timber filled the rest of the pit.

Leaving Londinium burning, Boudica's trail of destruction headed north, and within days Verulamium was similarly looted and in flames. Boudica's decision to destroy it was probably based on the fact that its inhabitants, members of the Catuvellauni, were sympathetic to Rome and had been granted the right to govern themselves. Tacitus' claims that about 70,000 Roman citizens and native sympathizers were mass-

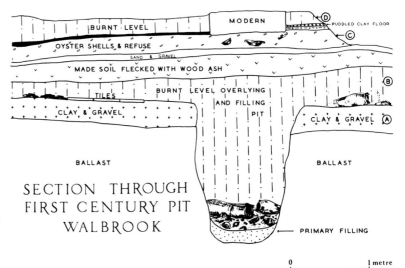

SECTION THROUGH
FIRST CENTURY PIT
WALBROOK

The burnt debris of AD 60 from a nearby building filling a rubbish pit in which a complete amphora lay. Found in Walbrook street.

acred by Boudica's forces in three towns, must be regarded as
an exaggeration. It is difficult to see how even half this number
can be justified, especially as two of the towns were probably
almost deserted. Nevertheless it is a fact that three major
Roman towns had been destroyed, and if Suetonius Paullinus
was to retain the province, Boudica had to be defeated. We do
not know where the final battle took place, but somewhere
beyond Verulamium Paullinus gathered his army, nearly
10,000 strong, and awaited the Britons. Behind him lay the
barrier of a wood, while in front lay open country without any
cover for the enemy to hide behind. According to Tacitus the
army of Britons was at least 80,000 strong, for he claims that
almost all of that number died that day. Led by the Queen, the
Britons were no match for the highly skilled Roman soldiers
who surged ahead in wedge formation to strike deeply into the
midst of the enemy, while the cavalry with lances at the ready
speared into the battle. The Britons fled but were followed by
the soldiers who did not even spare the women. 'Baggage
animals too', wrote Tacitus, 'transfixed with weapons, added to
the heaps of dead.'

The battle was over, the revolt all but ended, and Boudica
had killed herself to avoid capture. For some Romans it was a
rather hollow victory – particularly for the Procurator Catus
Decianus who, horrified at the havoc his staff had caused, had
fled to Gaul. In spite of the defeat, 'the savage British tribesmen
were disinclined for peace', wrote Tacitus, and Paullinus
undertook massive troop movements to subdue them. New
forts were built as Paullinus was bent on a campaign of repression and punishment, and it is just possible that the temporary fort built at Aldgate, close to the main road to
Camulodunum, was one of these. Discovered in 1972, the only
remaining sign was its small defensive V-shaped ditch only 2 m
wide and 1 m deep. There was no silt in the bottom of it and it
had been backfilled with the clean clay that was excavated just
a short time before – signs that the camp had been in use for
only a little while. Unfortunately there was no dating evidence,
such as coins and pottery, in the ditch; one of the main clues to
its date was a Roman rubbish pit, that may have been filled up
as late as AD 70, for it had been dug through the filled-in ditch.
Because its filling was of clean clay, perhaps from a demolished
rampart, it is more likely that the fort was constructed before
AD 60, since none of the rubbish and building debris of the
occupation on the site at that time was mixed with the filling of
the fort ditch. But whatever its date, the fort indicates troop
movements, and its position outside London, beyond the
Billiter Street cemetery, suggests that it was not one of the
earliest features of Roman London.[14]

In AD 61 Nero sent a new Procurator to Britain, Gaius Julius
Alpinus Classicianus, a Roman noble of provincial origin probably from the Trier region in Gaul, whose association with
London was to be particularly important. It is uncertain why
he was chosen, particularly as Nero must have known that
Classicianus and Paullinus were old enemies. Tacitus, who was
pro-Paullinus, wrote that Classicianus had allowed his personal animosities to damage the national interests by advising
the Britons to wait for a new Governor who would be kind to
those who surrendered, without an enemy's bitterness or a
conqueror's arrogance. But Classicianus considered that
oppression would not win peace, and that it was in the best
interest of Rome to take a statesmanlike attitude by trying to
win the support of the Britons. When Classicianus reported to
Nero that there could be no hope of peace until Paullinus was
replaced, the Emperor sent someone to investigate the situation, and in due course Paullinus was removed on the pretext of
a mishap to some ships.

As Classicianus had predicted, the new Governor, Publius
Petronius Turpilianus, also took a statesman's attitude and was
concerned with building a peaceful future rather than allowing
the war to continue – particularly as it was not necessary for
Rome to demonstrate her military prowess again. Tacitus was
disgusted, and wrote that Turpilianus 'neither provoking the
enemy nor provoked, called this ignoble inactivity peace with
honour'. Between them, Classicianus, Turpilianus and his successor M. Trebellius Maximus, did much to heal the old
wounds during the nine years following the revolt. Not least of
all was the redevelopment of the three devastated towns, and it
was in one of these, Londinium, that Classicianus probably
decided to make his headquarters.

In London there is no evidence of any immediate rebuilding,
though the upper part of the burnt debris often shows signs of
having been disturbed by digging, presumably to level the land.
On a site in Fenchurch Street the debris was left lying on the
edge of the main street until a new layer of gravel metalling was
laid down.[15] Presumably the shock and the destruction had
removed all incentive for traders to reopen business until they
could see that the peace was to be lasting. There is no clue as to
how long this situation remained but, as at Verulamium where
there are also signs of a slow recovery, it seems likely that
Londinium may have taken some years to regain its former size.

An important factor in the rebuilding of Londinium must
have been the presence of the Procurator, Julius Classicianus,
who no doubt encouraged the resettlement of merchants and
traders. It is just possible that there is some connection between
the Procurator and the earliest known stone building in

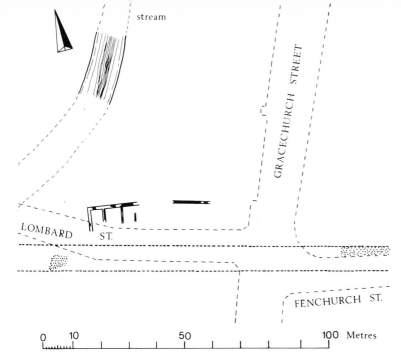

stream

GRACECHURCH STREET

LOMBARD ST.

FENCHURCH ST.

0 10   50   100 Metres

Traces of a stone building, perhaps official, that was probably built during the period AD 60–80 before the construction of the first forum.

London, apparently constructed before AD 80, after which the first forum was built on its site in Lombard Street. Only a small part of the building has been recorded beside the main street and just west of the market area, and so its plan is insufficient to determine its purpose. In spite of this it represents a degree of wealth and permanence that was probably exceptional in London at that time, and so it could have been an official building.[16] Although it is not known where the headquarters of the Procurator lay, it is clear that his ashes were buried by his wife Julia beneath a monumental stone tomb in a cemetery north of the present Tower of London.

The tomb had been broken up in the fourth century AD and used as building material in the defences of the city. When the first piece was found on a building site in 1852, Charles Roach Smith suggested that it was part of the tomb of the famous Procurator mentioned by Tacitus. Unfortunately, the inscription only recorded his name, 'Gaius Julius Alpinus Classicianus, son of Gaius, of the Fabian voting tribe', and specialists naturally felt that it would be too fortunate to have found the tomb of such a great personage. It was not until 1935 that more of the monumental inscription was found by Frank Cottrill on another building site, '. . . Procurator of the Province of Britain: Julia Pacata Indiana , daughter of Indus, his wife, had this built'. Charles Roach Smith was right, and Julia, daughter of a Gaulish cavalry commander who had taken the Roman side in a rebellion in Gaul in AD 21, had built this monument that lies restored in the British Museum, where it is a treasured national possession.[17]

Fragments of the tomb of the *procurator*, Julius Classicianus, as restored in the British Museum.

37

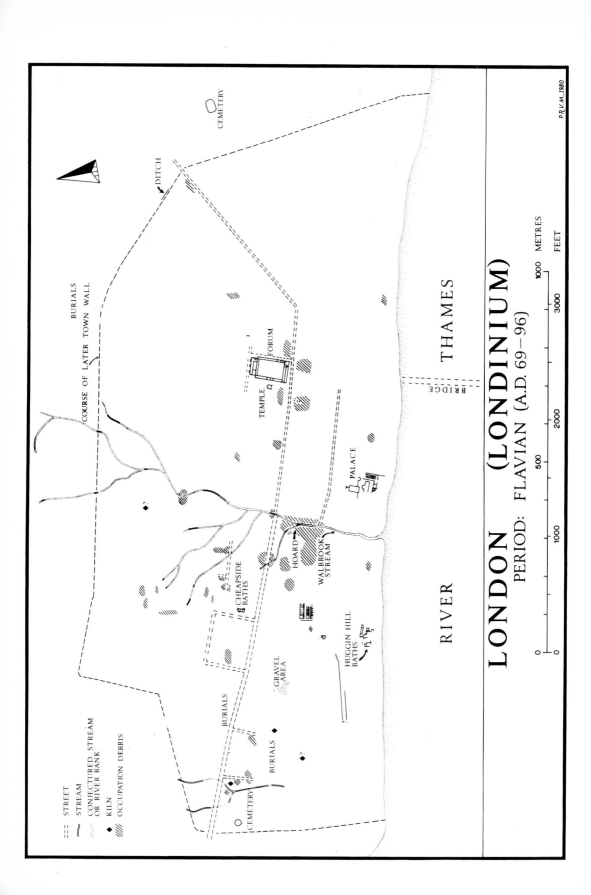

LONDON (LONDINIUM)
PERIOD: FLAVIAN (A.D. 69–96)

STREET
STREAM
CONJECTURED STREAM
OR RIVER BANK
KILN
OCCUPATION DEBRIS

CEMETERY
BURIALS
COURSE OF LATER TOWN WALL
DITCH
BURIALS
BURIALS
CEMETERY
GRAVEL AREA
HUGGIN HILL BATHS
CHEAPSIDE BATHS
HOARD
WALBROOK STREAM
PALACE
TEMPLE
FORUM
BRIDGE
THAMES
RIVER

P.R.V.M. 1980

METRES
FEET
0   1000
0   1000   2000   3000
500   500

The first Roman forum

Although the growth of Londinium during the two decades
following the devastation of A D 60 is little understood, it seems
that eventually the citizens of London were granted a charter of
self-government which entitled them to elect a local council and
to construct public buildings. This is shown by the discovery of
the remains of the Roman basilica, the town hall, and adjacent
to it the forum or public market-place.

From the seventeenth century onwards antiquaries have
wondered where the basilica and forum lay, believing that a
Roman city of this large size must have been self-governing and
administered from the *curia*, the council chamber, in a basilica
or forum. Various suggestions were made as to its location,
such as the site occupied by some massive Roman walls that
were found during rebuilding in Bush Lane, off Cannon Street,
just after the Great Fire of 1666; two centuries later, the anti-
quary Charles Roach Smith expressed the view that it might
have been situated in Clements Lane close to the spot where
part of an official Roman building inscription had been found
by labourers constructing a new sewer. These ideas proved to
be wrong when in 1923 Professor W. Lethaby positively
identified some massive Roman walls found about forty years
earlier under Leadenhall Market, off Gracechurch Street, as
the east end of the missing basilica.[1] Drawings of these walls
had remained undiscovered in Guildhall Library and in private
hands until just before 1915, when a copy of some of the details
was prepared for publication. The identification was confirmed
in 1928 when the Royal Commission on Roman London published its findings, and since then much more has been found.[2]

By the 1960s it was clear that the basilica and forum together
formed a huge block of buildings about 152 m square; and it
seemed that by the end of the first century London had completely recovered from Boudica's destruction, and had become
the capital of the province of Britain, with an enormous forum
and basilica to match its status. Just as specialists were becoming used to this idea, the remains of an older public building came to light under the forum, which recent discoveries
have shown was an earlier but much smaller basilica and
forum, apparently also dating from the late first century A D.[3]

This discovery meant that ideas about the later stage of the
second and larger forum, as well as the status of Londinium in

Opposite, planned streets and
public buildings characterize
the Flavian city, and the
burials lay beyond the city
limits at that time. The map
shows that the main
archaeological discoveries
have occurred in the western
half of the city away from the
Roman city centre around
the forum.

the late first century, had to be reconsidered to take account of the new information.

The identification of this first basilica and forum was something of a surprise for two main reasons: firstly, it was in use at a time when both the Governor and Procurator apparently had their headquarters in London, and yet its small size contrasts with what one might expect in a provincial capital; and secondly, its size is in such striking contrast to the second basilica and forum, which was more than five times larger, that it is hard to believe that London could have had two such contrasting forum buildings. In spite of this, the identification of the first basilica and forum has solved an increasing number of problems that gradually developed as more and more discoveries in recent years could not be fitted into a coherent forum pattern. One of these, for example, was a strange set of brick piers, near the entrance to the second forum, which now seem to belong to a reconstruction or addition to the first forum.[4]

The general picture that emerges of London in the late first century is that, as trade was booming throughout the Empire in the 70s, the increasing wealth of London brought an influx of people and a rapid expansion of the city. Under the governorship of Agricola (AD 78–84) a particularly positive effort was made to develop the towns in Britain, and the building of fora about this time indicates that several towns, such as Chichester, Winchester, Silchester, Exeter and Cirencester, were constituted as capitals of self-governing communities; and an inscription from the forum at Verulamium definitely shows that he was responsible for its dedication.[5]

Since the first basilica in London seems to have been built at about this time, it may be inferred that Londinium too received self-governing status, perhaps as a *municipium*, in recognition of the status of its inhabitants. Regarding Britain generally Agricola's biographer and son-in-law Tacitus wrote, 'Agricola gave private encouragement and official assistance to the building of temples, fora, and private mansions', with the result that the native population grew enthusiastic about becoming Roman citizens, and in addition to having 'a passion to command' the Latin tongue, 'our national dress came into favour and the toga was everywhere to be seen. And so', adds Tacitus, 'the Britons were gradually led on to the amenities that make vice agreeable – arcades, baths and sumptuous banquets. They spoke of such novelties as "civilization", when really they were only a feature of enslavement.' This is reflected in London by the discovery of temples, baths and fine houses, as well as evidence that education was such that even artisans could write in Latin. But pride of place went to the new forum that was built on the site of the old market-place beside the main street.

The Roman town council met in the *curia*, or council chamber, that was usually to be found in or close to the basilica and forum. They built or authorized such public buildings as the basilica, forum, baths and temples, while at the same time they were expected to construct roads, and even to regulate industries. Revenue for this came from various sources such as taxes on goods entering the town and on rents paid by tenants occupying such council property as the shops in the forum. The responsibility of the town council extended beyond the limits of the town into the surrounding *territorium*, and this region no doubt included the industrial area on top of Ludgate hill around the site of modern St Paul's Cathedral, where potters and metal- and leatherworkers operated, as well as the region across the Thames where Southwark Cathedral now stands. Since industries often needed running water, metal- and leatherworkers were also permitted to operate close to the town centre along the banks of the Walbrook stream close to the modern Bank of England and Mansion House.[7]

By the 80s and 90s Londinium was a vigorous town of merchants, shopkeepers and manufacturers reacting to the generally rising prosperity by trying to satisfy the aspirations and demands of the new province for consumer and luxury goods. Because of their international contacts, many of the traders had no doubt come from across the English Channel and from provinces around the Mediterranean and Aegean basins – people like Aulus Alfidius Olussa from Athens, who died in London at the age of seventy before the end of the first century, and was probably buried in the same cemetery as Julius Classicianus, north of the present Tower of London.[8] It was Roman citizens like him who probably served on the first town council.

The first basilica and forum with an area of 5459 sq. m was small compared with others in Britain. The basilica and forum complex at Silchester, near Reading, for example, was 8455 sq. m in area, while that of Verulamium covered 18,415 sq. m.

Just outside the forum in London there was also a small municipal classical temple standing on a low podium, which was clearly part of the whole complex of public buildings.[9] The basilica was only 104.5 m long and 52.7 m wide, which contrasts with the enormous but coeval basilica at Cirencester, a tribal centre, where the corresponding measurements were 167.6 m and 103.6 m.

The basilica in London was also small, considering that it served the dual role of town hall for public meetings, and law court from which local justice was administered. It lay along one side of the forum square or piazza, while shops and offices of the forum formed the other three sides.

Tombstone of Aulus Alfidius Olussa from Athens, found in 1852 on Tower Hill. Height 2 m.

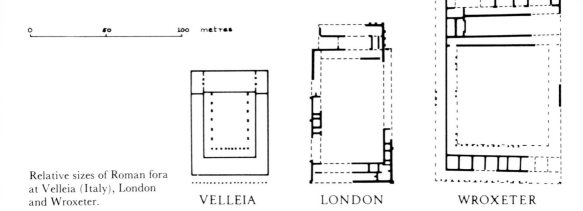

Relative sizes of Roman fora at Velleia (Italy), London and Wroxeter.

VELLEIA   LONDON   WROXETER

Judging from what is known of Roman town councils elsewhere, particularly in Spain where parts of actual town charters have been found, it is clear that the council, the *ordo*, was composed of up to 100 councillors who qualified for election to office on a wealth and property basis. Each year the council appointed two pairs of magistrates from among their number to act somewhat as a chief executive does today, overseeing council meetings and minor legal and judicial matters. Fortunately, a description of an example of an actual situation that could have resulted in a hearing was found some years ago in the waterlogged filling of a first-century well on the site of Temple House in Queen Victoria Street. This site lay close to the west bank of the Walbrook stream, where a wooden writing tablet was found on which were preserved traces of ink letters. Photographs in infra-red light deepened the contrast which enabled this letter to be partly read.

It had been written by someone at Durobrivae (Rochester) to someone in London (Londinii), giving details of how a boy, perhaps a slave, had run away with a waggon that had been entrusted to him.[10] The outcome of the situation is not known, but had this developed into a serious criminal, or major financial case, involving, say, murder, it could not have been dealt with by the civic authorities; instead, it would have been remitted for trial in the Governor's assize court.

It was through the system of local administration that the Roman government gained the loyalty of the wealthy ruling classes and spread the cost of government on to the shoulders of the local population. But it was partly because a considerable number of towns and other communities in Britain had been granted self-government during the last twenty years of the first century, that it was necessary to appoint a law officer, the *legatus iuridicus*, to assist the Governor in tackling the extra legal and judicial work involved. An inscription found in Walbrook street suggests that he may have been based in London, presumably close to the Governor's headquarters.[11]

The basilica in London had a simple layout somewhat like that of a church, comprising a large central hall with a raised dais or *tribunal* at the east end where the magistrates presided over meetings; on each side of the nave a row of columns or brick arches separated the nave from the side aisles. It was different from other buildings in Britain in that its adminstrative offices, including the town treasury and the prison, were not placed next to one of its aisles. Instead it resembled a Continental basilica, where the administrative offices, including the *curia* or council chamber, were sometimes to be found in the forum, or even possibly elsewhere in the town.

The forum was an impressive building probably with a portico of columns supporting a tiled roof on the south side which fronted the main street of the city, and behind this there was a range of shops and offices. The entrance archway probably lay in the middle of this south wing, and gave access to the long rectangular open courtyard with the basilica along the far end. To the right and left were rows of shops possibly with porticos in front, providing shoppers with welcome shelter from the winter weather.

The length of the entire basilica and forum complex was exactly twice its width. As this elongated type of forum was like those at Wroxeter and Leicester, and unlike the square fora at

Suggested reconstruction of the first Roman forum and basilica beside the main street of Londinium, and also the adjacent small classical temple.

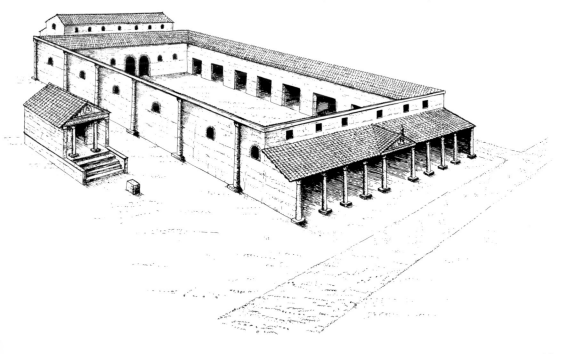

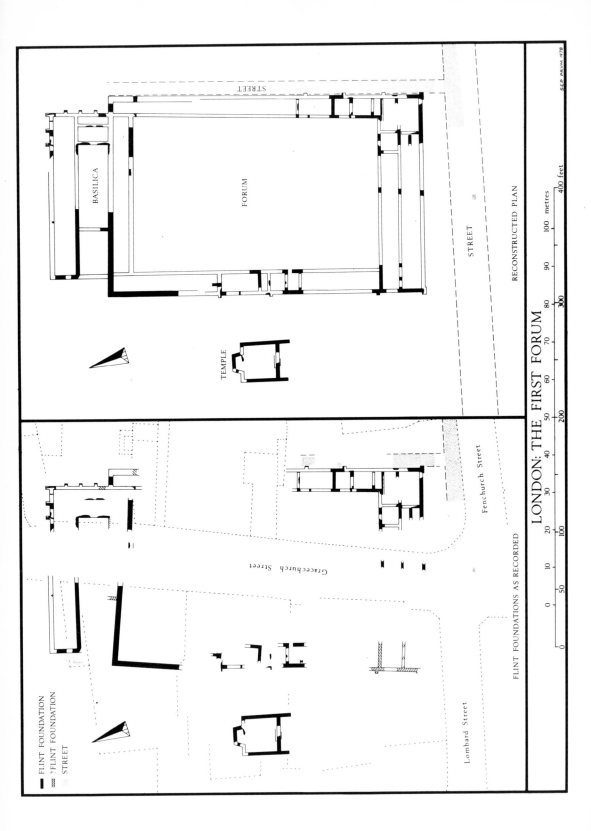

LONDON: THE FIRST FORUM

FLINT FOUNDATIONS AS RECORDED

RECONSTRUCTED PLAN

Silchester and Caerwent, it might have had a path or avenue crossing the courtyard, such as was apparently a feature of some of the elongated fora in Gaul. Although no clear evidence of this path has been found in London, that it once existed is suspected from the position of the temple just outside the middle of the west wing, and from the butt end of a wall in the west wing of the forum at that point, indicating a former side entrance.

Traces of gravel streets have been found around all four sides of the forum, and apart from the main street bounding the south wing, the only other street about which we have full details is that to the east of the forum. When this was discovered in 1968 it was found to be no more than 3.3 m wide; it seems, too, that in all the long time it had been in existence, it was never resurfaced. Clearly, therefore, it was a road that was not much used.[12]

These streets are crucial to our understanding of the remains of the first basilica and forum, for they give the ground level of that period; below this level are the distinctively deep wall foundations of flint and brown mortar, while above are survivals of the bottoms of the walls themselves, built of ragstone with courses of tiles. Projecting into the edges of the roads was a succession of brick buttresses with deep foundations of flints and brown mortar. These existed only on the east, west and north sides of the basilica and forum, for the south side had the portico fronting the main east-west street. The buttresses perhaps supported pilasters, and reflect the degree of architectural pretension required by the wealthy traders of Roman London.

The date of the first forum has been the subject of careful scrutiny since 1968 when its south-east corner was excavated. It then seemed likely that the building had been constructed in the decade immediately following the destruction of AD 60; but in fact a study of the partly unpublished discoveries of 1934 shows that the south wall of the basilica had been built across an earlier rubbish pit in which was found pottery of the Flavian period (AD 69–96), and a coin almost certainly of the Emperor Vespasian which had been minted in AD 71.[13] How much later than this the basilica was built, is uncertain, though under the small north-south street to the east of the forum were found dumps of rubbish deposited to raise the land level for the new road, and in these was a large amount of closely dateable pottery, particularly samian ware, of the period AD 75–85.[14]

As the road was clearly part of the forum layout, and as it is unlikely that the rubbish had been dumped much before the forum was built, it seems reasonable to conclude that the date of this rubbish is in fact the same as the date of the forum, and that

Opposite, the basilica beside the first Roman forum seems to have comprised a nave, side aisles, and a tribunal at the east end. The forum may not have had an inner portico facing the courtyard, though a portico apparently fronted the main Roman street.

the Governor Agricola was possibly responsible for its construction.

The limits of Londinium before A D 70 are uncertain, but after that date the location of cemeteries provides a very important clue. According to Roman law it was unlawful to bury or burn the dead within the city and so cemetery sites were set aside just outside the towns. In London, several cemeteries have been found dating from the first century A D, particularly to the north of the present Tower of London, around Bishopsgate and to the north and west of St Paul's Cathedral. If one draws a line inside these cemeteries as a hypothetical boundary, the interesting fact emerges that the forum lies nearly in the middle of the enclosed area.[15] It seems therefore that the planners of the new self-governing town had decided to place the forum roughly in the centre. It is even possible that what was a boundary ditch may have been found recently to the north of Aldgate, on a line immediately in front of the later Roman city wall, and also just inside the wall on a site in Crutched Friars.[16] On the latter site the ditch was 2.4 m wide and 1.8 m deep, and was clearly too wide to have been used merely for drainage.

Within the town itself a major effort seems to have been made during the late first century to lay out a grid pattern of streets, not only by resurfacing the old main east-west street, but also by constructing new ones like the north-south road found just east of Milk Street,[17] and others found in King Street and Newgate Street. Built of hard rammed gravel metalling, occasionally mixed with cement to form a very hard concrete

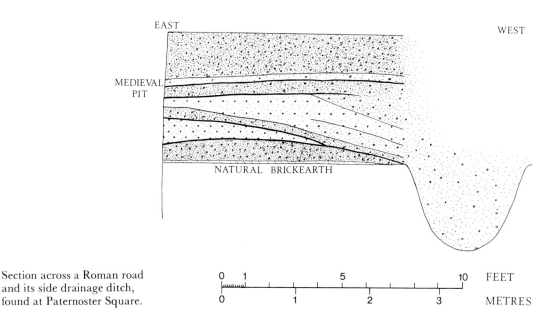

Section across a Roman road and its side drainage ditch, found at Paternoster Square.

surface, these roads were usually cambered to allow surface water to drain off into side ditches. Although traces of the road system have been discovered on various sites, the overall plan is still far from complete, and is complicated by the fact that the regular grid is broken around the forum, where there seems to have been a diagonal road crossing the main street, presumably leading from London Bridge northwards towards the site of Bishopsgate. This road probably lay on the west side of the forum where it caused the odd alignment, not only of the forum itself but also of buildings immediately to the south of it. In Roman towns there were usually two principal streets, the *decumanus maximus* and the *cardo maximus*, crossing each other at a right angle in the town centre where the forum lay. In Londinium the main east-west street under Lombard Street and Cheapside was the *decumanus*, and although the *cardo* has not yet been found, it presumably took the form of the missing diagonal road.

An important clue to the topography of Roman London is that the basic measurement used in planning its main street is now known to have been the *actus* (120 Roman feet, or 35.5 m). This was commonly used in land division in the planning of streets in new Roman towns in other parts of the Empire, and sometimes in dividing up the surrounding countryside to form land plots for retired soldiers to cultivate.[18] That the *actus* was used in London is shown by three facts: first, the early-second-century Roman fort at Cripplegate was positioned exactly 6 *actus'* north of the main east-west Roman street now under Cheapside; second, a grid 3 × 3.5 *actus'* square of land bounded by streets to form an *insula*, as it was called, has been discovered north of that main street under Cheapside and west of modern Milk Street; and third, the two parallel main east-west streets south of the forum, under Lombard Street and Eastcheap respectively, were also 3.5 *actus'* apart. Thus it seems likely that 3.5 *actus'* (124 m) was a basic module used in forming the street grid. Unfortunately, not all of Roman London was built on the same grid alignment, for, although little is yet known of the main streets south of Cheapside, the alignment of the Roman buildings there is different from those to the north of the Cheapside road. This is illustrated by a recent excavation at the south end of Bow Lane which has also shown how an *insula* was subdivided into individual house plots, each building being separated from its neighbour by narrow streets and paths. The walls of the buildings had been built from mud brick or puddled clay, usually filling in a timber frame, and then plastered over. In spite of the mud bricks the quality of the buildings was such that traces of eight mosaic floors were found, both plain and patterned, these being the earliest mosaics known in London.[19]

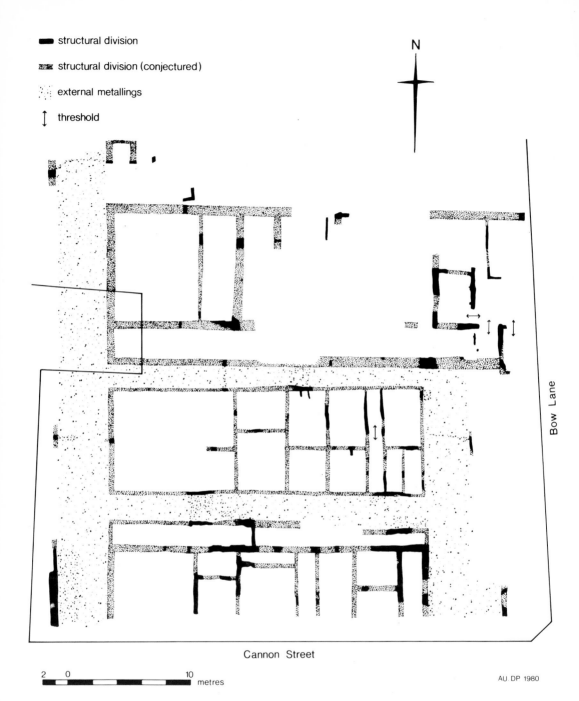

Temples were mentioned by Tacitus as one of the important signs of civilization, and Londinium had at least two before the end of the first century. Only one, that next to the forum, has been found; but the existence of a temple or shrine of Isis is known from a rough graffito scratched on the side of a jug of late-first-century date found in Southwark long ago.[20] *Londini ad fanum Isidis* (London at the temple or shrine of Isis) are the words which preserve one of the oldest known references to London, and they introduce a strange and sophisticated cult, a mystery religion which must reflect the cosmopolitan background of those first citizens of London, and might well have puzzled the comparatively simple Britons with the elements of mystery in the story of the goddess.

Central to the story is the search by Isis for the body of her brother and lover Osiris, killed by her other brother Set. Could the Britons understand the mystery of how Isis later brought Osiris back to life, and could they understand why her son Horus turned on her and cut off her head because she would not allow him to kill Set? This basic story underlay the religion that had originated at Philae in southern Egypt, spread to the cosmopolitan port of Alexandria, and then through traders and

Opposite, Roman houses destroyed in the Hadrianic fire of about AD 130. Found at the south end of Bow Lane in 1979, they are typical of town houses, two heavy corridors giving access to living rooms. The central house, without a corridor, was probably built after the corridor houses in a gravelled courtyard.

A graffito reference to a temple or shrine of Isis in London, on a late-first-century jug from Tooley Street, Southwark.

49

sailors to Greece and Rome. Eventually temples of Isis were to be found in Athens and Tithorea, near Delphi, in Greece; and in Italy in ordinary towns like Pompeii, and in Rome itself where Emperor Gaius Caligula built a temple in the Campus Martius. As trade spread so did the worship of Isis, and temples were built in Asia Minor, North Africa, Sardinia and Spain, and eventually northwards through Switzerland into Germany. Since Mediterranean traders, of whom Aulus Alfidius Olussa from Athens was probably one, were presumably operating in late-first-century London, it is not surprising that a temple or shrine of Isis should have been built so far from the homelands of the religion, and only half a century after Caligula built his temple in Rome.[21]

If the Britons in Roman London found it difficult to understand the belief that, just as Isis had given life to the scattered limbs of Osiris, so she might give life after death to those who worshipped her, they would have been more at home with Isis as a manifestation of the Great Mother, the creator of life, and therefore another form of the Mother Goddesses that were well-known to Celtic peoples in their own religion.

We do not know where the temple stood, but almost certainly it was not in Southwark where the jug was found. A possible site in the City is suggested by a massive stone altar of later Roman date, presumably from the same temple, that was recently found built into a late Roman defensive wall at Blackfriars.[22] Elsewhere in the City evidence of the religion has been found in the form of a bronze steelyard weight in the shape of Isis herself, of a clay statuette of Horus her son, and perhaps of three iron rattles or *sistra* that were an important element in the worship of the goddess.[23] Clearly the temple of Isis is one of the important monuments of Londinium that has yet to be discovered.

Although the temple built of tiles that Frank Cottrill found in 1934 next to the forum in Gracechurch Street was recognized long ago,[24] its importance remained obscure until recently when a careful study was made, for the first time in over forty years, of Cottrill's meticulous archaeological records. This has enabled us to identify it as a small classical temple standing on a low podium or platform, with a flight of steps leading up to the portico on its south side. This type of temple was rare in Britain because it represented a wholly Roman religion in a land where Celtic religion was particularly strong, and where the memory remained of the destruction in AD 60 of that other classical temple, the temple of Claudius at Camulodunum. Nevertheless, the type was common in other provinces of the Roman Empire, such as in Gaul and even in Dalmatia (modern Yugoslavia) where similar temples in the town of Doclea were found dedicated to Diana and to Dea Roma.[25]

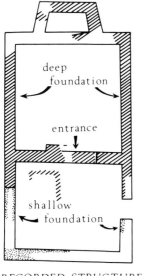

RECORDED STRUCTURE

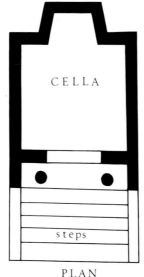

CELLA

steps

PLAN
RECONSTRUCTION

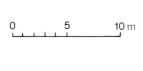

0   5   10 m

ELEVATION

Plan and suggested
reconstruction of the
first-century temple adjacent
to the first Roman forum.

Because the foundations of the temple in London had exactly
the same and unusual construction of flints and brown mortar
as those of the basilica and forum, there is little doubt that it
was planned as part of the new civic centre of late-first-century
Londinium. No trace of the dedication has been found, but it is
possible that it was sacred to the Imperial House and that the
temple would therefore have contained imperial statues and
other official civic dedications. The altar would not have lain
inside the temple but in an enclosure outside, near the foot of
the stairs where a forecourt of hard rammed gravel was found
on the site of Barclays Bank, Lombard Street, in 1961.[26] Unfortunately, the altar site could not be excavated and was
destroyed during rebuilding operations. The architectural
description of the temple is *distyle in antis*, which means that at
the top of the flight of steps there was originally a portico with
two columns, and behind them a doorway leading into the

Walls of tiles forming a corner inside the temple adjacent to the first forum.

sacred chamber, the *cella*, which, measuring about 8.5 sq. m, contained the principal cult image in an apse in the far wall.

This classical temple in London, like the basilica and forum, the temple or shrine of Isis and the quality and quantity of imported goods, yet again reflects the importance of Roman merchants probably from the Mediterranean region as the principal planners and builders of late-first-century Londinium. They were no doubt trying to build a city that would have the facilities and give them the life style that they were used to in their homelands: a town that Aulus Alfidius Olussa would recognize as home.

Tacitus classes public baths as 'an agreeable vice', and the fact that he listed them alongside temples underlines the view that cleanliness was indeed considered as next to godliness in Roman times. But the baths served the equally important function of a meeting place for a social occasion with friends, and Roman Londoners could probably boast having two such establishments before AD 100. The first of these was discovered in 1955 on the site of the Sun Life Assurance Offices in Cheapside opposite the church of St Mary-le-Bow, while the second was found in 1964 at Huggin Hill, on the north side of Upper Thames Street just west of Southwark Bridge.[27] Although frequently financed by private benefactors, public baths were usually the responsibility of the town council; for a small fee both rich and poor could use the facilities during daylight hours when the baths were open. Since the basic design of baths was the same all over the Roman Empire, a Greek trader, for example, could expect and find the same arrangements anywhere between London and Palestine. The baths were not like modern swimming baths with large pools of water, but instead like Turkish baths with rooms of varying degrees of heat, and with small baths of cold and hot water.

The usual procedure for visiting baths like those found in London was for the bather to enter the *palaestra*, the exercise court, which was sometimes surrounded by a colonnaded path where one could walk with friends, and where one could 'limber up' in the central area with one of the popular ball games. The next step was to enter the baths proper through the undressing room, the *apodyterium*, where clothes were stored in lockers or niches in a wall. It was but a short walk from here into the *frigidarium*, which, as the name suggests, was a cold room. Here exercise stimulated the circulation before the bather walked into the *tepidarium*, the warm room. Being farthest from the furnace which heated the baths, this room had a comfortable temperature from its underfloor heating, that must have been welcomed by the poorer folk who suffered at home during the cold, damp winter months. Next was the *caldarium*, the hot room, humid and steamy, with a small hot-water bath along one side. Here, when the skin pores were open, the bather scraped himself with a blunt sickle-shaped tool called a strigil to remove the sweat and dirt; and after a dip in the bath to wash himself he returned to the warm and cold rooms where, if he could afford it, he was massaged with perfumes. Olive oil stored in green glass flasks was rubbed into his skin to replace the lost natural oils before he at last took a dip in the cold water bath, the 'cold plunge', to close the pores. Finally, after a drink and a snack, the invigorated bather was ready to face the world again.

Men and women were eventually supposed to bath separately though this was not always the case. From time to time there were even scandals. In spite of this, public baths were immensely popular, as the first-century writer Seneca found to his cost when staying in a provincial town next to the *frigidarium* of a bath building.[28] His comments about the excessive noise were clearly written with great feeling, and probably reflect the usual happenings in the London baths. There were the grunts and wheezes of the man exercising with lead weights, the

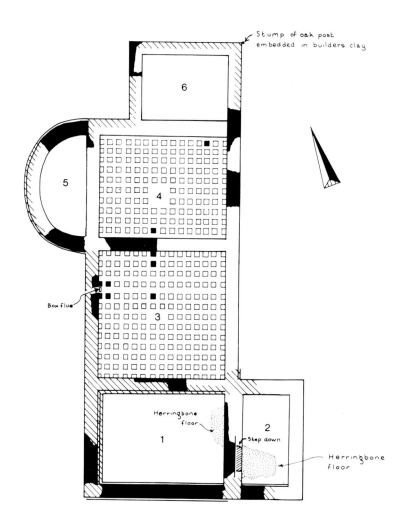

Stump of oak post
embedded in builders clay

6

5

4

Box flue

3

Herringbone
floor

1

Step down

2

Herringbone
floor

CHEAPSIDE BATH–HOUSE

PHASE 1   (FLAVIAN?)

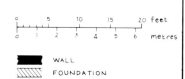

0   5   10   15   20 feet

0 1 2 3 4 5 6 metres

■ WALL

▨ FOUNDATION

■ ☐ PILAE FOUND & CONJECTURED

VKM, INH, PRVM. 1975.

changing sounds of the masseur's hands as he slapped and pummelled his victim, depending on whether they were flat or cupped, the shouts as a thief was chased through the building, and the man singing unmelodiously only to be interrupted by the great splashes of those who jump into the cold bath. Add to this the cries of the food vendors selling cakes, sausages and sweetmeats, and one has a picture of a lively establishment.

Because both the Cheapside and Huggin Hill baths were extensively rebuilt and enlarged during the second century there is only an outline of their original layout and little dating evidence, though such as there is shows that they were probably constructed before the end of the first century. Unfortunately, the bath in Cheapside has been completely destroyed so we shall never be able to check when it was built, but the Huggin Hill bath mostly survives, though still buried, and is now a protected ancient monument.

The Cheapside bath, a small building 21.6 m long and 13.7 m wide, was found at a depth of about 4 or 5 m where it lay beside a main north-south Roman street and just 30 m from the main east-west street of the Roman city which here partly lies beneath modern Cheapside. No trace of an exercise yard or an undressing room could be found, but as it was a small building it may not have had these separate facilities. Instead, the *frigidarium* could have served as a changing room even though it measured only 4.4 m by 6.2 m. Traces of red paint were found on the walls of this cold room, which at least gave an impression of warmth, while at the east end there was a step leading down into a small cold-water bath with a herringbone-pattern tiled floor, only 4.3 m long and 2.3 m wide. This cold bath could have been no more than about half a metre deep, so clearly the bather must have merely splashed himself to cool off rather than lying down in the water. After this, the bather entered the *tepidarium*, and beyond that the *caldarium* where the concrete floors rested on brick pillars, which allowed hot air from the furnace to circulate underneath. On the north side of the *caldarium* was a chamber measuring 3 m by 4.3 m that was probably a hot water bath, for it was heated by the main flue leading immediately from the furnace. Although small, the bath probably served the people entering Londinium along the main road to the west, and it is even possible that it was a privately owned venture, perhaps attached to an inn situated between the bath and the main street where traces of another Roman building have been found.[29]

The Huggin Hill baths were built on a much larger scale on terraces dug deeply into the hillside overlooking the Thames, where a constant flow of clear spring water fed the baths. Little of its original plan has been identified as it was so extensively

Opposite, plan of Cheapside bath house 1, *frigidarium*; 2, cold water bath; 3, *tepidarium*; 4, 5, *caldarium*; 6, hot water bath.

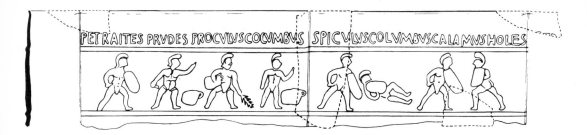

PETRAITES PRVDES PROCVLVSCOCVMBVS SPICVLVSCOLVMBVSCALAMVSHOLES

Gladiatorial decoration on a glass cup from Southwark.

rebuilt later, but its size can be gauged by the fact that its cold bath measured 5.87 m by 3 m and was entered by a flight of steps, and its *caldarium*, 8.2 m wide and over 11 m long, was more than three times larger than that in the Cheapside baths. This large building clearly required a considerable staff of public slaves, attendants, stokers and maintenance men, all of whom would have been organized by an agent (*conductor*) employed by the town council.

Roman London, like other major towns, probably had at least one more public building, an amphitheatre, where on certain days gladiators entertained the population by fighting either each other or wild animals. The amphitheatre is likely to have been built on the outskirts of the city, but in spite of its size it has proved difficult to find because, even though large and expensive, it probably had few stone walls. Judging from amphitheatres found elsewhere in Britain, it presumably had a large, oval, sandy or gravelled arena surrounded by a high earth bank provided with tiers of seats for the spectators. A wooden or stone barricade will have separated the spectators from the arena, while an external wall no doubt supported the back of the embankment. Travelling groups of gladiators, with their wild animals, such as bulls, bears and wild boars, together with acrobats, wrestlers and boxers, would parade in the arena before drawing lots and commencing the games. One such troupe that may have been popular in first-century Britain included Petraites, Prudes, Proculus, Cocumbus, Spiculus, Columbus, Celamus and Holes, who were all represented with crested helmets on glass cups; three such cups have been found, in London in Cheapside, Cornhill and Southwark, others at Colchester, Leicester and Wroxeter, and on sites in France, Germany and Spain.[30] Gladiators like these fought each other with sword and shield, while others were armed with only a net and a trident, and it is likely that the three-pronged point of an iron trident found long ago in Stoney Street, Southwark, was used in the arena.[31]

The shows in the amphitheatre, usually freely open to the townspeople, were often financed by city councillors or magistrates to celebrate their holding office or entering the council;

for this reason it was essential that those who held civic responsibilities were wealthy men. It is difficult to believe that Londinium did not conform to the usual pattern of western cities of
the Roman Empire in having an amphitheatre, and it is likely
that it was built in the late first or early second century, like
most amphitheatres in Britain. It therefore remains another
major monument of Roman London that has yet to be found;
like the other public buildings, it will have been administered
by the town council from the basilica and forum which have
been so recently identified under Gracechurch Street.

Lead curse on Tretia Maria found in Telegraph Street.

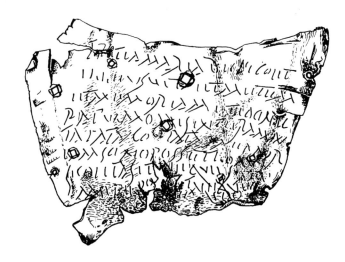

Fragments of wooden writing tablets, found in Lothbury, describing (1) an oath or promise, (2) part of a deed concerning Crescens, and (3) the sale of an object from a shop, and the construction of a ship.

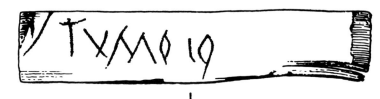

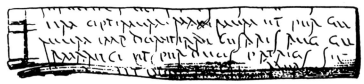

1

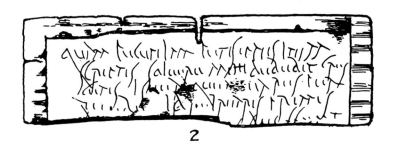

2

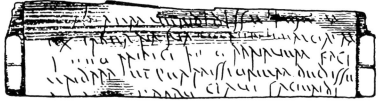

3

The people of early Roman London

A scrap of lead found on a building site near Moorgate in 1934 has revealed a curious situation in the private lives of two people living in Londinium eighteen centuries ago. The lead has Latin words scratched on its surface, conveying a message that transcends the centuries:

I curse Tretia Maria and her life and mind and memory and liver and lungs, mixed up together, and her words, thoughts and memory; thus may she be unable to speak what things are concealed, nor be able . . . nor . . .

Could it be that 'Tretia Maria' was a blackmailer? Certainly her secret had placed her memory, and power of speech, in grave danger. With the magical number of seven nails, the lead sheet had been fastened face downwards, with the writing hidden, to a wooden surface, perhaps of a shrine standing beside Walbrook stream where it was found, and from then on the writer no doubt hoped that the gods would silence her.[1]

Throughout the Roman Empire, society was stratified like the layers of an archaeological site, and Tretia Maria, was presumably a Roman citizen. She had certain privileges: if she was a married woman, her marriage would have been recognized in Roman law, and her family prosperity and the inheritance rights of her children would have been protected. She and her husband would have been able to enter into contracts with other Roman citizens that would have been legally binding in Roman courts. Fortunately part of such a contract, although nearly 2,000 years old, has been found in London preserved in the peat and waterlogged mud of the Walbrook stream. Originally incised with a pointed stylus on the now decayed waxed surface of a wooden writing tablet, the writer had scratched the wood surface beneath sufficiently clearly to show the Latin script: '. . . which money by the terms likewise of the claim shall be paid to me by Crescens or by the person concerned . . .'[2] It is interesting that such a document should have been found in the heart of the business centre of modern London.

Roman citizens, are known by the style of their names inscribed on tombstones, writing tablets, pots and so on; and although some were wealthy merchants, and government officials like Julius Classicianus, most were probably of more modest means. These included the considerable number of soldiers serving on the Governor's headquarters staff, like the legionary centurion Sempronius Sempronianus, as well as local traders and specialists in various professions like Publius Julius Sura, a leather merchant, and Gaius Silvius Tetricus, an oculist. Others were poor, such as Lucius Aelius Festus, who had scratched his name on such a treasured possession as an ordinary samian ware cup.[3]

It was from the wealthy Roman citizens that the rulers of Londinium, the magistrates and town councillors, were drawn. Since there was no substantial indigenous population, it is likely that during the first century the settler families from abroad held much of the land and controlled most of the trade, but during the second century the native landowners and traders may have tended to dominate the scene. This could explain the flourishing later Roman economy in Britain, which was increasingly based upon British manufactured goods, and the general spreading of Roman culture. In Londinium it is possible tentatively to identify the homes of some wealthy residents because they were at least partly built of stone, Kentish ragstone, brought by ship from quarries on the river Medway, near modern Maidstone, since there is no local building stone near London. Although their building plans are usually incomplete, what is known so closely resembles parts of Roman town houses found elsewhere in Britain that it can be assumed they had the normal layout of living rooms, bedrooms and kitchen at ground level, in one or more wings opening off a corridor which probably overlooked a courtyard or garden. Two of the houses recently excavated in Bow Lane were of this type.

One of the more substantial buildings lay south of the forum and was found in 1956 in Plough Court, off Lombard Street; another was found in 1880 just north-east of the forum under a later Roman road, and all that was recorded was a plastered wall of ragstone with courses of tiles, and beside it a floor of tiles laid in herringbone pattern;[4] and a third building, some distance away from the forum, was found in 1974 on the site of St Mildred's church, Bread Street, where a range of rooms, one with a pink mortar floor, was discovered probably behind a corridor.[5]

Little of the interior decoration of these houses has survived, but a clue to the type of wall paintings used at that time was found in a dump of building debris containing only late-first-century pottery, which overlay the Bread Street building.[6] Dozens of fragments of painted wall plaster from the interior were sufficient to show that one of the walls had a white background, upon which there was probably painted a large rectangular panel bordered by narrow green lines. A corner of the panel survived and in it was a scroll design of green leaves and red flowers painted over a blue-green background, giving a colourful and attractive design.

Judging from the extensive areas of late-first and early-second-century occupation rubbish in the City where no trace has been found of buildings with stone walls, it seems that Londinium at that time consisted mostly of timber-framed buildings with wattle-and-daub and mud-brick walls resting on timber foundations. Unless one of these buildings was destroyed by fire, it would leave little trace other than a scatter of painted wall plaster over its floors of clay, concrete and sometimes mosaic. About A D 130 such a major city fire occurred leaving a thick and extensive layer of burnt daub-and-mud brick, but traces of individual late-first-century building fires have also been found from time to time, particularly at Nos 143–147 Cannon Street and No. 7 King Street.[7]

Accidental losses such as these give us valuable clues to the lives of the citizens of Londinium, and could explain why a hoard of silver coins was buried about A D 80, at a time of comparative peace, close to the west bank of the Walbrook stream. The hoard was found by a Polish labourer in 1958 about 4.9 m below street level on the site of Temple House in Queen Victoria Street. The workman thought that the coins were a 'nest of buttons' and happily shared the collection with his workmates until someone realized what they were. The seventy-four coins that were surrendered comprised a remarkable collection ranging in date from 130 B C to A D 78–79, and included issues of Julius Caesar, Mark Antony, and the Emperors Tiberius and Claudius. In fact fifty-one coins were earlier than the invasion of A D 43, which would indicate that the hoard may have been the savings of several generations of a Roman settler family, perhaps hidden at a time of personal crisis, after which the owner was unable to recover the hoard.[8]

Seldom have the finds from Roman London been so spectacular. Apart from the usual household goods, such as crockery, cutlery, lamps, door hinges, keys and even locks reflecting how people lived, various items of dress, jewellery and cosmetics have been uncovered indicating how people, particularly the women, were dressed. Leather shoes and sandals, sometimes carefully decorated and even bearing the cobbler's stamp, are frequently found, but other garments rarely. More common are the dress and hair fittings. Hairpins of bone and bronze are particularly prevalent, and some are beautifully decorated; two, for example, show the bust of a Roman lady with her hair piled high in the style of the period, and wearing a tiara-like decoration on top. Combs of wood and bone are sometimes found, but the bronze mirrors used by Roman ladies are very rare indeed. Finger rings are among the most interesting objects, not merely because they were commonly of bronze, iron, and occasionally of gold, but because they sometimes held stone or glass inserts decorated with various deities and figures from mythology: such as Sol, the sun god; Mars, god of war; Theseus holding a sword; and Diana, goddess of hunting.

Green glass beads from necklaces appear frequently, but the neck ornament called a *torc*, like a huge bracelet, used by British women, is uncommon. One of the most beautiful antiquities yielded by a London site was part of a Roman necklace of gold with emeralds, recently found in Cannon Street.

Brooches, dress hooks, buckles and manicure sets are among the objects that are found, particularly in the Walbrook stream; there are also small pottery bottles, originally containing cosmetics, from which ointments and powders were extracted by a long narrow spoon whose rounded end was used for mixing the powders on a small stone palette.

There were three classes of people in Londinium apart from Roman citizens – the free, the freed and the slaves. The native Britons, who were free but had none of the special rights of a Roman citizen, were known as *peregrini*, and probably formed the bulk of the population, filling such jobs as local craftsmen, shopkeepers and even farm labourers. Small-time local manufacturers sometimes stamped their names on their products; hence we know that among this class were the cobblers Burdonius, Sammicus and Verus, all of whom were possibly based on the banks of the Walbrook where their rubbish was found, close to the site of the present Mansion House. Aprilis and

Austalis graffito on a tile from Warwick Square.

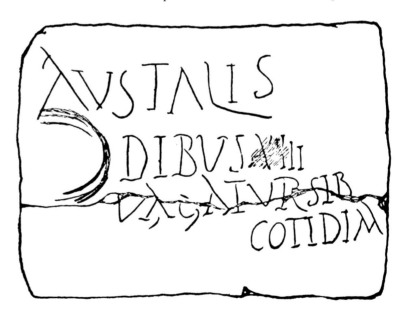

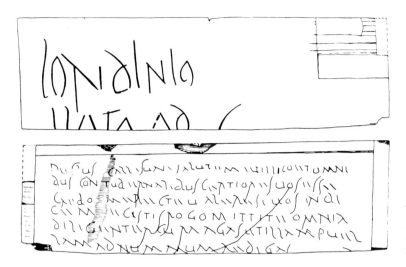

Wooden writing tablet of
Rufus, son of Callisunus,
apparently sent to an address
in London (Londinio).

Titulus made tools, while Basilius was a cutler. Undoubtedly
the most interesting personality in this class was Austalis, who
worked in a tile factory perhaps not far from modern St Paul's
cathedral. He had upset one of his workmates who, thanks to
Roman education, was able to express his feelings in positive
and lasting terms. In large capital letters he wrote with a stick
on a tile before it was fired in a kiln, the Latin words 'Austalis
has been going off by himself every day these last thirteen
days!'[9] Absenteeism is clearly no new problem, and ironically
the tile was dug up near Old Bailey, on a site close to the
Central Criminal Court.

The ordinary free people could be quite wealthy, as is known
from a letter written on a wooden tablet by Rufus, son of
Callisunus, to his bailiff in London about selling a slave girl,
perhaps because he was moving out of Londinium. Certainly
the letter was written from elsewhere as it was addressed on the
back to 'Londinio'. The letter began:

Rufus, son of Callisunus: greetings to Epillicus and all his fellows.
You know me to be very well I believe. If you have the list please send.
Carefully look after everything. See that the girl thou turnest into
money...[10]

Epillicus was probably a slave, and represents a notable part of
the population of Londinium in the first and second centuries.
Another possible slave is represented by the leather trunks of a
young girl acrobat or dancer that were found in a first-century
well on the site of the Bank of London and South America in
Queen Street. Originally laced up on both hips, one side was
found still fastened with a 'granny knot'. The other objects
recovered from this well included a ladder more than 4.2 m

63

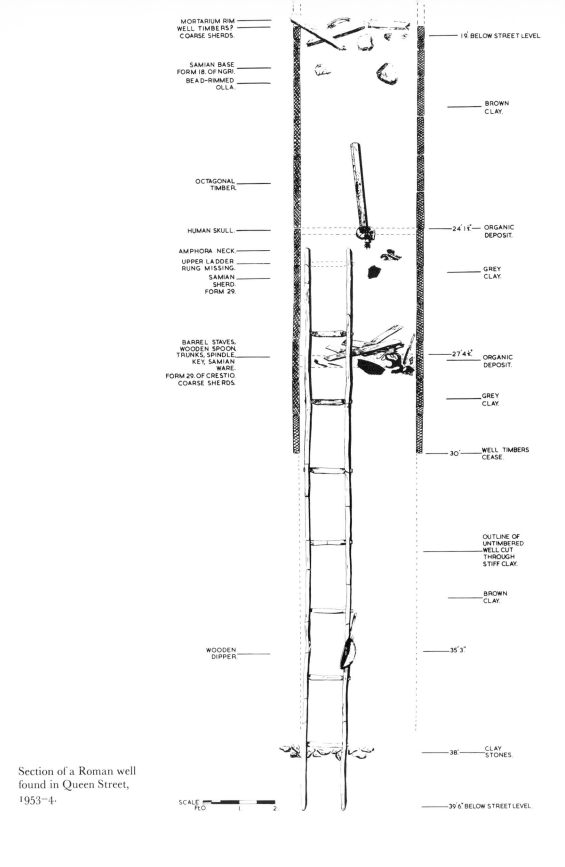

MORTARIUM RIM
WELL TIMBERS?
COARSE SHERDS.

SAMIAN BASE
FORM 18. OF NGRI.
BEAD-RIMMED
OLLA.

OCTAGONAL
TIMBER.

HUMAN SKULL.

AMPHORA NECK.
UPPER LADDER
RUNG MISSING.
SAMIAN
SHERD.
FORM 29.

BARREL STAVES,
WOODEN SPOON,
TRUNKS, SPINDLE,
KEY, SAMIAN
WARE.
FORM 29. OF CRESTIO.
COARSE SHERDS.

WOODEN
DIPPER.

19'. BELOW STREET LEVEL

BROWN
CLAY.

24'1½"— ORGANIC
DEPOSIT.

GREY
CLAY.

27'4½"— ORGANIC
DEPOSIT.

GREY
CLAY.

30'— WELL TIMBERS
CEASE.

OUTLINE OF
UNTIMBERED
WELL CUT
THROUGH
STIFF CLAY.

BROWN
CLAY.

35'3"

38'— CLAY
STONES.

Section of a Roman well
found in Queen Street,
1953–4.

SCALE
Ft.O.   1   2

39'6" BELOW STREET LEVEL.

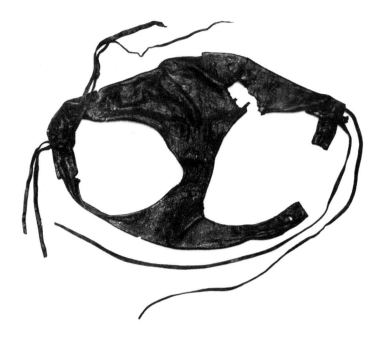

Leather 'bikini'-type trunks
from a first-century well
found in Queen Street,
1953–4.

long, a wooden bowl with a handle, and a human skull with a post rammed through its side.

Although these slaves were owned by their masters, their safety was protected by law, ill-treatment being a punishable offence. In fact it was illegal to force a slave either into immoral ways or to fight in the arena, and when a slave was old or sick the master was responsible for his care. Nevertheless, a slave who might run away could be restrained and an iron shackle from the Walbrook shows how this was done. But not all slaves were given menial tasks and, as the letter from Callisunus to Epillicus shows, the relationship between master and slave could be a pleasant one. Many slaves were therefore educated and responsible people, like Anencletus who, as a slave of the Provincial Council, seems to have worked in an administrative office in Londinium.[11] A slave could buy his freedom, but then his former master became his patron watching over his affairs, in return for which the freed man was required by law to render certain services. One of these was to ensure the proper burial of his former master, as a tombstone of Purbeck marble from Bishopsgate shows. The burial was of the centurion Sempronius Sempronianus and his two brothers, and 'his freedmen had this [gravestone] set up for their well deserving patrons'.[12]

Until recently little was known about the homes of the more humble folk of Roman London, but excavations have now revealed parts of the many clay and timber-framed buildings in

Southwark that crowded around the south end of the Roman London Bridge. Most were no doubt houses, and some even shops, especially as there is little evidence of industrial activity among the local population. But of special interest has been the study of the animal bones which, apart from reflecting the diet, show that the people of Roman Southwark preferred dogs as pets, and had very few cats. None of the dogs quite resembled any modern breed, though their sizes did range from that of today's terrier to the labrador.

It is in the study of the contents of Roman rubbish pits and dumps that some of the major advances in knowledge have occurred, and at last we are beginning to determine the diet of Roman Londoners. With a large town population to feed in the late first and early second centuries, agriculture was organized on a massive scale, backed up by a considerable fishing industry and by the import of specialist foods such as figs, grapes and olives, all of which have been found.[13] In the City various agricultural tools have been discovered in the Walbrook valley where they may have been made for sale to farmers living in the countryside. Hoes and mattocks were used for clearing the ground before cultivation, while a ploughshare, the iron tip of a wooden plough, indicates the planting of crops. The ploughs were no doubt pulled by oxen whose bones are very common in rubbish dumps, and iron goads, spikes fastened to sticks, were used to urge the animals along. Sickles were used to reap the crops when they were ripe, pruning hooks, curved blades on the ends of long poles, to trim fruit trees. In addition to major crops like wheat, other vegetables were produced which needed more individual care, and for this, wooden spades with iron edges and rakes with iron spikes were used. Curiously, a hand-dug garden bed has actually been found in Warwick Square, close to St Paul's, where a row of deep spade cuts into the natural brickearth edged the bed, while beyond where the person digging the edge would have been standing there was a concentration of root holes from the cultivated plants.[14] This example of gardening in the late first and early second centuries is so far unique in London, but it does show how and where such market-garden plants as cabbages, carrots and cucumbers, traces of which have been found, could have been produced. The seeds of other plants have also been found in London, many no doubt locally grown and others clearly imported. The list is impressive: apples, blackberries, raspberries, strawberries, cherries, plums, mulberries, dill, millet, coriander and walnuts. A single well-preserved pit of the late second century in Southwark contained a particularly impressive list: fig, raspberry, blackberry, plum, cherry, damson, apple or pear, cabbage, peas, lentils, coriander, mustard and dill.[15]

Spade cuts into the natural brickearth at Warwick Square formed the edge of a garden bed (left) of the late first century.

Meat from cattle, sheep and pigs, like grain, was a major part of the diet of the townspeople. As in later times, the animals were presumably driven from the farms to Londinium, and, perhaps after being fattened up for a short while on the outskirts of the town, they were slaughtered there. The debris from a slaughterhouse has been found in a pit at Aldgate beside the road to Camulodunum,[16] while 47 lambs' skulls were found in a ditch in Southwark close to the junction of roads leading from Sussex and Kent. It is only in Southwark that a major study of Roman animal bones has so far been completed, though a similar study is in progress in the City. Of 452 animals represented by the bones from Southwark, it has been found that over 80 per cent were of domesticated livestock, and that cattle, sheep and pig predominated, whereas domestic fowl were relatively scarce. The remaining creatures, red deer, roe deer, hare, wild boar, badger and woodcock, were all hunted but were not very important in the local diet. But because a high percentage of the cattle and sheep were adult before being slaughtered, they had obviously been useful in the economy, as draught animals pulling waggons and as providers of milk and wool; and although there is little evidence of these benefits, dairy products in general and milk in particular must have been of outstanding importance.[17] From the archaeological evidence there is little trace of this other than a pottery cheese press from the City and several baby's feeding bottles made of pottery.

This varied diet was supplemented by seafood; all Roman sites in Britain, including London, however far from the sea, produce an abundance of oyster shells showing that the farming, distribution and sale of oysters was one of the major, but least studied, industries of Roman Britain. Mussel shells are rarely found in Roman London and, like oysters, each shell represents a small amount of actual food compared with, say, a fish. Fish bones are notoriously difficult to find because they are so small and thin. Recently, however, appreciable quantities have been recovered, indicating the existence of a major sea- and river-fishing industry which brought fresh herring, mackerel, smelt, eel, plaice or flounder and even pike and dace to London.[18]

As a major international Roman port of the late first and early second centuries, Londinium no doubt made the import and export of goods its main source of income in an entrepôt trade aimed at supplying other cities of Britain along the excellent road system, and by sea along the coast. It is no wonder, therefore, that the provincial administration, especially the Procurator who controlled finance, settled there to monitor trade. But also many local service industries and trades developed both in the town and in the surrounding countryside to serve the merchants and government officials, and these too are represented by the finds. Rubbish pits of the period AD 60–130 usually contain evidence reflecting this most vital period in the history of Londinium, where fragments of wine jars from as far afield as Rhodes and Palestine are found with local cooking pots from Highgate and Brockley Hill. In fact wines, olive oil and even much valued fish-sauce from the Mediterranean were evidently an important part of the daily life of London. A fairly typical rubbish pit of late-first-century date was found some years ago on the site of Gateway House in Watling Street, containing a quantity of locally made kitchen cooking pots and tableware, together with samian ware from Gaul, and parts of amphorae from southern Spain, Italy and Palestine.[19] Elsewhere in London just a few sherds of North African red ware, probably from Tunisia, have been found; these, however, are too few to represent trade goods, and were perhaps the personal possessions of traders from Mediterranean lands who were working in Londinium for a while.[20]

For less than a century, therefore, the life style of Londinium somewhat resembled that of a classical city, where before AD 79 it was even possible to buy red-slipped kitchen cooking dishes which had been made within sight of Vesuvius. Detailed analysis of the volcanic minerals in these dishes has shown that the industry was probably based around Pompeii and Herculaneum; hence it would have been no surprise to the citizens of Londinium, on learning from traders that Vesuvius had erupted in 79 and buried the two cities, that the dishes would no longer be available in their shops.

Pompeian-red ware was just one of London's many small-scale Mediterranean imports. By good fortune the probable site of a shop that sold another commodity, wine, has been found. An excavation immediately east of the entrance to Cannon Street Station revealed rubbish pits of the period AD 60–80, in which there was such a concentration of amphora fragments that we may assume a shop had stood adjacent to this spot fronting on to the main east-west Roman road beneath Cannon Street. Parts of about ten amphorae from southern Spain were found, together with five or six from Italy, three or four from the Greek island of Rhodes, one from southern Gaul, and one from Palestine.[21] There was clearly a complex administration involved in getting the wines from the vineyards in Spain and elsewhere to the shops in Londinium, but of this we know little except for the rough scratches or inked inscriptions that are sometimes found on amphorae. For example a date was written on one, V(KAL A)PRILIS (5 April), while on another is recorded the quantity, M VIIS VIMI ($7\frac{1}{2}$ measures of wine). But wine also arrived in wooden barrels nearly 2 m high and made of fir probably from Spain. It is thanks to their reuse in London as linings for wells, their tops and bottoms having been knocked out, that they have survived.[22]

Roman well comprising a square frame and reused barrels, found in Lime Street.

Bronze figure of an archer found in Queen Street. Height 280 mm.

Other trade imports included an enormous quantity of red glossed samian ware, mostly from Gaul and often decorated with a range of designs from the rural to the blatantly erotic. Glass, too, was imported in considerable quantities from as far away as Italy and Syria, one of the finest glass vessels found being a two-handled cup probably from Syria. Pottery lamps from Gaul, millstones of basalt lava from Mayen in Germany, bronze tableware from Italy, and even amber from the Baltic for making jewellery, are all included in the many imports to Londinium before AD 150. Bronze statues such as the figure of an archer unearthed in Queen Street, and life-size figures that might have stood in the forum area, underline the quality of some possible imports.[23] Perhaps it is in the imported marbles that we can best see the range of trade, for rare fragments of high quality marbles used in building decoration had been imported from Synnada in Turkey, and from the Greek island of Paros, while the more ordinary marbles came from Carrara in Italy and from the Campan valley in the French Pyrenees.

Opposite above, glass bowl, imported from the eastern Mediterranean region, found in a rubbish pit of about AD 60–80, in Walbrook.

Opposite below, writing equipment from London, including inkwells, a pen, a seal box, wooden writing tablets and stili.

Goods of British origin also flooded into London: pottery from the nearby kilns at Brockley Hill and Highgate, and from Ludgate hill, lead from the Mendips, tin from Cornwall, and iron from the Weald of Kent and Sussex all contributed to the wealth of Londinium. With such a diverse trade, reading and writing were essential to commerce in London, and it is not surprising that commercial documents have been discovered.

In addition to the fragment of a wooden writing tablet found in the Walbrook stream, which records the payments of Crescens, another tablet records a formal oath or promise part of which reads: '... by Jupiter Best and Greatest, and by the Genius of His Imperial Majesty Domitian Conqueror of Germany, and by the Gods of our fathers ...' Yet another tablet has a reference to the purchase of something from a shop (taberna), and deals with an order to build a ship, the rudder in particular being mentioned.[24] A great deal of writing was by pen and ink both on parchment and on wooden tablets, and there are examples of pens as well as inkwells of pottery, glass and bronze, though these are rare. So many people could read and write, that an oculist in Gaul found it worth his while to advertise his eye ointment in London and elsewhere by having the base of samian ware cups manufactured in Gaul stamped L. IVL. SENIS. CROCOD. AD. ASPR. ('Lucius Julius Senis's ointment for roughness of the eyes'[25]). Perhaps it was possible to order the ointment through the samian ware importer.

Local businesses were aimed at producing goods and services. Though there is little evidence of the actual shops, a group of brick ovens just east of the forum may mark the site of a baker's shop;[26] and what appears to have been the rear living, storage and workshop rooms of timber-framed buildings with clay walls, possibly shops, were found in 1978 in Newgate Street.[27] Bread was clearly a major item in the diet of Roman Londoners, to judge from the frequent discoveries of millstones for grinding the grain. Although small handmills were sometimes used in homes to make flour, the bulk of flour production seems to have been on a commercial scale and centred around watermills using the flow of the Walbrook stream. Large millstones of German lava for watermills have been found on the site of Bucklersbury House in Walbrook street, and it was there that the site of what may have been a watermill was found in 1955. At one point near the middle of the site the revetted banks of the stream were found to narrow suddenly from a width of 4 m to 2.4 m, and a hollow in the stream bed at this point suggests that the resulting greater flow might have been used to turn a waterwheel.[28] But this was not the only type of commercial mill, for a large hourglass-shaped millstone has been found in Princes Street that was originally turned by a donkey. The mills used grain supplied by farms probably up to some considerable distance from the town, and it was necessary to store it in granaries. A building which may have been used for this purpose was found in Fenchurch Street in 1923, and although the walls were built of bricks, its floor was possibly ventilated from underneath by being raised up on a series of low supporting walls.[29]

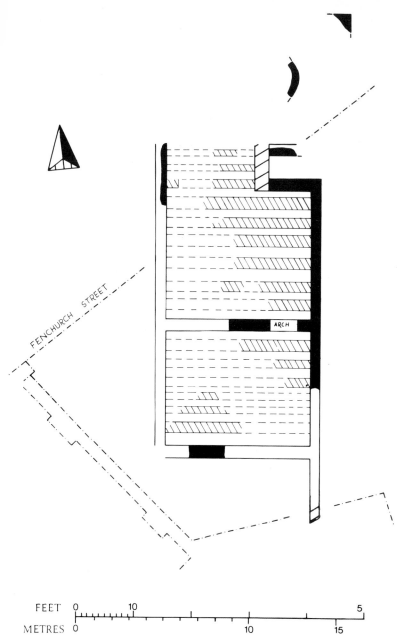

FENCHURCH STREET

ARCH

FEET 0   10   5
METRES 0   10   15

Plan of a Roman building, possibly a granary, found in Fenchurch Street in 1923. The many cross-walls supported a raised floor.

Tools of many trades and occupations have been found: those of builders, carpenters, weavers and spinners, dockers, potters, a lamp-maker, a goldsmith, an oculist and even physicians. The range of surgical implements, for example, is considerable and extends from curettes to catheters and from scalpels to spatulae, but what is so interesting is the fact that most of them are remarkably similar to comparable modern surgical instruments, the major difference being that while modern ones are of stainless steel the Roman ones were of bronze. Metalworking in iron, bronze and pewter seems to have been particularly important, and, to judge from the sites where concentrations of iron slag has been found, the industry was widely spread. Along the Walbrook stream, blacksmiths left a great amount of slag together with such tools as tongs, punches, hammers, an anvil and a large furnace bar. But slag has also been found elsewhere, mostly near the outskirts of the Roman town in Old Jewry, behind the present Guildhall, in Warwick Lane and in Bread Street. Jewellery-making is indicated not only by evidence of goldsmiths having worked in Suffolk Lane and in Southwark, but also by small marble-sized balls of royal blue coloured frit, a coke-like substance used in enamelling, which have been found at the west end of Cheapside, in Lombard Street and in Aldermanbury.

The names that people scratched on pots give us some clues to those that were commonly heard in Londinium: Alexander, Audax, Felicula, Felix, Gaius, Glycera, Julius, Optatus, Paullus, Petronius, Restituta, Titullus and Verecundus. These people would have been among those who joined crowds of thousands to visit the largest undiscovered building in Roman London – the amphitheatre. They would also have enjoyed other sports and games, such as hunting the wild boar (whose tusks are so frequently found), or fishing with bronze fish-hooks. At home, the gaming counters and dice that are found were used in a board game like modern backgammon, and children had their own games which included playing ball; one such scene is shown on the tombstone of a child about five years old that was dug up during the rebuilding of Westminster School in Great College Street. A surprising toy is the wooden yo-yo, two of which have been found in Roman London, along with simple musical instruments like the flute and whistle.

Although little is known about the children of Roman London, a good deal can be said about the private religious ideas of the adults and of their hopes for the afterlife. Their polytheistic belief may seem strange, but in general it was a fairly simple mixture of Roman and native Celtic ideas, based largely on the belief that the offering of gifts would induce the god to grant certain favours. The gift would take a variety of forms – the dedication of an altar; the sacrifice of an animal or bird; a small object like a brooch, coin, or statuette of the god or goddess; or even something of practical use like a tool. Particularly important in Londinium was the worship linked to the water spirits of gods associated with the Thames and the Walbrook. In both cases an enormous quantity of complete and usable objects were thrown into the water, both from the banks of the stream and from the Roman London Bridge. Coins, tools, statuettes, jewellery and much besides have been found on such

Part of a tombstone depicting a child holding a ball. Found at Westminster School, Great College Street.

building sites as the Bank of England and Bucklersbury House on the site of the Walbrook stream, and also during dredging in the Thames – especially during the 1830s when London Bridge was being rebuilt. Objects obviously linked to religion are rare in the Walbrook, but among them are many fragments of incense burners,[30] and a number of phallic neck pendants that presumably had been used as a charm against the evil eye. On one site there was even a child's gold finger ring decorated with a phallus to ward off evil. Nor is the curse on Tretia Maria the only reminder of the shrines that seem to have stood in the Walbrook valley, for another curse, also on a lead sheet, exists which reads, 'Titus Egnatius Tyrannus is cursed, and Publius Cicereius Felix is cursed.'[31]

In addition to this, votive offerings at various undiscovered shrines in London include small stone altars to Mercury, god of commerce, and Diana, goddess of hunting; elsewhere have been found bronze and pipeclay figures of Mercury, Hercules the patron of merchants and soldiers, Mars god of war, Apollo god of song and music, Venus goddess of love, Selene the Moon goddess, and Demeter goddess of the earth and corn, shown seated in mourning for her daughter Persephone.

Hades was the underworld where most likely the people of Roman London believed they were to wander in the afterlife. During the late first and early second centuries it was the normal practice for the dead to be cremated on a pyre, in order to leave the soul free and purified. The ashes were collected and placed in a container, usually an ordinary domestic pot, but sometimes in something more elaborate like a glass jar, lead box, or even a beautifully carved stone vase such as the one found in Warwick Square in 1881. In this a coin of Claudius was found, no doubt the fee to pay the grim old ferryman Charon to carry the soul across the great rivers of the underworld.[32] The container was nevertheless believed to be the home of the spirit of the dead, and so was furnished, and the departed given food and drink in pots to help sustain the spirit in the afterlife.

The burial place of the dead covered a wide area, and were most numerous near the main roads leading to other towns. In some areas, however, burials were grouped together to form what were clearly planned cemeteries that may originally have been enclosed by a wall or fence. One group was found in St Clare Street off the Minories; another lay just north of Warwick Square. But of the many burials that have been found dating from this period, only one has been fully investigated.

It was found in Warwick Square in 1966 and is one of the most curious burials so far encountered. That an elaborate ritual had taken place before burial was proved by an examination of the cremated bones. Fortunately, they had not been entirely destroyed in the pyre and enough remained to show that two persons had been buried here. One was an adult at least twenty years old, and the other a young child of between eighteen months and two years. Could this have been a mother with her child? The discovery of a long bone spindle in the furnishing of the grave suggests that the adult was a woman.[33]

The burial of two people in one grave was curious, but the arrangement of the 'grave furniture' was even more unusual. After the bodies had been cremated their ashes, including wood ash from the pyre, were collected up and shovelled into a large globular amphora that had originally contained wine or olive oil from southern Spain. This was not an uncommon secondary use of an amphora, which was then carefully lowered into a pit no more than some 1.5 m deep; in this instance two small and much used pottery lamps were placed on top of the ashes inside, perhaps to provide the two souls with light.

The entrance to the amphora burial chamber was then closed with a tile, two more tiles being placed in the pit as if to form three sides of a box in front of the chamber. Up against the tile closing the entrance, those who buried the dead placed three complete pot lids as if ritually to seal in the spirits of the latter; and then, instead of burying food in the three pots to sustain the dead, they deliberately smashed them, and placed the fragments up against the lids in the box of tiles, as if to deny the spirit sustenance to the underworld.

The explanation for this curious burial, where the living seem to have been trying to deny the dead a chance of happiness in the afterlife, will never be known, Nevertheless it illustrates one aspect of the importance of burials, for it is through them that a direct contact is made with the people of Roman London.

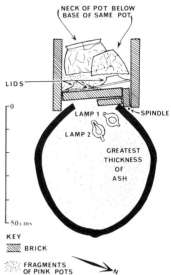

Plan of the late-first-century cremation burial found in Warwick Square in 1966.

Cremation burial of late-first-century date, found in Warwick Square in 1966. A tile and pot lids sealed the burial chamber, an amphora, in front of two deliberately smashed pots.

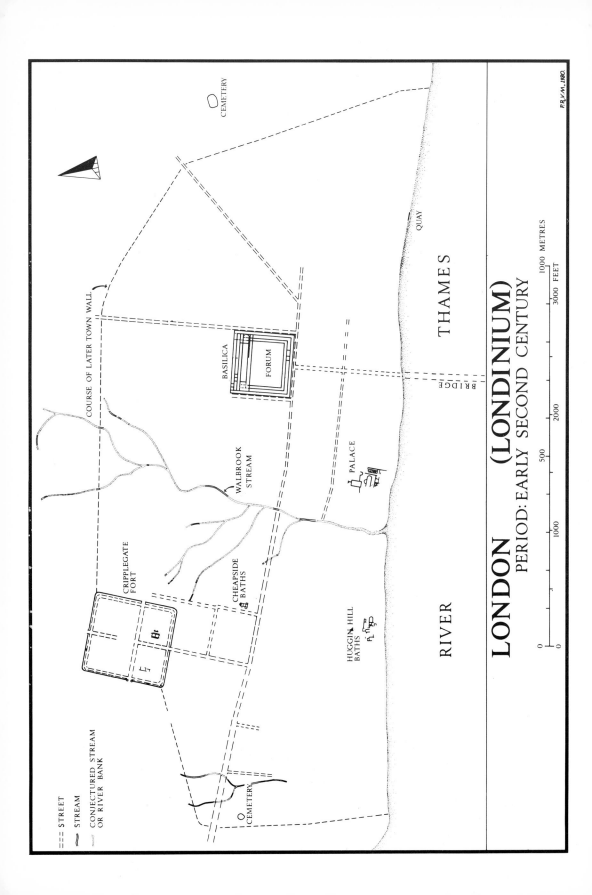

CEMETERY

COURSE OF LATER TOWN WALL

BASILICA

FORUM

QUAY

BRIDGE

THAMES

RIVER

PALACE

WALBROOK STREAM

CRIPPLEGATE FORT

CHEAPSIDE BATHS

HUGGIN HILL BATHS

CEMETERY

=== STREET

STREAM

CONJECTURED STREAM
OR RIVER BANK

P.R.V.M. 1980.

LONDON (LONDINIUM)
PERIOD: EARLY SECOND CENTURY

0   500   1000   2000   1000 METRES

0   1000   3000 FEET

The Roman Governor in London

The discovery in 1935 of the tomb of the Imperial Procurator, Julius Classicianus, just north of the Tower of London, was a landmark in the study of Roman London. It provided the first clear evidence that, from a very early date in the conquest of Britain, Londinium was at the province's administrative centre.

But this find made it difficult to decide what was the precise status of Londinium in Roman Britain. Was it ever the provincial capital, whatever that may mean, and, if so, when? As further discoveries were made, it became evident that the Governor had his headquarters in the town, and that the Provincial Council, representing all the tribes in Britain, was based there in some form. In fact, soon after the end of the first century, Londinium had all the features of a capital city – the central administration of the province. But the basilica and forum dating from that time were so small that it is difficult to understand the contrast with its presumed capital status. Perhaps Londinium, as a vigorous trading centre, was considered before AD 100 as a completely separate entity from the provincial administration, as is the modern City of Westminster, whose administration, and status are totally separate from Parliament. In fact, in view of its unique place in Roman Britain it may be wrong to compare the size of the forum in London with others in Britain until more is known about the Roman city.

The setting up of the provincial administration in Londinium seems to have been a slow process, the Procurator probably becoming the first to be established there, about AD 60 if not before, to deal with the financial affairs of the province. By about the end of the first century, the Governor also settled there; now that the conquest of Britain was complete, it was no longer necessary for him to be constantly mobile, engaged in battle during the summer months, and touring the new province in the winter.

Unfortunately there is little evidence in the form of coins and pottery sherds to date the major public buildings of Londinium. But such indications as do exist, together with the apparent sequence of public buildings enable a reconstruction of the development of London as the home of the provincial government to be attempted. That which follows is therefore offered in full knowledge of the imperfection of the evidence, and with a

Opposite, major public buildings were either built or enlarged during the early 2nd century, suggesting an elevation in the status of Londinium. New buildings include the Cripplegate fort, a new basilica and forum, a new Cheapside bath building, and an enlarged Huggin Hill bath building.

79

Imaginative reconstruction of Roman London just before the Hadrianic fire of about AD 130. The second basilica and forum dominates the hill above London Bridge, the palace of the Governor lies beside the mouth of the Walbrook stream, while beyond there lies the Cripplegate fort which housed the Governor's troops.

plea to future archaeologists to tackle the many problems of dating and identifying the known buildings.

Although no inscription has yet been found in London stating that the Governor had his headquarters there by the early second century AD, there is so much other evidence, both of his staff and of his palatial residence, that there can be no serious doubt as to his presence. As the representative of the Emperor his duties were considerable, ranging from the command of the army to keeping a list of all Roman citizens. He decided where roads were to be built, he supervised the British tribes and their leaders, and made legal judgments concerning Roman citizens and natives and in all cases requiring capital punishment. For this he had a considerable headquarters staff of perhaps two hundred people who, apart from the senior adjutants, registrars and so on, included men whose duties ranged from clerks and grooms to prison guards and executioners.[1]

His staff of carefuly picked men was drawn from each of the legions in the province. Ten men, for example, were taken from each legion to be given the special rank of *speculator*, which is only found on the immediate staff of the Governor. These men were responsible, among other things, for the execution of prisoners condemned by the Governor's assize court; thus the discovery of a tombstone in 1843 in Playhouse Yard, Black-friars, of a *speculator* called Celsus of the II Augusta Legion is most important evidence that the Governor resided in London.[2] The fact that it was set up by certainly one man of this rank, but probably also by two more from the same legion, shows that Celsus had died while living in Londinium rather than while passing through. Theirs was an unpleasant job, a curious benefit of which was to be allowed to keep the cheap possessions of the people they executed – as did, for example, the soldiers who drew lots for Christ's clothing.

Stone figure of a Roman legionary soldier, originally from a tomb, but found reused as building material in Bastion 10, in Camomile Street, 1876.

A *speculator* was also responsible for carrying dispatches from the Governor to places as far afield as Rome itself. The documents were confidential, and tied with cord threaded through a small box containing an official seal. Three of these official seal boxes have been found in London, two in the Walbrook stream close to Cannon Street, of which one was decorated with the imperial eagle and the other with a portrait of Emperor Domitian (AD 81–96); the third seal box from Aldgate, lost beside the road to Camulodunum, has a portrait of Emperor Vespasian (AD 69–79).[3]

The presence of the Governor's staff no doubt explains why so many tombstones of soldiers have been found in Roman

London. The II Augusta, VI Victrix and XX Valeria Victrix Legions are all represented even though the legions themselves were based at Caerleon in south Wales, York and Chester. It also probably explains why two of the tombstone sculptures depicting the deceased soldiers in full military dress, show them holding objects reflecting their administrative duties. The tombstone of the centurion Vivius Marcianus of the II Legion was found at Ludgate in 1669, and shows him holding a scroll of parchment; the other, an almost life-size sculpture found reused in the late Roman town defences in Camomile Street near Bishopsgate, shows the soldier carrying a case of wooden writing tablets.[4]

In addition to his headquarters staff, the Governor had a guard of 1,000 soldiers called *singulares*, five hundred being infantrymen and the remainder cavalry, all of whom were commanded by centurions seconded from the legions. The tombstone of a soldier who may have been one of these auxiliary infantrymen has been found in London, and gives us some indication of what they looked like. Unfortunately his name is not inscribed on the fragmentary stone, but he is shown wearing a helmet, a cloak and tunic, and he is armed with a spear and oval shield.[5] It is believed that the twelve-acre fort, beside Cripplegate on high ground at the north-western edge of the Roman town, was the headquarters of the guard, because it was apparently built at a time of peace, perhaps during the reign of Hadrian.[6] The fact that it was large enough to house about 1,500 men does not invalidate this interpretation, since Londinium was at the centre of communications and extra barracks space may have been required for troops in transit.

The discovery of the fort in 1949 was a notable achievement of Professor W. F. Grimes, for it was the result of carefully thought-out research rather than a mere chance discovery. The first clue came to light when he dug a trench across the line of the later Roman city wall near Cripplegate, and instead of the usual stone defensive wall 2.4 m thick, he found two Roman walls lying side by side each about 1.2 m wide. Puzzled by this, he had more trenches dug near by, until a point was reached where the walls diverged, one of them curving through a right angle. In the corner lay a nearly square turret, and it was this that gave the answer to the puzzle: it was the south-west corner of a military fort whose north and west walls had been thickened much later when the town wall was built, hence the double wall. This discovery was so important that the west wall of the fort, part of its west gate, and the sites of the curving north-west and south-west corners have all been preserved by the Corporation of London, in sunken gardens in Noble Street and opposite the Museum of London.

Tombstone of an auxiliary Roman soldier with an oval shield.

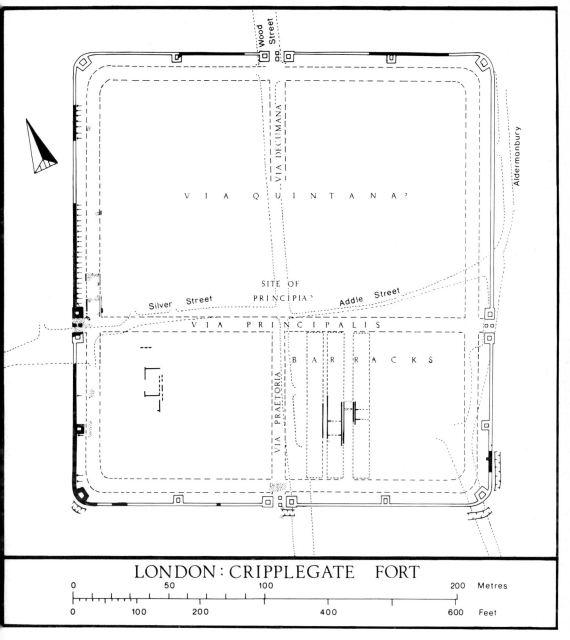

LONDON : CRIPPLEGATE   FORT

| 0 | 50 | 100 | | 200 | Metres |
| 0 | 100 | 200 | 400 | 600 | Feet |

Shaped in plan like a gigantic rectangular playing card with rounded corners, the London fort has proved to have a standard layout of defences, with a gate near the middle of each side, the plan of its defences being very similar to the fort at Housteads on Hadrians Wall. Few traces have been found of the barracks, stables and other interior buildings, since the basements of the bombed office buildings were very deep in this part of the City. Even the fort's defensive wall on the eastern

Plan of the Cripplegate fort, built during the first half of the second century.
Opposite above, south-west corner of the Cripplegate fort with its tower, as found in Noble Street.
Opposite below, the north tower of the west gate of the Cripplegate fort, looking south-west.

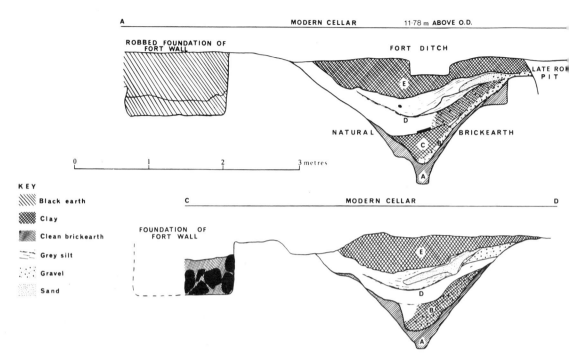

WEST   EAST

A   MODERN CELLAR   11·78 m ABOVE O.D.

ROBBED FOUNDATION OF FORT WALL   FORT DITCH   LATE ROM PIT

E

D

NATURAL   C B   BRICKEARTH

A

0   1   2   3 metres

KEY

▨ Black earth

▨ Clay

▨ Clean brickearth

≈ Grey silt

⋯ Gravel

▨ Sand

C   MODERN CELLAR   D

FOUNDATION OF FORT WALL

E

D

B

A

Sections across the east wall and defensive ditch of the Cripplegate fort, Aldermanbury. Deposits B, C and D are silt and rubbish accumulated during the second century, and E is a dumped clay filling of the late second century, all suggesting that the fort may have been abandoned during that century.

The defensive ditch of the east side of the Cripplegate fort, Aldermanbury, excavated in 1965. The start of the curve of the south-east corner is clear. On the right is the foundation trench of the fort wall, robbed of stone during the twelfth century.

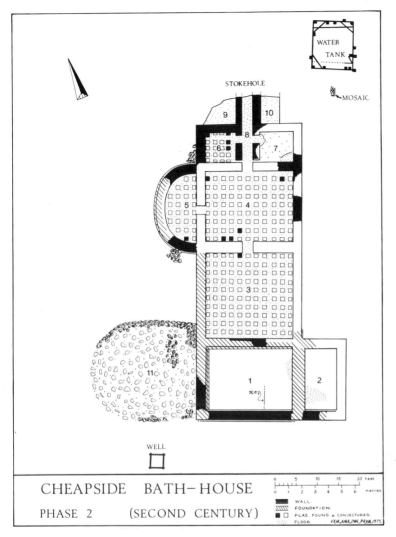

WATER TANK

STOKEHOLE

MOSAIC

9 10

8

6 3

7

5 4

3

11

1 step

2

WELL

CHEAPSIDE BATH–HOUSE

PHASE 2 (SECOND CENTURY)

0 5 10 15 20 feet
0 1 2 3 4 5 6 metres

WALL.
FOUNDATION.
PILAE FOUND & CONJECTURED.
FLOOR. VKM, AMA, JNH, PRVM, 1975.

Cheapside bath house: the rebuilt public bath building included the following: (i) *frigidarium*; (2) cold water bath; (3) *tepidarium*; (4, 5) *caldarium*; (6, 7) Hot water bath; (8) flue from stokehole; (9, 10) base for hot water tank; (11) *laconicum?*

and southern sides has been mostly destroyed, though the small regulation defensive ditch just beyond, with its characteristic V-shaped cross-section, is a vital clue to the position of the wall. Indeed, almost all trace of the south gate had been destroyed when its site was excavated, but it was possible to establish its position by the holes left by the decayed wooden bridge supports crossing the ditch.

Roman soldiers were evidently a common sight in the town, not only around the Governor's palace on the site of Cannon Street station, but also probably when visiting the baths in Cheapside while off duty. These were discovered in 1955 on the site of the Sun Life Assurance offices opposite St Mary-le-Bow church, which produced evidence that the building had been

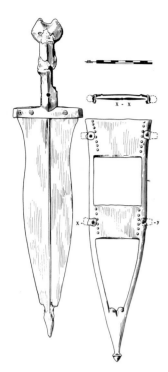

Legionary soldier's iron dagger and sheath from Copthall Court.

reconstructed some time during the first half of the second century. This perhaps took place at the time the fort was built in the early second century, in order to provide the soldiers with bathing facilities. Less that five minutes' walk from the fort gates, the baths had in the second century a distinctly military appearance, with an uncomplicated arrangement of cold, warm and hot steam rooms, and with cold- and hot-water baths. A room was added next to the *frigidarium* probably at this stage, this too being typical of military baths. It was the curiously popular 'Spartan room', the *laconicum*, in which the bather vigorously sweated in dry heat before taking a dip in the cold-water bath in the adjoining *frigidarium*.[7]

The soldiers soon became involved in the religious life of the town, for they too left their offerings of military equipment in the Walbrook stream. The objects therefore probably help to illustrate the dress and armour of the soldiers who served the Governor, the dress items including buckles and supports for crests on helmets, the weapons including parts of swords, daggers, scabbards, bows, and bolts fired from a kind of catapult called a *ballista*. Several iron spearheads have also been found, including one inscribed C.VER.VICT., showing that it belonged to the Century or section of the auxiliary unit commanded by the centurion Verus Victor.[8]

Military life in Londinium was presumably centred around the fort and the Governor's palace, and it was in the latter that the daily administration of the province was no doubt punctuated from time to time by impressive occasions of state. That these occasions involving visiting high-ranking officials and dignitaries took place is reflected by the existence of the state rooms, and by the fact that they enjoyed the outlook over the spectacular garden terrace with its gigantic ornamental pool.

It was not until the 1960s that the palace itself was found on sites just east of Cannon Street station, and even now its identification as the residence of the Governor is not confirmed by an inscription; it is, however, extremely unlikely that it belonged to any other official.[9]

The palace was not found by chance, but, like the fort, was the result of the intensive archaeological investigation of a known major Roman public building whose purpose was in doubt. Its plan was the only clue to its function, and in the event it took six years to collect the necessary information. Earlier discoveries of mosaics and massive Roman walls, particularly in Bush Lane during the 1840s, and of tiles stamped with the name of a department of the provincial Roman government, showed that a major public building probably stood there. But when Cannon Street station was built in 1868 the importance of the Roman building became more apparent, for an enormous

Roman wall some 61 m long, 3 m high and 3.6 m thick was found, and near it a sequence of large rooms, one of which measured 15.2 m by 12 m.

Mosaic pavements were also recorded and paintings on the walls which were apparently divided by lines and bands into panels, while others had a trellis pattern and a 'powdering of fancy-coloured spots'. The plan made in 1868 of the remains was never published and has since been lost; but it should be possible to reconstruct the plan eventually because a great deal survives beneath the station. John Price, an archaeologist who examined the walls, wrote in 1870 that 'it was interesting to observe how completely the old walls defied the appliances of modern engineering, the necessary dislodgements being only affected by the aid of gunpowder; in some cases, I believe the veritable Roman walls now form foundations for the support of the railway arches.'[10]

In 1960 an archaeological investigation was carried out on the site of Elizabeth House, between Bush Lane and the station, right in the middle of the area of massive walls. As the contractor erecting the new office block started clearing the north end of the site with a mechanical excavator, substantial Roman walls even larger than the 2.4 m thick Roman city wall were soon exposed. Three metres wide and with foundations descending 3 m below the Roman ground level, they proved to have been part of one of the state rooms, a hall 13 m wide and 24.38 m long.

Just south of the hall, the contractor's men met no more obstructions and so were able to speed up the excavation. No one realized that they were digging out the north side of the ornamental garden of the palace – until the mechanical excavator suddenly hit a new wall extending right across the site. This turned out to be a mere 0.9 m thick, but it sat on the edge of a concrete raft 1.8 m thick and 12 m wide, extending to the southern edge of the site. The workmen had found the ornamental pool.[11]

There was still some doubt as to the significance of these Roman structures, but in December 1964, permission was given for an archaeological excavation to take place on a neighbouring site just eight weeks before it was to be redeveloped, and although mostly only the surviving tops of the Roman walls and foundations were examined, a meaningful plan of the Roman building was uncovered together with some pottery and coins to help date its construction. More walls and floors were recorded during the development work that followed, when almost all trace of the Roman building on this large site was destroyed. Nevertheless, by 1966 there was enough information to show that a Roman palace of monumental proportions had

An imaginative reconstruction of the ornamental garden and state rooms of the Roman palace, now partly beneath Cannon Street Station.

Opposite, plan of the Roman palace in Bush Lane, Cannon Street, and an important adjacent building in Suffolk Lane.

once stood there, apparently built in the late-first or early second century AD.

It was the central range of huge 'state rooms', evidently used for large-scale receptions, and the magnificent formal garden that proved this was a palace. Although the remaining wings had walls of more modest size, their arrangement around the garden and beside the river also confirmed that this was a palatial residence. Its sheer size and plan are unlike anything that either a private individual or a town council would have built, and so it was not surprising to find that many of the tiles set in its walls bear the stamp of a provincial government department. Similar stamped tiles have also been found in the Cripplegate fort region, and it seems likely that they were issued by the Procurator who was perhaps responsible for financing government buildings in Londinium. The size and grandeur of the palace are such that the only possible official

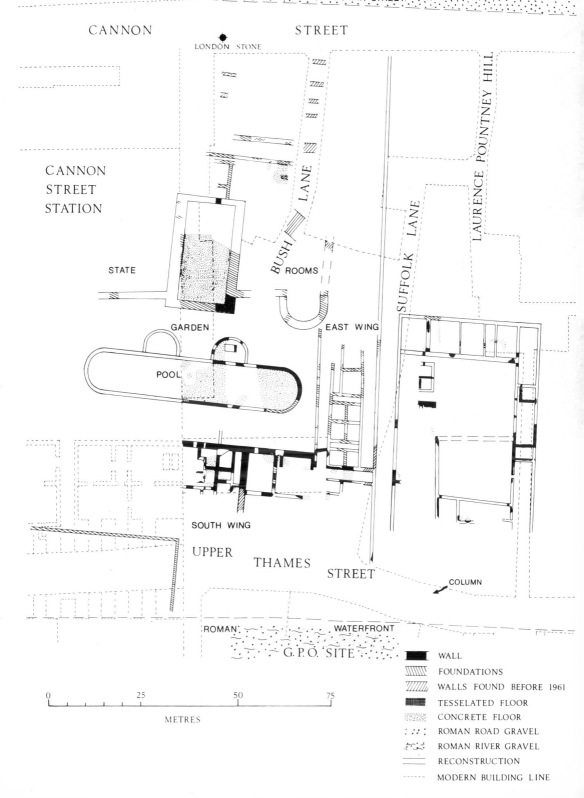

ROMAN STREET.

CANNON   STREET
• LONDON STONE

CANNON
STREET
STATION

STATE

ROMAN STREET

BUSH LANE

SUFFOLK LANE

LAURENCE POUNTNEY HILL

ROOMS

GARDEN

EAST WING

POOL

SOUTH WING

UPPER   THAMES   STREET

COLUMN

ROMAN   WATERFRONT
G.P.O. SITE

	WALL
	FOUNDATIONS
	WALLS FOUND BEFORE 1961
	TESSELATED FLOOR
	CONCRETE FLOOR
	ROMAN ROAD GRAVEL
	ROMAN RIVER GRAVEL
	RECONSTRUCTION
	MODERN BUILDING LINE

0   25   50   75

METRES

who could have resided there was the representative of the Emperor – the Governor.

The palace probably measured about 130 m by 100 m, and extended down the hillside from the major Roman street under Cannon Street, to the waterfront just south of Upper Thames Street. It was terraced on three levels and the landward entrance was probably situated on the upper terrace, on the south side of modern Cannon Street, though deep modern basements have destroyed almost all trace of this. It is here that possible remains of an entrance courtyard were found leading off the main Roman street beneath Cannon Street, and it is now thought likely that the enigmatic monolith that has been called London Stone for at least the past 800 years belonged to the palace entrance.[12]

Being part of such an important building could explain why the Stone was venerated so long ago, despite the fact that it stood as an inconvenient stump in Cannon Street roadway until 1742. But as traffic increased and vehicles kept knocking into it, it was decided to break off the top and place it in the south wall of St Swithin's Church in Cannon Street. This church was bombed during the Second World War and, when the site was sold for office development, it was on the understanding that London Stone would be preserved in the south wall of the new building.

During the rebuilding, when the Guildhall Museum housed the Stone, all that could be ascertained was that it was merely its top, and that it was shaped like a tea cosy and was made of Clipsham limestone from the Chiltern Hills. More important was the fact that when the original site of the Stone was plotted on to a map of the Roman palace, it lay not only on the main axis of the garden and state rooms, but also beside the main Roman road under Cannon Street, where the entrance to the palace may have been situated. This double coincidence makes it even more likely that the Stone was part of the palace.

It is on the middle terrace that the choice of the hillside location is best appreciated; this part of the palace being clearly designed to impress, the garden and the state rooms were planned to receive the maximum light, air and scenic view. Built in the style of wealthy Roman residences at that time, the principal rooms and the garden were outward looking, across the river and countryside, instead of in the older tradition of looking inwards to a garden or court. The gradiose proportions of the state rooms were aimed at enhancing the dignity of the office of Governor of the province; and on entering the garden court the visitor would see the enormous pool 10 m wide, probably 55 m long, and holding about 200,000 gallons of spring water. This, together with the minor pools and ornamental monuments, would have given an impression of Imperial luxury almost unequalled in Britain. The visitor would rightly have felt that this was the hub of Roman Britain.

The lower terrace is perhaps where the private apartments of the Governor were to be found, and there is some evidence that a colonnaded river frontage framed a view of the Thames, with its shipping from many lands. Beyond, the scene of the riverside marshes of Southwark, no doubt teeming with wild life, contrasted with the formal arrangement of the palace; and it is this scenic aspect and the general size and plan of the palace that made it so closely resemble Governors' palaces in other parts of the Empire—at Cologne overlooking the Rhine, at Aquincum above the Danube, and at Dura Europos in Syria commanding a view of the Euphrates.

Among the dignitaries entertained in the palace were no doubt members of the Provincial Council who had perhaps established some form of headquarters near the Governor's palace by the early second century. Representing the interests of all the British tribes, the Council was primarily responsible for maintaining the Imperial cult, the worship of the divinity of the Emperor at the annual festival, which after A D 60 probably continued to take place at the rebuilt temple of Claudius at Colchester. The Romans apparently established some form of temple in London too, for part of its dedicatory inscription on a block of stone was found reused in a later wall in Nicholas Lane in 1850. Charles Roach Smith managed to save it at his own expense and get it moved up to Guildhall Library, where it was lost soon after, but not before he had made a detailed drawing of its inscription which read: NUM (INI) C(AESARIS ...) PROV(INCIA ...) BRITA(NNIA), signifying 'To the Deity of the Emperor, the Province of Britain set this up.'[13] In what form the Council was established in London is not known, though it may have been little more than an administrative headquarters. It has been suggested, however, that the annual festival and the worship of the Emperor was perhaps transferred from Colchester to London, but more evidence is required before we can be sure. The Council had its own staff of slaves, and one of these, called Anencletus, is known to us because he buried his young wife Claudia in a cemetery near Ludgate. The tombstone of oolitic limestone is massive, and its hexagonal shape, originally perhaps supporting a statute of his wife, bears the inscription, 'To the Spirits of the departed, and to Claudia Martina, aged 19; Anencletus, slave of the province, set this up to his most devoted wife; she lies here.'[14]

Within about three minutes' walk from the place where the inscription was found in Nicholas Lane, there was another large Roman residence. It was discovered in 1969, in Suffolk

Part of an inscription on stone dedicating a temple to the divinity of an Emperor, set up in the name of the Province of Britain. Found in Nicholas Lane.

Lane immediately east of the Governor's palace; measuring roughly 70 m by 40 m, it was rather large for a town house. Since no road separated this building from the palace, it may have been the private residence of the Governor or of another official, or indeed the accommodation for officials visiting London on government business. Like the palace, it too was terraced but only on the middle and lower levels overlooking the river, its four wings apparently surrounding a large terraced garden or courtyard. In its east and west wings were found mosaics and traces of hypocausts for central heating; the discovery of a stone column in Upper Thames Street suggests that the south wing perhaps had a colonnaded frontage overlooking the river.[15]

There were at least two officials, other than the Governor, who were probably based in London and could have resided in the Suffolk Lane building. One of these was the *Legatus Iuridicus*, the juridical legate, whose job was first established in Britain by Vespasian about A D 79 to deal with the increasingly complicated legal codes in use, Roman citizens being bound by Roman law and free native Britons by native laws. Although responsible to the Emperor, the *Legatus Iuridicus* was subordinate to the Governor and acted as his deputy in legal matters. Possible evidence that he resided in London was found in 1954 in Walbrook street just north of Cannon Street, close to the Roman palace site. It was a broken building inscription on stone, which mentions the '. . . Imperial Juridical Legate of the Province of Britain, on account of the Dacian victory.' It seems that the *Legatus Iuridicus* had built or donated something in London to commemorate the emperor Trajan's victory over Dacia in A D 102 or 106.[16]

The other official who might have resided in the Suffolk Lane building was the Procurator who, although of slightly lower rank than the Governor, was not subordinate to him. Indeed he was directly responsible to the Emperor. and although the Governor was at the head of the army and the provincial administration, it was the Procurator who was responsible for government income and expenditure in the province. Therefore, it was, with doubtless one eye on the floundering economy of Britain in A D 61, that Julius Classicianus managed to convince Nero of the wisdom of recalling the Governor, Suetonius Paullinus, soon after the rebellion of Boudica. Had Suetonius Paullinus been allowed to continue his uncompromising repression of the Britons, there could be no hope of further revenue to the Imperial treasury. Fortunately there are a few clues, other than the tomb of Julius Classicianus, to show that the Procurator's office, the *tabularium*, was based in London. One of these is a wooden writing tablet on the back of which are

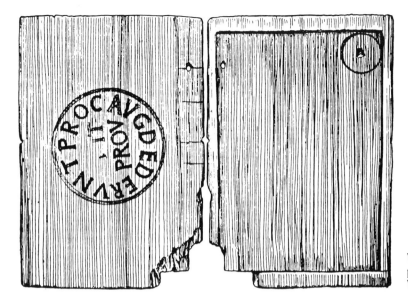

Writing tablet with a procuratorial stamp, from Walbrook. Length 152 mm.

branded the words PROG. AVG. DEDERVNT. BRIT. PROV. ('Issued by the Imperial Procurators of the Province of Britain'). This was probably found in the Walbrook stream, unlike the next clue, a series of bricks and tiles bearing the stamps P.P. BR. LON, PR. BR. LON or P. PR. BR. These amount to just four words, and we can be sure of the meaning of only the last three – 'Provinciae Britanniae Londinii' ('... of the Province of Britain in Londinium'). Clearly , this refers to a department of the provincial administration that was based in London alone, since tiles with these stamps occur in no other town in Britain, though they have been found at Brockley Hill, Stanmore, where they may have been made. Although these were government bricks which we now know were for government buildings, the crucial meaning of the first 'P', the initial of the name of the government department, has been the cause of much debate. It now seems most likely that it refers to the Procurator, not only because we know that he was in London, but also because it was probably his responsibility to pay for government buildings.[17]

Roof-tile stamped P P BR LON, from Leadenhall Street. Length of stamp 98 mm.

95

In addition to administering finance, the Procurator was responsible for various valuable natural resources such as lead and gold, and it is possible that an iron punch found in London was used by one of his departments for stamping ingots of soft metal like gold. It bears the letters M.P. BR. which are believed to mean METALLA PROVINCIAE BRITANNIAE ('Mines of the Province of Britain'), and was presumably stamped on ingots by the official responsible for refining and checking the metal.[18] The Dolaucothi gold mine in Carmarthenshire, Wales, is believed to have been in Imperial ownership, and this was a likely source of the gold that was refined during the late first century in London at Bush Lane, before the Governor's palace was built on the site. In fact it is possible that the palace was built there because the land was already in Imperial ownership, and although goldsmiths are known to have worked in Southwark, Verulamium and Cirencester, it seems that in each place they used only refined gold, and so the fact that refining actually occurred in London does suggest that the Procurator was involved.[19]

The evidence of refining was particularly interesting, for it comprised two large gold-impregnated crucibles and three matching crucible lids, found in a rubbish pit dating from AD 80–100. With them were pieces of baked clay that had been used to seal the lids to the crucibles during the refining process, and it was from these that a specialist was able to reconstruct the probable method of refining. First, the impure gold was placed in the crucible with a mixture such as brick dust and

Clay luting to seal gold refining, from a late-first-century rubbish pit in Bush Lane.

Bronze head of Emperor
Hadrian found in the
Thames at London Bridge,
1834.

urine; next, the lid was hermetically sealed to the crucible with
a layer of clay, various designs being stamped in the clay to
ensure that nobody drained off any refined gold. The crucible
was then heated for a considerable time, and as the gold became
molten the impurities were absorbed by the brick dust and
dissolved by the acid fumes from the urine, so that the pure
molten gold could be poured off into a smaller crucible, an
example of which was also found. Some months after the pit
was excavated, a Roman well was found close by which was
evidently linked with the work of the goldsmith for in it were
traces of gold dust.

Even though the town that the merchants had created had by
the early second century become the home of the government of
the province of Britain, the continuing use of the small forum
suggests that Londinium had not been formerly recognized as
the capital. This situation apparently changed during the early
second century, perhaps when the Emperor Hadrian toured
Britain in AD 122 and presumably visited Londinium. Perhaps
it was he who authorized demolition of the first forum, basilica
and temple and sanctioned their replacement by a new forum

97

and basilica more than five times as large. It is almost as if the Emperor had recognized the fact that London was the capital, and formally elevated its status perhaps from *municipium* to that of *colonia*, and gave it a forum to match its rank. Although this is speculation, it would explain why the new basilica included government-stamped bricks in its walls, and why an impressive life-size bronze statue of Hadrian was set up in London, possibly in the new forum where the arm of a statue of similar scale has been found. As it happens, the head of the statue was fished out of the Thames at London Bridge in 1834, and is now in the British Museum.[20]

Of Hadrian's visit little is known except that it was in the course of a tour of the western provinces that he eventually arrived in Britain, where 'he instituted many reforms and was the first to build a wall eighty miles long to separate the barbarians from the Romans.' Apart from this, he probably sanctioned a forum at Wroxeter which was completed in 129–130, and probably the forum at Leicester. In his general policy of consolidating the Empire, the rebuilding and enlarging of the forum in London would not be surprising.[21]

The second basilica and forum complex of London was first recorded in 1880 by Henry Hodge, an architectural artist working on the site of Leadenhall Market, off Gracechurch Street. When he visited the site on various occasions he carefully sketched and measured the remains of the large Roman building whose purpose was completely unknown to him, together with the ruins of the medieval Leadenhall.

Most of his drawings are beautifully rendered in water colour, and show views of the site, sections and elevations of ancient walls, and even sections through the Roman strata–all carefully drawn to scale. These drawings remained unpublished for many years, and were unknown to the authors of the Victoria County History whose excellent volume on *Roman London* was published in 1909. Some of them were eventually published in 1915, though the significance of the walls was generally not realized until 1923 when Professor W. Lethaby correctly interpreted them as the east end of a basilica.[22] It was not then clear on which side of the basilica the forum lay, though it was certain that it must have been to either the north or south. Most people favoured the south, though by 1926 the uncertainty was still so great that one authority, describing various Roman chambers found during the previous year in Lombard Street, wrote: 'What now has been found may be a fragment of the forum wall and its sheltering arcade. It may be that or half-a-dozen other things. It may be a portion of a row of shops in Roman Lombard Street, outside the forum wall. It may be a gateway, not necessarily of a public building. It may be part of some inconspicuous person's house. There is ample room for speculation.'[23] Ample room indeed! In fact the walls belonged to two separate forum buildings.

It is thanks to a number of subsequent discoveries that sufficient proof existed by 1965 to show positively that the forum lay to the south, and recently there have been other major finds which disclosed a considerable amount of the south wing of the forum. The most unusual investigations, however, took place in 1977 in a small tunnel only 1.2 m high, dug by Post Office workmen along the whole length of Gracechurch Street, mostly at the level of the basilica and forum floors 3 m below the modern street. Many important features were recorded for the first time, such as the forum courtyard floor and the two concrete floors of the basilica. For a short while it was even possible to walk, uncomfortably crouched, across the entire width of the nave and side aisles of the basilica while examining its floors.[24]

The general plan of the second basilica and forum is now clear, for instead of being a large rectangular group of buildings as was the first, it was about 167 m square, and therefore much larger than the other which had an area of about 5459 sq. m. Indeed the area of the second forum was about 29,392 sq. m, which made it far larger than any other in Britain. In the centre there was a large unroofed courtyard originally surrounded on three sides by an inner portico 9 m wide where, it may be assumed, stone columns were once supported on the founda-

Recording archaeological features in the Post Office tunnel dug through the Roman forum beneath Gracechurch Street in 1977.

tions. A range of large rooms, probably shops, lay along the centre of each of the three wings of the forum, and beyond these there was an outer portico 5.5 m wide. On the fourth, northern side of the courtyard, stood the basilica whose vast hall (more than 30 m wide) was divided, like a church, into a long central nave, with side aisles separated from the nave by rows of brick piers that no doubt once supported arcading. At the east end, and most likely at the west end also, there was a semicircular tribunal whose floor level was raised above that of the nave to form a dais for the magistrates presiding over meetings. Although it has been suggested that a piece of Roman wall plaster, painted with foliage and found on the basilica site long ago, was part of the decoration of the building,[25] in fact no sign of wall plaster could be found in the recent excavations in the tunnel which also disclosed the destruction debris of the basilica. It is unlikely, therefore, that it was decorated in that way. The tunnel also entered a range of rooms on the north side of the hall, rooms that have been found on nearby sites, and which may have housed the offices of the Roman city council, probably including the *curia* or council chamber, the treasury and prison.

Section of the thick white concrete floor of the nave and side aisles of the second basilica. A later floor can be seen above. Scale shows centimetres. Found in the Post Office tunnel beneath Gracechurch Street, 1977.

Opposite, reconstructed plan of the second basilica and forum, probably built during the first third of the second century. The basilica comprised a nave, tribunals and side aisles, with office rooms to the north. The forum included a large courtyard surrounded by shops and a wide portico.

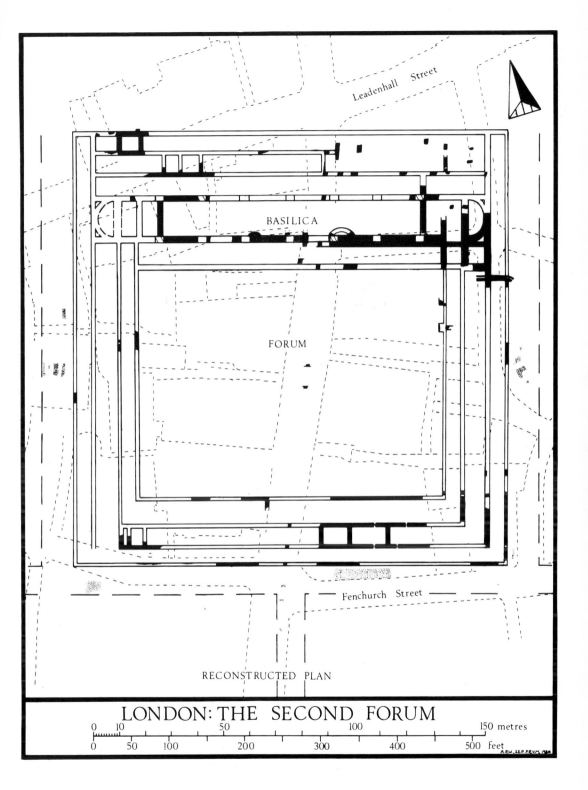

Leadenhall Street

BASILICA

FORUM

RECONSTRUCTED PLAN

LONDON: THE SECOND FORUM

Fenchurch Street

0   10   50   100   150 metres

0   50   100   200   300   400   500 feet

A.R.W. SEP PRVM 1980

Probable stages in building
the second basilica and
forum.

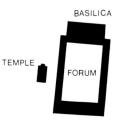

BASILICA

TEMPLE

FORUM

1. First Basilica and Forum in use.

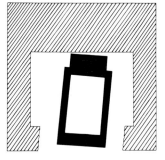

2. Second Basilica and Forum built around
first Forum.

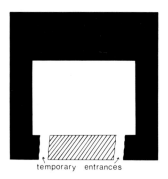

temporary entrances

3. First Forum demolished. Second Forum
entrance built.

BASILICA

FORUM

4. Temporary entrances blocked

Reconstruction of Stages in the Redevelopment of the Forum Site.

▨ New Construction

Because the entire new basilica occupied a much larger plot of land than had the first forum, it had been necessary to demolish the old forum, the temple and several stone and timber-framed houses. The presumed diagonal road from London Bridge upon which the first forum was aligned, was, like the demolished buildings, buried under a metre-thick dump of clay and rubble, not only on the forum site but also probably to the south. Two new north-south roads were built, one on each side of the new forum, that on the east being the new *cardo maximus* leading north to the site of later Bishopsgate. What is interesting is that the first forum continued in use until the new basilica and most of the new forum had been completed, because it was essential for the town to have the continuing facilities of the civic centre. The care with which one or other of the buildings was always kept in use is evidence – if still needed – of their equal importance and common utility.

The date of the second forum is still uncertain because no inscriptions have been found and very few coins and datable pottery sherds recovered from the layers of soil and rubbish associated with its construction. The most important finds were discovered by Adrian Oswald of Guildhall Museum on a site in Lombard Street in 1939. He found a white cement floor, assumed to be that of the second forum, which overlay the demolished walls of the first.

Beneath the floor was a dump of builders' rubbish 0.6 m thick, which contained pottery apparently dumped when the second forum was built, the latest samian ware sherd of which was datable to the period AD 120–50. This floor lay flush against a stone and brick pier of the second forum in the mortar of which Owald found a coin of Hadrian (AD 117–38) in excellent condition. On the basis of this uncertain evidence, none of which survived the Second World War, it seems that the second forum could not have been completed before AD 120. But its construction may have started some time earlier for on several other sites the dumped deposits that levelled up the ground before the second basilica and forum were completed, contain many sherds, none of which need be dated any later than AD 100.[26]

Just as it is to Hadrian that we may perhaps attribute the second forum and regard his statue as commemorating his visit to London in AD 122, so it is to him that Londinium may owe yet another monument – the enlargement of the already huge public baths at Huggin Hill. Scandals had been so rife in Roman towns in various provinces, due to mixed bathing in the public baths, that the Emperor banned it throughout the Empire. In most cases this meant that many men and women had to bathe at different times; at Vipasca in Lusitania, for example, the baths were used by women from the first hour of the day to the seventh, and by men from the eighth hour of the day to the second hour of night.[27] Elsewhere, as at Huggin Hill, the baths were enlarged with the addition of a second suite of bath rooms for the women. The additional rooms were found at Huggin Hill in 1969 to the east of the original suite, the new *caldarium* being 16 m long and 8.81 m wide. Which of the two parts of the baths was used by the women is not known. The fact that someone had scratched the man's name QVINTVS on the red painted wall-plaster found in the western *caldarium* is unfortunately no clue.[28]

What is interesting, however, is the huge size of the new *caldarium*, both *caldaria* in these baths being among the largest

Overleaf:
Plan of the large public bath building at Huggin Hill, before its demolition probably during the late second century.

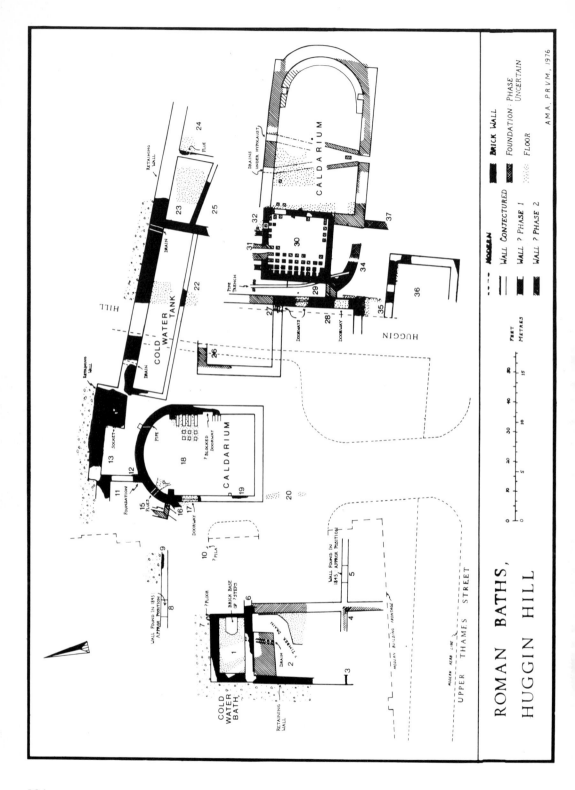

ROMAN BATHS,
HUGGIN HILL

known in Roman Britain. They obviously catered for a large increasing population, but what brought the crowds to this part of the town? A concentration of government-stamped bricks just west of the baths in the Lambeth Hill area suggests that there may have been a public building there to draw the crowds.[29] But more certain traces of a public building lie on the hilltop just north of the baths in the form of two enigmatic parallel walls extending in an almost straight line for nearly 200 m. The walls are 9.7 m apart and each foundation is 1.2 m wide, extends 1.5 m below the Roman land surface, and is exceptionally hard. The walls are undated within the Roman period, but in fact similar ragstone and rock-hard white concrete foundations are to be found only in the second basilica, in the Huggin Hill baths and in the Governor's palace, all public buildings of late-first to early-second-century date. So what could this long structure be? Having two parallel walls, it is unlikely to have been a boundary, though there are no other fully satisfactory explanations.[30]

A large heated room, perhaps a *tepidarium*, in the Huggin Hill baths excavated in 1969.

Flue leading from a furnace into a large heated room in the Huggin Hill baths. The brick pillars originally supported a concrete floor, thus allowing hot air to circulate beneath.

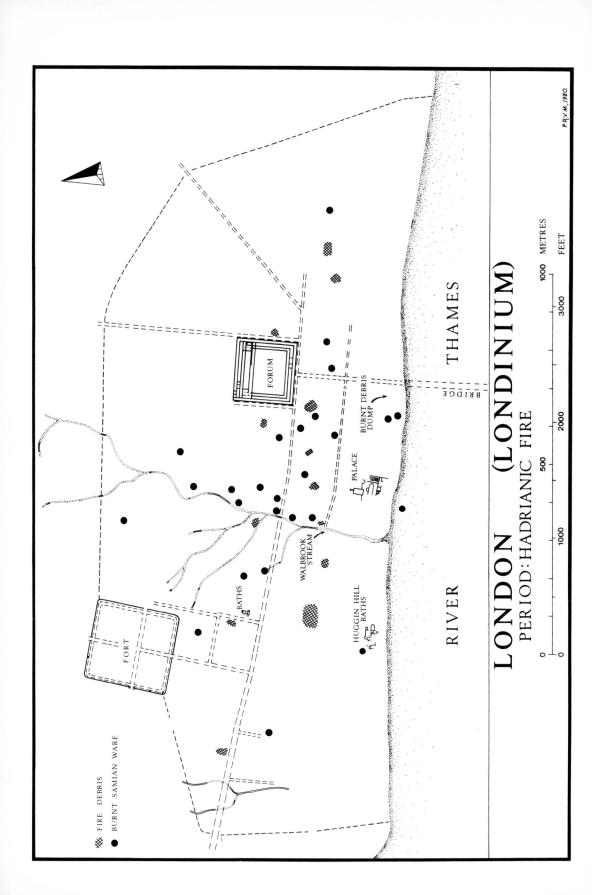

LONDON (LONDINIUM)
PERIOD: HADRIANIC FIRE

FORUM

PALACE

BURNT DEBRIS
DUMP

BRIDGE

WALBROOK
STREAM

FORT

BATHS

HUGGIN HILL
BATHS

THAMES

RIVER

FIRE DEBRIS

BURNT SAMIAN WARE

P.R.V.M, 1980.

METRES
FEET

1000

3000

500

2000

1000

0

0

The second great fire of Roman London

When Gerald Dunning discovered a 2.4 m thick layer of burnt red Roman building debris close to London Bridge, during the construction of Regis House in 1930, it was the first recognized clue to a major disaster that had befallen Roman London about AD 125–30. The thickness of debris of this conflagration, which is now called the Hadrianic fire of London, was astonishing, but by carefully sifting the rubble, he established that the fire had not occurred on that site, for the debris at Regis House had been dumped on the hillside behind the Roman riverside wharves in a clearing-up operation after the fire. The date, too, was easily determined, for in the debris were found hundreds of blackened sherds of samian ware from Gaul, including 124 potters' stamps, some of which could be closely dated to the reign of Emperor Hadrian.[1]

Dunning's first step was to find out if the fire had been restricted to the London Bridge area, or if it had extended over a much larger part of the Roman city. The clues lay amongst objects preserved for the most part in the Guildhall Museum, though since then there have been new sightings of the early second-century fire layer, and it now seems that the fire must have devastated a large part of the Roman city. But unfortunately, because the fire layer has been seen on only a comparatively few sites, it is still essential to consider the burnt samian ware of early second-century date that had been handed in to museums from building sites where there had been no archaeological recording; the assumption being that most of the burnt pottery from those sites was probably derived from unrecorded exposures of the burnt layer.

What does all this careful cataloguing tell us? First, it shows that more than 100 acres of the city were apparently devastated, traces of the fire having been found as far west as Newgate Street, and as far east as All Hallows Barking church by the Tower of London – a distance of almost a mile. Secondly, it shows that the greatest concentrations of debris lay to the south of the forum in the region around King William Street, and to the west of the Walbrook stream in the area south of Cheapside. In these regions the fire layer ranges from 0.1 m to 1.2 m in thickness, though generally all that is seen is a 0.50 m thickness of red burnt clay, tiles and wall plaster.

Opposite, the extent of the great fire of about AD 130 as suggested by the fire debris and burnt pottery. No trace of the fire has been found in the Cripplegate fort, forum, palace or in the two public baths.

Collapsed debris of roof tiles, wall plaster and burnt clay against the scorched clay wall of a house burnt in the Hadrianic fire. Excavated in Bow Lane in 1979.

The fire was so extensive that it is likely that the majority of the houses were made of inflammable materials, and that they had been built so close together that the blaze could spread with ease. Analysis of the debris shows that the buildings had a timber framework, some with carefully built walls of sun-dried mud bricks and others probably with wattle and daub. Wall plaster had been applied to this, often painted in red and white. The internal walls were sometimes merely partitions, as was found on a site in Mincing Lane where a charred upright post only 0.09 m wide was seen to have been plastered on both sides.[2] Floors were commonly of white mortar, and of pink cement made with crushed red tiles to form an *opus signinum* floor. Also there were occasionally mosaics like those recently found in a house at the south end of Bow Lane, to show that, despite their clay and timber construction, the houses were sophisticated Roman buildings. Indeed, this is confirmed by traces of the many roofs that had collapsed into the fire, for, instead of being of thatch, they were of tiles which left a thick layer of debris on many sites. The common use of clay was occasioned by the absence of any building stone near London, a situation which even today results in London's houses being built mostly of bricks, in contrast to the stone houses that commonly exist in the rocky areas of Britain. Kentish ragstone was brought from the Maidstone district for use in Roman public buildings in London, and in the more substantial houses, but its expense clearly restricted its use.

Although the fire debris reflects not only where the fire occurred but also approximately when it happened, what is impossible to discover in the ground is *why* it occurred. Contemporary written records show that there had been some trouble with the Britons during the reign of Hadrian, but apparently not in the south of the province; thus there is no reason to believe that this caused the destruction of London. Indeed, nearby cities like Verulamium, Silchester and Colchester were all flourishing at this time, which leads one to the conclusion that the fire was accidental. Perhaps it began in the city centre, and, like the fire in Rome in 64 and the Great Fire of London in 1666, soon spread among the densely packed shops containing inflammable wares, until it was driven by the wind to the fine houses in the more distant parts of the Roman city. Fire was certainly a serious hazard in Roman towns, and a similar major conflagration devastated Verulamium about 155 and another occurred at Wroxeter somewhat later. But in spite of its severity, the fire in London did not destroy the entire city, for no definite trace of it has been found in the area of the Cripplegate fort.

Did the fire reach the basilica and forum? It was certainly found nearby, to the east in Lime Street, to the west in Birchin Lane and to the south in Plough Court, but although fire debris has been recorded on the basilica and forum site its relationship to those buildings remains unknown.[3] In fact it could have been the debris from earlier fires, for in the recent investigations in the basilica and forum under Gracechurch Street, no trace of the fire could be found. Perhaps the stone walls saved the buildings. Because it is not known exactly when the first forum was demolished, it is also just possible that the Hadrianic fire was the reason for building the second. This is most unlikely, however, for three reasons: firstly, nowhere in and around the first forum has any debris been found to suggest that it was burnt down; secondly, such meagre dating evidence as exists indicates that the second forum was probably built before the fire; and thirdly, it is clear in any case that the first basilica and forum remained in use while the second basilica and forum were completed and built around it.

The fire devastated Londinium, and although there was some rebuilding, it seems that this may have been a period of economic decline in the port, for particularly during the latter half of the century the town seems to have been undergoing a fundamental change in its character. Even though there was a certain amount of clearing-up in the London Bridge area, on many sites investigated in Roman London there is little evidence of renewed occupation until after the end of the second century. Indeed, on some sites there is no trace of any later Roman usage at all. It is as if many businesses, particularly those based on trade with the Mediterranean region, had ceased operating and the traders had decided to leave. When the economy of London is strong, as after the fires of AD 60 and 1666, its rebuilding presents no long-term difficulty, but the recovery after the Hadrianic fire seems to have been relatively feeble and even some of this later declined, and so it is likely that factors other than the fire were at work. In other words it is probable that the conflagration merely hastened the otherwise inevitable end of the city as the main importer and distributor of goods in Britain. A possible cause is that with no large local native population to supply, the merchants of London depended upon the demand for goods from other towns of Roman Britain, and that demand was now probably in decline. Soon after the invasion it had been essential to establish Londinium as a supply centre for the province, but in due course it was just when the native Roman towns and ports became successful centres of trade and industry in their own right and able to supply their own requirements in the second century, that their need for Londinium declined.

After the fire the rebuilding of London seems to have been only fitful and ultimately the people even in areas it had spared, such as Southwark (the suburb at the south end of London Bridge), left their homes. By about 150 their clay and timber buildings beside the roads leading to the bridge had been mostly abandoned and were left decaying during the 160s and 170s. Within the suburb a channel, believed to have been a canal with substantial revetments, was allowed to silt up.[4]

Although after the fire Londinium was apparently a shadow of its former self, it was not until recently that this declining phase was recognized, and so helped to explain a number of puzzling features. As long ago as 1927 the amateur archaeologist Gordon Home called attention to what he considered an archaeological puzzle on a site in Cheapside at the south end of King Street, near the modern Guildhall. There he discovered that an accumulation of more than 1.2 m of Roman deposits overlying the natural gravel contained only objects dating from the period 50 to about 130. But it was the medieval deposit overlying this that left him wondering where the remains of later Roman London were. He could not understand why it was that, if the thickness of layers below represented merely eighty years of occupation, there were no deposits representing the last 270 years of Roman London. With no solution at hand he suggested that perhaps the dating of pottery from layers had been incorrect![5] In fact the dating was correct, for Gordon Home had noted in the sections the contrast between the intensive early Roman occupation debris of Londinium, and the start of the long subsequent period of relative decline.

This change in the fortunes of Londinium has important implications for our understanding of its status. It raises the question why, if London continued to be the capital of the province after the fire, there was apparently no major effort to restore the city. It is hard to find a convincing answer, but maybe this was a direct result of the changing situation in Britain following the death of Hadrian in July 138. Soon after his successor, Antoninus Pius, took the throne there was an outbreak of troubles in northern Britain, which included revolts by the Brigantes and raids from the peoples beyond Hadrian's great wall. These troubles, which continued until the late second century, were tackled by the construction of the turf-built Antonine wall in southern Scotland, and by a major movement of troops to the north. With government resources heavily committed in northern Britain, perhaps there was no need to support devastated London as the administrative headquarters of the province.

Evidence of the decline of Londinium has been found on various sites in addition to the abandoned buildings in the suburb in Southwark. It affected public and private buildings alike, presumably reflecting a decline in civic and provincial authority in the town. Most sites that have been investigated show little trace of immediate rebuilding after the fire. Very few pits and rubbish layers have been found dating from the middle of the second century, and there is a marked absence of dumps of rubbish in the bed of the Thames after the early second century, rubbish that up to then had been dumped from boats in very large quantities.[6] However, recent excavations in Bow Lane off Cannon Street, in Milk Street and in Newgate Street, have all shown some initial sign of rebuilding after the fire, but then of subsequent decay. In Bow Lane houses burnt in the fire had been replaced by less substantial buildings which seemed to respect the old property boundaries, but these were destroyed by yet another fire perhaps not long after the middle of the second century. No later Roman activity was found on the site, and objects of the third and fourth centuries were rare. In Milk Street a building with a fine mosaic pavement was erected after the Hadrianic fire, but by the end of the second century this seems to have been abandoned and there is little trace of later Roman occupation on the site. On the Post Office site in Newgate Street two long timber-framed buildings with clay walls were found to have been burnt in the fire, and these

Superimposed Roman buildings recently found on the Post Office site in Newgate Street. The similarity of their plans before (left) and after (right) the Hadrianic fire suggests a reconstruction by the same owner after the fire. By the end of the second century, however, the latest buildings had been abandoned in the decline of Roman London.

Opposite, a fine mosaic, unfortunately damaged by medieval pits, found in a Roman building in Milk Street in 1977. It was constructed soon after the Hadrianic fire, but the building had been abandoned before the end of the second century. No later Roman buildings occupied the site.

had been immediately replaced by buildings of identical character and very similar plan. By the end of the second century these too had gone out of use, and were merely overlaid by a stratum of dark earth in which there were few later Roman objects.[7] Just as the waterway in Southwark had silted up, so did the Walbrook stream in the City, for with little or no industry probably operating on its banks, the timber embankments became neglected and gradually decayed until they collapsed during the middle of the second century. Ralph Merrifield, who wrote the last general study of Roman London, suggested that the reason for this neglect was that the level of the Thames had risen so much that it flooded the embankments; but recent excavations beside the Thames suggest that the river level did not rise sufficiently at that time for this to occur.[8] The decay of the town may reflect a decline of the local authority, and out of this situation could have grown trouble, which would account for the burial of a hoard, found at 146 Fenchurch Street, of at least twelve silver coins some time after 166, the date of the latest coin.[9]

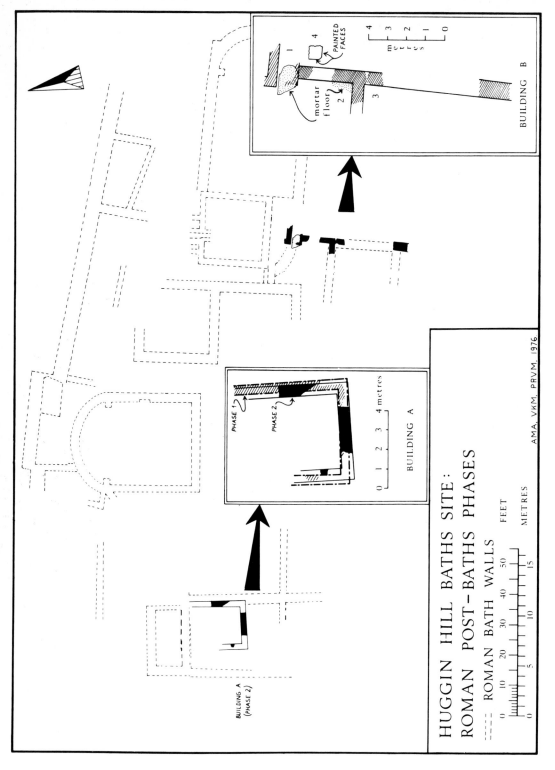

HUGGIN HILL BATHS SITE:
ROMAN POST-BATHS PHASES

--- ROMAN BATH WALLS

BUILDING A

PHASE 1
PHASE 2

BUILDING A
(PHASE 2)

BUILDING B

PAINTED FACES

mortar floor

AMA, VKM, PRVM, 1976

The decay and abandonment of buildings presumably reflects a decline in the population of London and this must have had a serious effect on the pottery-producing centres at Brockley Hill, Stanmore, and Highgate, especially after the fire at Verulamium, for they were forced by a dwindling market more or less to close down about A D 160.[10] Instead, the inhabitants of London in due course had to buy their pottery from centres much farther away, mainly in Dorset and Oxfordshire.

Religious life in Londinium was also neglected, and even the casual offerings thrown into the Walbrook stream stopped at about 154–155, the date of the latest of hundreds of recorded coins recovered from the stream bed.[11] Elsewhere in London, two temples were perhaps at this time allowed to decay, one being the temple of Isis, and the other possibly a temple of Jupiter. Their eventual restoration during the third century after having been in ruins was recorded on massive altars found at Blackfriars in 1975.[12] Another inscription, also perhaps dating from the third century, records that a temple or shrine, dedicated to the Mother Goddesses, had been restored probably after a period of neglect.[13] Even the public buildings of Londinium decayed; the baths in Cheapside and at Huggin Hill, once so alive with people, became deserted and were demolished by about the end of the second century. No trace of any later Roman building was found on the site of the Cheapside baths, and since the Huggin Hill baths were replaced by a flimsy building constructed from the rubble of the ruins, it is clear that it had not been demolished because the site was required for other important purposes.[14]

It is not certain that the Governor moved his administrative headquarters out of London at this stage, but at Aldgate the ditch which could be part of a formal town boundary, had been filled in probably before the middle of the second century.[15] By the middle of the century the defensive ditch around the Cripplegate fort was simply being allowed to silt up, nobody apparently bothering to clear out the silt and rubbish. When the eastern defences of the fort were excavated in Aldermanbury, just west of the medieval Guildhall, the silt layers were found to be clearly preserved, the silting and rubbish possibly suggesting that the fort had been abandoned by this time. Since it is likely that there were Roman military regulations controlling the care of fort defences, the apparent total disregard for the ditch of the Cripplegate fort could be significant. One particular mid second-century layer in the ditch, excavated in Aldermanbury, included a large portion of a human skull, a scatter of large animal bones, and three almost complete, but smashed, cooking pots – all of which had been left in the open until eventually buried by the silt.[16]

Opposite, traces of insubstantial Roman buildings, constructed from demolition debris of the Huggin Hill public baths, indicate that the baths were not demolished so that they could be replaced by other important buildings.

Mid-second-century pottery and other rubbish lying in the half silt-filled fort ditch in Aldermanbury in 1965, suggesting that the Cripplegate fort might have been abandoned by this time.

The possibility of the fort having been abandoned by about 150 raises the question: was it at this time too that the Governor's palace was abandoned? It was definitely abandoned at some stage during the Roman period, for its state rooms were demolished and the great pool was filled in, only to be replaced by a far less substantial Roman building – though one with some pretensions, since it had hypocausts for central heating.[17] Despite a most careful search, however, no clue to when this happened has been found, though there is convincing evidence that the south wing of the palace by the waterfront continued in use until the fourth century.[18] The deliberate demolition of the prestige state rooms and ornamental garden presumably reflects a change in the status of the entire building, and a down-grading of its use, but the identity of its occupants at that later date remains unknown.

In fact even though we may not now understand what was happening to Roman London, it is clear that the city was undergoing profound changes during the second century, and that these probably meant that it no longer remained the great trading centre of the province as it had been during the first century.

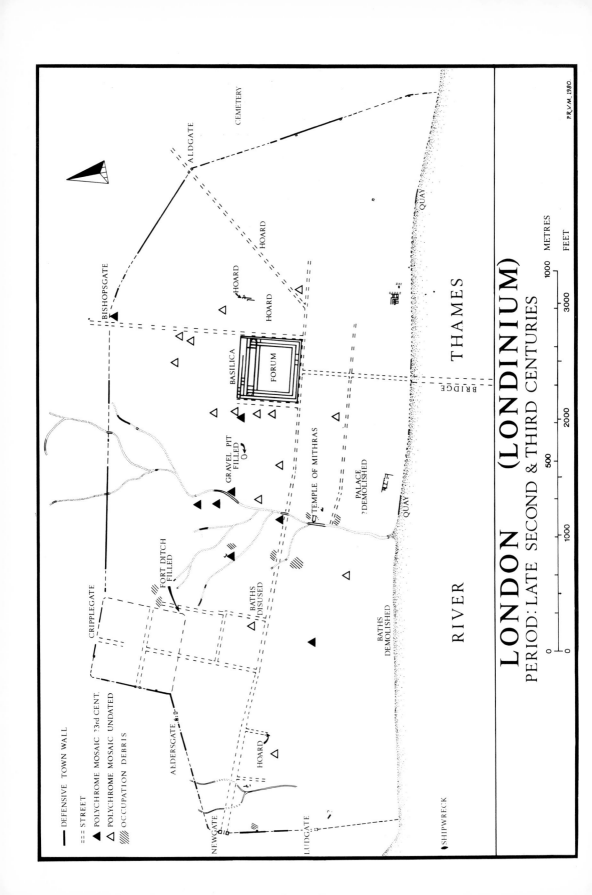

LONDON (LONDINIUM)
PERIOD: LATE SECOND & THIRD CENTURIES

DEFENSIVE TOWN WALL
STREET
POLYCHROME MOSAIC 23rd CENT.
POLYCHROME MOSAIC UNDATED
OCCUPATION DEBRIS

CEMETERY

ALDGATE

BISHOPSGATE

HOARD
HOARD
HOARD
HOARD

BASILICA

FORUM

CRIPPLEGATE

GRAVEL PIT FILLED

FORT DITCH FILLED

TEMPLE OF MITHRAS

PALACE ?DEMOLISHED

BATHS DISUSED

BATHS DEMOLISHED

QUAY

QUAY

QUAY

ALDERSGATE

NEWGATE

HOARD

LUDGATE

SHIPWRECK

THAMES

RIVER

BRIDGE

1000   METRES
3000   FEET

500
2000
1000
0   0
1000

P.R.V.M. 1980

Traces of Roman London between AD 180 and 450 are peculiarly elusive and the evidence is frankly confusing. The one thing that seems to have happened, however, is that from the late second century onwards there was a major effort to restore Londinium, presumably as a provincial capital. The town that emerged was decidedly different in character from what it had been. It was probably no longer occupied by large numbers of overseas merchants, but instead housed a much smaller population. Judging from the huge area enclosed by the new town defences, it seems that it might have been intended around AD 200 to restore Londinium to its former vast size; but in the course of the third century it did not meet those expectations. Such evidence as there is suggests that Londinium may have remained a comparative shell of its former self, until abandoned by the Roman administration two centuries later.

The dating evidence of coins and pottery suggests that the town's restoration may have begun a little before the end of the second century, and continued on during the third, after which time it gradually declined in size and quality. In Southwark, however, renewed building activity does not seem to have generally started until well on into the third century, perhaps as late as the middle of the century. The third-century city was characterized by fine houses with patterned mosaic floors, by the restoration of old and the construction of new temples, by the demolition of unwanted public buildings such as the Huggin Hill public baths in a major tidying-up programme, and by the construction of a formal timber quay over half a mile long. But one of the first projects was the construction, about AD 200, of a defensive wall and ditch, two miles long, encircling the landward side of the city; it was this which formed the basis for the defences of London for the next fourteen centuries. In fact, even though little of the wall now survives above ground level, its former course is indelibly marked on the face of modern London through street alignments and property boundaries.[1]

Third-century Londonium was perhaps a somewhat formal city with major public buildings and monuments, and it seems to have exhibited a wealth which, as far as one can see, was not based on the sure foundation of extensive trade, for there is a surprising absence of traces of trade and industry, a situation that is in contrast to its abundance during the late first and

Opposite, the demolition of some public buildings and the construction of the city defences, a quay and other buildings all reflect a major restoration of London mainly during the third century. The many polychrome mosaics may be of this period, but their dating is generally highly uncertain.

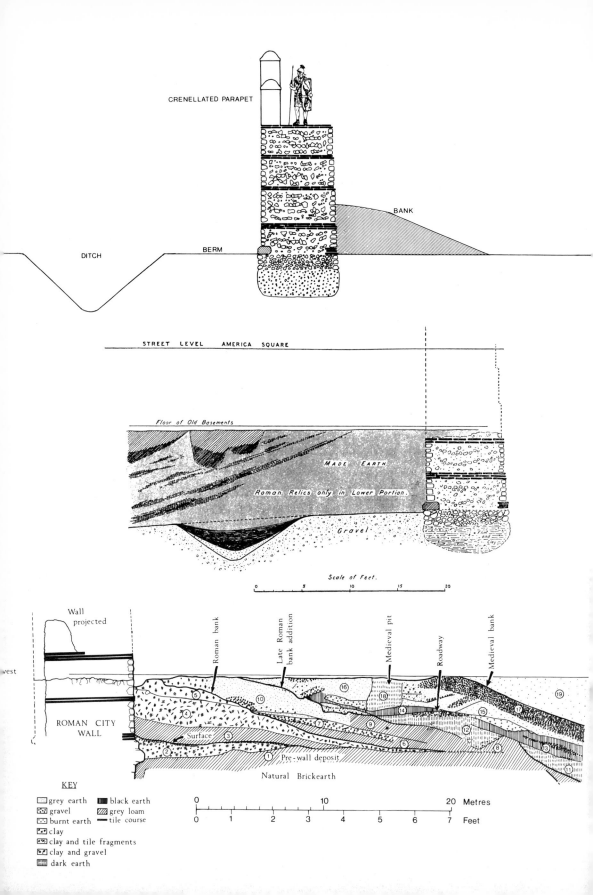

CRENELLATED PARAPET

BANK

DITCH

BERM

STREET LEVEL AMERICA SQUARE

Floor of Old Basements

MADE EARTH

Roman Relics only in Lower Portion.

Gravel

Flint and Clay

Scale of Feet.

0   5   10   15   20

Wall
projected

Roman bank

Late Roman
bank addition

Medieval pit

Roadway

Medieval bank

west

ROMAN CITY
WALL

⑤

④

③

②

Surface

①

Pre-wall deposit

⑩

⑦

⑨

⑯

⑱

⑭

⑥

⑫

⑮

⑧

⑬

⑰

⑲

Natural Brickearth

KEY

grey earth   black earth
gravel   grey loam
burnt earth   tile course
clay
clay and tile fragments
clay and gravel
dark earth

0   10   20 Metres

0   1   2   3   4   5   6   7 Feet

early second centuries. The discoveries relating to this period therefore raise several fundamental questions: for whom was the city rebuilt, and why? Who organized and financed the restoration? Why did the new defensive wall enclose a larger area than the earlier city, particularly when there is no trace of a large urban population? Indeed, how reliable is the archaeological evidence?

Archaeology can only give an indication of what *might* have happened, and can rarely establish why and how events occurred. For a possible answer we must turn to the contemporary historical records, but first the date and magnitude of the restoration must be defined. The defensive wall is the most distinctive symbol of the restored city, and is more closely dated than almost anything else, since associated coins show that it was built between about 190 and 225.

The city wall was 2.4 m thick, probably about 6 m high, and enclosed a roughly semicircular area of 330 acres beside the Thames, from the site of the Tower of London in the east, to Blackfriars in the west.

Just a short distance beyond the wall there lay a roughly U-shaped ditch about 4.5 m wide and 1.8 m deep, the earth from which had been neatly piled up against the inner face of the wall to form a bank about 4.9 m wide and 1.8 m high.[2] A close examination of the wall shows that it was built of several types of stone: flints quarried from the chalk were mixed with very sticky puddled clay to form the foundation, while Kentish ragstone was used with mortar in the wall above ground level. At ground level a plinth carved from red sandstone lay along the outer face of the wall, while at vertical intervals of roughly 0.76 m the wall had horizontal layers of red tiles through its entire thickness to give it added stability.

Opposite, reconstructed section through the Roman defences of London in the third century.

Section showing the lower part of the Roman city wall, and also the Roman defensive ditch found in America Square, 1908.

Section of the Roman city defences, recorded at the Central Criminal Court in 1966, showing successive banks of earth against the inner face of the Roman wall.

The internal clay bank, here surviving in its entirety, partly removed in 1966 to reveal the inner face of the Roman city wall at the Central Criminal Court, Warwick Square. The square piers are modern foundations.

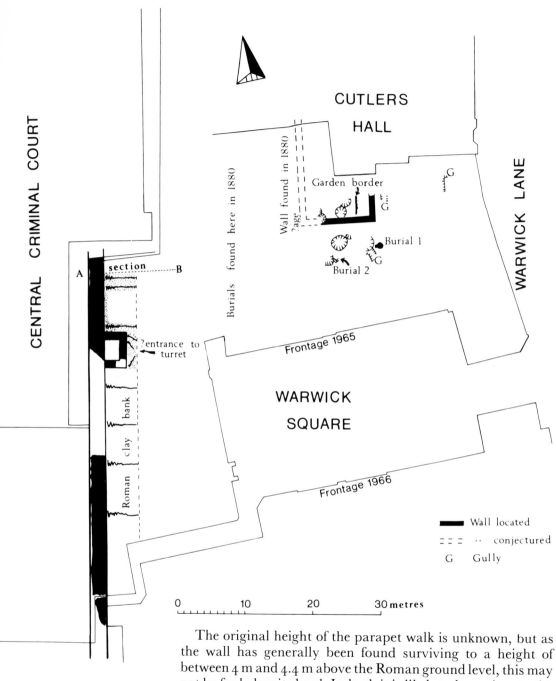

CUTLERS HALL

CENTRAL CRIMINAL COURT

WARWICK LANE

Wall found in 1880

Burials found here in 1880

Garden border

G

G

G

Burial 1

Burial 2

A section B

?entrance to turret

Roman clay bank

Frontage 1965

WARWICK SQUARE

Frontage 1966

Wall located

= = = " conjectured

G Gully

0 10 20 30 metres

Plan of the Roman city wall, turret and clay bank excavated at the Central Criminal Court in 1966.

The original height of the parapet walk is unknown, but as the wall has generally been found surviving to a height of between 4 m and 4.4 m above the Roman ground level, this may not be far below its level. Indeed, it is likely to have risen to the next tile course, which is missing, above which there was presumably a narrow parapet wall, perhaps about 0.6 m thick and 1.8 m high, with crenellated openings through which defenders could shoot arrows and spears.

Internal turret of the Roman city wall (right) found in Warwick Square in 1966. The coin forger's equipment lay in the bottom of the turret close to the city wall.

It has been suggested that various bolster-shaped stones found in the later Roman bastions may have been capping stones from the top of the parapet.[3] The wall was extremely carefully built, and contained no reused building materials, though a small piece of broken mosaic pavement once found in its core in the street of London Wall, was clearly a chance inclusion.

Two other features need to be mentioned in order to complete the description of the wall, namely the internal towers and the gates. Four small rectangular towers have been found built on to its inner face and these presumably contained timber staircases leading to the parapet. Three of the towers were found on the length of wall between the Tower of London and Aldgate, and one more was between Newgate and Ludgate.[4] In spite of the fact that there seems to have been no regular spacing in their position, and their dimensions vary, it is clear that other internal towers have yet to be found.

Only four gates seem to have been built initially in the city wall: Aldgate, on the road leading north-east to Camulodunum; Bishopsgate, on the road leading northwards to York; Newgate, on the road leading west to Silchester and Gloucester; and Ludgate, on a road leading towards the south-west of Britain. Parts of the Roman gates at Aldgate, Newgate and Ludgate have been found, and, although only small portions of Aldgate and Ludgate have been examined, it is clear that each opening was flanked by two substantial square towers.[5] Fortunately, enough of Roman Newgate has been

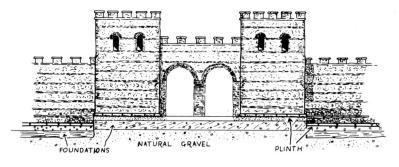

RECONSTRUCTION

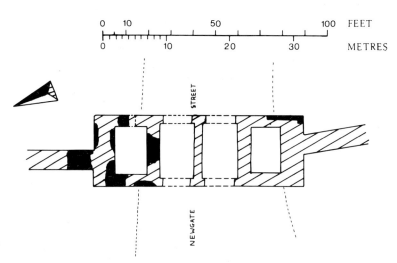

Plan and reconstructed
elevation of Roman Newgate.

found for its entire plan to be reconstructed, showing that it had
a double carriageway 10.5 m wide. The plinth of the gate,
however, lies some 1.4 m above the plinth of the city wall on
each side, suggesting that the discovered gate was built at a
different date in the Roman period; indeed, judging from its
style and construction, it is possible that it was originally a
free-standing arch earlier than the defensive wall, as was the
Balkerne Gate at Colchester, and stood on the high ground
overlooking the valley of the Fleet River.[6]

Aldersgate seems to have been a later Roman gate in its
entirety, for its foundations, discovered by Adrian Oswald in
1939, were apparently cut into the clay-and-flints foundation of
the city wall below. It too had a double carriageway, for
between the two solid masonry gate towers, only one of which
was found, there were stone piers to carry the central support of
a double archway.[7]

The fort walls at Cripplegate were incorporated into the new
town defences, and we know that its north and west gates were

retained, since the west gate has been excavated, and the north gate continued in use into the Middle Ages and was then known as Cripplegate.

Cripplegate itself has not been excavated, though its plan was presumably like that of the west gate of the fort which was uncovered and preserved for public display under the modern street named London Wall during 1956. This had a small double carriageway between two square towers, and thus was a small version of Newgate. The gate had been blocked at some stage, though this is unlikely to have occurred until after the city wall was built, since the blocking foundation of ragstone and mortar is completely different from the flints and clay of the Roman city wall.[8]

In spite of the fact that the fort wall was only 1.2 m thick and therefore much smaller than the town wall, the planners wanted to include the fort walls in the town defences. Perhaps this was to save labour and building materials, or possibly it was with a view to housing soldiers within its twelve-acre enclosure. Whichever was the case, however, both its north and west walls were incorporated in the new defences by being thickened up with the addition of another wall also 1.2 m thick, against the inner face of the fort wall. This addition reduced the size of the original earth bank behind the fort wall, and so, when the new town ditch was dug, a new bank was piled up over the remains of the fort bank.

It was as recently as 1956 that the first true indication of the age of the city wall was ascertained, when a coin of Commodus, minted in 183–84 was found in a deposit below the town wall addition to the fort wall.[9] The wall thickening must have been built after that date, but how much later was at first uncertain. Careful cleaning of the coin showed that it was worn and therefore had been in circulation long enough for it to be unlikely to have been lost before 190. On the reasonable assumption that the addition to the fort wall was made at the same time as the construction of the city wall, we can therefore say that the city defences must have been built after 190. This date was confirmed by pottery of the late second century found in other excavations both in and under the bank of the city wall on sites in Coopers' Row, just north of Tower Hill underground station, and at the Central Criminal Court, in Old Bailey.[10] Strictly, the little worn coin formed one end of a time bracket showing the date *after which the wall had been built*; and, in spite of the pottery dating evidence, it was possible that the defences were built considerably later. It was particularly important, therefore, to search for the other end of the time bracket by finding a closely dated deposit that had been buried soon after the wall was built.

It is thanks to the efforts of a Roman coin forger that the evidence exists, and it is an ironic coincidence that it was found on the site of the Central Criminal Court, Old Bailey. The evidence came to light in January 1967, in a layer of rubbish on the gravel floor of a small Roman tower on the city wall. The most important finds were two clay moulds for casting copies of official silver coins, the forger probably intending that the copies should be cast in bronze, and then be given a silver wash to coat the surfaces. In the layer, which otherwise contained a large dump of early third-century rubbish, there were also four coins that presumably belonged to the forger, and which suggested that he was disposing of incriminating evidence, perhaps in an emergency. Certainly, the dark corner at the base of the tower was a convenient place in which to lose the evidence![11]

The coins and moulds show that the forger was at work about 215–25, for the two double-sided moulds in fine terracotta were for producing copies of silver *denarii* of Septimus Severus (minted 201–10), of Geta (minted 210–12), and of Caracalla (minted 215). The three bronze coins, an *as* and a *sestertius* of Antoninus Pius (minted 143–44 and 145–61), and an *as* of Commodus (minted 180–92), were perhaps for melting down; a silver *denarius* of Caracalla in perfect condition (minted 213–17) may have been a coin from which the forger was making a mould. The fact that in addition to this coin, the forger had in his possession and was copying three new silver coins issued between 210 and 217 strongly suggests that he was working within a few years of 220, not earlier than 215, when one of the coins was minted, but probably not later than 225. The time bracket was now closed and we knew that the city defences had been built before about 225. There is a curious postscript to this, however, for in the deposit that contained the coins there was an unusual collection of bones which included those of several dogs, and pieces of an adult human skull.

No other town in Roman Britain had defences enclosing such a huge area, the largest being Cirencester (240 acres), Verulamium and Wroxeter (both about 200 acres). London was also larger than most Roman towns on the Continent, being about the same size as Milan (329 acres) and Lyon (about 318 acres). Indeed it was exceeded in size by only four towns in Gaul and Germany – Nîmes, Autun, Avenches and Trier.[12]

The magnitude of the task in building the city defences at that time can best be judged by considering what would be required to construct the wall today. It was about 2,956 m long, and assuming that it was about 4.5 m high to the parapet walk, and that it had a narrow parapet wall 1.8 m above that, we can work out the volume of the wall. Allowing for the amount of the concrete used, the wall would require roughly 5000 standard seven-cubic-yard tipper-lorry loads to bring the stone from the quarries near Maidstone in Kent to London. It would require a further 700 lorry loads of flints to be transported from the chalk quarries; and about half a million tiles, measuring 0.3 m by 0.45 m would be needed for the tile courses.

The stone was brought to London in ships, and so a large labour force was necessary at the quarries, breaking up the stone and transporting it in waggon loads to the embankment of the River Medway, where it was loaded into barges ready for the 70 mile water voyage to London, via the Thames estuary. Another large work force will have been employed in London making tiles, digging the foundation trench, puddling clay till it was exceptionally sticky, mixing mortar, and dressing more than a million facing stones until they were neatly square. It must have taken at least two years to build the wall; but curiously little trace of the construction debris has been found to reflect the magnitude of the task. However, one of the mortar-mixing areas was found some years ago as a thick layer of buff-coloured mortar preserved beneath the bank behind the city wall, just south of Tower Hill underground station.

By good fortune one of the ships bringing Kentish ragstone to London, perhaps for building the walls, was wrecked in the late second century, and was found in 1961[13] It was a large sailing vessel that had just completed the voyage from near Maidstone, when it was apparently involved in a collision. Although its shape as an elongated tub, roughly 16.75 m long, 6 m broad and more than 2.1 m deep was particularly stable, it could not survive a major collision. The ship was probably lying a little over 100 m off the north bank of the river when it was evidently struck by another vessel on its starboard side with such violence that, when it sharply heeled over to port, its cargo of building stone was thrown over to that side also. Its 0.025 m thick oak planking must have been damaged, for this is the only explanation for the fact that it filled with water and quickly sank.

No casualties were found in the wreck when it was excavated during the construction of a new embankment wall in the river. The Guildhall Museum was informed, and decided to carry out two excavations at low tide to discover the ship's age, construction and position. These gave a fair amount of information about the last two points, but nothing about the age.

During 1962 a cofferdam, an enormous watertight steel box with an open top, was sunk into the bed of the river to enable part of the new embankment wall to be built, and the placing of the cofferdam coincided with the forward half of the ship. It was dated by finds within the wreck, especially by a quantity of Roman pottery that had been dumped into the river nearby as

Coin forger's debris found in a turret in Warwick Square. *Above*, top to bottom; clay coin moulds for silver coins of Severus and Geta, and silver *denarius* of Caracalla. *Opposite*, worn bronze coins of Antoninus Pius and Commodus.

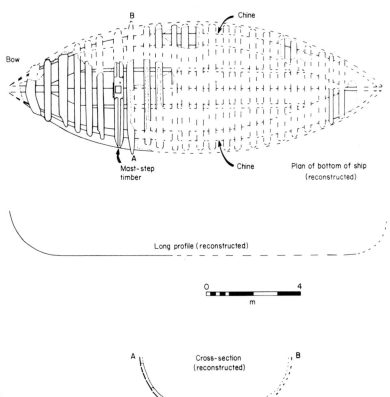

Partial reconstruction of the late-second-century ship found wrecked in the Thames at Blackfriars in 1962.

rubbish, and had been washed into the ship when its sides collapsed. Particularly important was a a large worn coin of the Emperor Domitian that had been minted at Rome in AD 88–89. This was found in the socket cut in a rib to hold the main mast, and was clearly placed there, as still happens in some shipbuilding yards, to purchase luck. In this case the coin lay reverse side up, so that the figure of Fortuna, goddess of luck, could touch the base of the main mast, through which came the power to propel the ship. Since this discovery, coins have been found beneath the masts of several Roman vessels in the Mediterranean, but not a single one in Scandinavian or Celtic ships in northern Europe, so it was presumably a Roman tradition to buy luck in this way. Yet another find was a large unfinished millstone carved from Millstone Grit quarried in Yorkshire, suggesting that perhaps on a previous voyage this vessel had been trading with the York region.

The timbers from the ship were raised from the site, and before any shrinkage occurred, each was carefully drawn to scale; so that when the plan and sections had been completed, the vessel was partly reconstructed on paper. This showed that it was unlike any of the Roman ships that divers were uncovering on the seabed in the Mediterranean, for it had a flat bottom and no keel, and its curving sides joined the bottom to form an angle. But particularly distinctive was the fact that its carvel-laid planks had been fastened to its skeleton of ribs with huge iron nails, unlike the Roman ships in the Mediterranean whose shell of planks had been constructed first, and held edgeways to each other by mortice and tenon joints so that the ribs could be added later. The Blackfriars ship was also completely different from the clinker-built ships (with overlapping planks) of the Scandinavians; thus it was clear that, although of Roman date, the ship must have been built by the native Celtic peoples of north-western Europe. It could have been built in south-east England, since its construction was similar to a river barge, also of second-century date, which had probably been built beside the Thames, and was partly excavated at Guys Hospital, Southwark, in 1959.[14] But the Blackfriars ship might have been built in many other places too, since other vessels of the same general native shipbuilding tradition have been found in Germany, Switzerland, the Netherlands and in Belgium, and

Votive offering of a bronze coin of Emperor Domitian, as found in a recess in the mast-step of the shipwreck at Blackfriars. The coin had been minted in Rome in AD 88–9, and lay with its reverse, showing the figure of Fortuna holding a steering-oar, uppermost.

Excavation of the forward part of the second-century Blackfriars ship inside a coffer-dam in the river, 1963. A, the bow; B, an unfinished millstone; C, rib containing the mast-step; D, part of the cargo of Kentish ragstone; E, the collapsed port side.

no doubt others will be found in Britain and in northern France.[15] The planks of the Blackfriars ship had been infested by the *teredo* 'shipworm', a marine creature that proves that the ship had been used primarily for sea-going. Presumably, therefore, the vessel and its crew had been hired for the task of transporting the building stone from Kent to London, and the fact that a similar vessel was found at Bruges in Belgium in 1899 suggests that these were normal coastal trading ships to be seen around the ports of north-western Europe at that time.[16]

The Blackfriars ship, interesting as it is, does not really answer the various questions raised by the building of the city wall. There are two events which occurred during the years 190–225 which might account for the building of the wall, though it is difficult to judge their respective merits. The first was the claim of the Governor of Britain, Clodius Albinus, to the throne on the assassination of the Emperor Commodus at the end of 192. Three other provincial governors were also claimants, but eventually it was Septimius Severus, Governor of Pannonia (now Hungary), who secured the throne with the help of sixteen legions. Initially Severus recognized Albinus as having a right to the succession, but this was merely a delaying tactic to enable him to defeat the other claimants first. By 194 Albinus realized that a confrontation with Severus was inevitable; two years later he led an army across to Gaul, but was defeated in 197 in a battle near Lyon.

It is possible that Albinus, before embarking on his confrontation with Severus, decided to develop and defend London as the capital of his province, because it lay at the centre of communications. Indeed an official list of routes, the so-called Antonine Itinerary, begins or ends at London seven of its fifteen routes in Britain, while the town was an intermediate station on an eighth. Several other towns, such as Dorchester-on-Thames, Chichester, Silchester and Verulamium, were also possibly defended at this time, and so, according to this theory, the city wall of London may have been built as a more general scheme of defence.[17]

On the other hand it may have been Severus himself who, as Emperor, authorized the town defences a few years later, even though he was heavily involved in restoring the northern defences of Britain after they had been depleted of troops by Albinus. Although it seems unlikely that he would have stretched his resources in northern Britain to build London's defences at the same time, it is still possible that during the early third century, when he divided Britain into the two provinces of Britannia Superior and Britannia Inferior, he encouraged the town to build its defences with a view to making it the capital of Britannia Superior.

The restored city

The investigation of the Huggin Hill baths near Southwark Bridge in August 1964 revealed a puzzle, because, although the identification of the baths was clear enough, it was its apparently short period of use that was so curious. Having been built not earlier than about A D 80, and possibly enlarged during the early second century to become one of the largest public baths in Roman Britain, it seems to have been demolished before 200.[1]

Presumably there was no further need for these baths, but why only halfway through the Roman period? In spite of our lack of understanding, there had in fact been such an enormous quantity of pottery to date the demolition of the baths, that the dating had to be accepted and fitted into our reconstruction of the history of Roman London. This could not be done for many years, and it is only now that it is recognized as an important clue to the second-century period of decline.

The destruction of the baths may have occurred about the time that the city defences were being built, possibly as part of an effort to tidy up the city at the end of the period of decline. But if London had had a large population at that time, it is unlikely that the baths would have been demolished, though they may have been replaced by some newer public baths elsewhere in the town. One possible site is the hilltop above the baths where a cold water bath, measuring 4.4 m by 2.6 m, was found in 1906 at the junction of Cannon Street and Queen Victoria Street. Another is in Lime Street, just east of the forum, where a rectangular room measuring 3.3 m by 2.4 m was found in 1932, and was believed to be part of a Roman bath.[2]

Traces of two other attempts to tidy up the city at that time have also been found, the first being to fill in the silted defensive ditch of the Cripplegate fort, and the second to fill an old gravel pit that had been used as a town rubbish dump for many years. At the time of Hadrian, during the 120s, when the fort defences were new, the fort ditch was about 3 m wide and 1.5 m deep; but by the end of the second century it was merely a silty hollow about 0.6 m deep. This was unsightly and unwanted, so the hollow was filled with loads of clay which fortunately contained a considerable quantity of pottery of the late second century.[3]

The gravel pit that had been used as a rubbish dump was found in 1841 while the Royal Exchange was being built. The pit measured 12 m by 15 m, and descended 5.8 m below the

D M
VIVIO·MARC
ANO·⅂LEGⅡI
AVG·IANVARIA
MARTINA·CNIVNX
PIENTISⓈIMA·POSV
IT·ME   MORAM

Tombstone of Vivius Marcianus of the Second Augustan Legion, found in 1669 at Ludgate Hill.

Roman ground level; and, as many of the objects recovered from it can be dated to the late first or early second century, the pit had obviously been a rubbish dumping area for some time and must have remained an unpleasant scar near the centre of Londinium for about a century. Nobody apparently bothered about this during the period of neglect in the middle of the second century, but after AD 200 the pit was filled in, the clue to when this occurred being the discovery of a coin of Septimius Severus beneath the upper filling of dumped gravel that sealed the pit.

Charles Roach Smith observed that the rubbish below

was composed almost entirely of animal and vegetable matter, apparently thrown in as refuse, from adjacent shops and houses. In one part of the pit were loads of oyster-shells, in another dross from the smith's forge, bones of cows, sheep and goats, matted together with ordure and interspersed with an abundance of broken pottery, pieces of leather, portions of sandals, fragments of glass, lamps, instruments of iron, fibulae, a strigil, coins and other objects.... The coins discovered in this pit ... are chiefly of the second brass of Vespasian and Domitian, to the amount of nearly 12, with only a solitary instance of a late date in a plated denarius of Severus; these coins must necessarily have been deposited previous to the pit having been covered in for building on.[4]

The tidying up of Londinium must have been the prelude to the town's reconstruction, but what evidence is there of a substantial population in the third century? Very little indeed. Inscriptions suggest that the Governor may have lived there, so we should expect his staff to have added to the population. But the fate of the Cripplegate fort which housed his guard is not known, even though its defensive ditch had just been filled in. If the fort was used by the Governor of Britannia Superior, then its east and south walls, now on the inside of the new city defences, must have remained standing. There is no evidence for or against this, but it is to be expected that if the fort remained as a fortified stronghold, it would have had a defensive ditch. Since no such ditch was ever dug during the third or fourth centuries, it is possible that the fort remained an unused shell. There is also no positive evidence to show that the Governor was based in London during the third century, though the undoubted presence of military personnel and civil administrators, recorded on inscriptions, may represent members of his staff.

The tombstones of two soldiers serving in third-century London have been dated by the fact that they were set up by their wives, for serving soldiers were not allowed to marry until Septimius Severus abolished this law after AD 197. Both are among the oldest discoveries of Roman London, the first having been found in 1669 during the rebuilding of St Martin's church in Ludgate Hill after the Great Fire of 1666. Its inscription records: 'To the spirits of the departed, and to Vivius Marcianus of the II Legion Augusta; Januaria Martina his most devoted wife set up this memorial.'[5] The second was found a century later, in 1787, near the Minories, north of the Tower of London, and reads, 'To the spirits of the departed: Flavius Agricola, soldier of the VI Legion Victrix, lived 42 years, 10 days; Albia Faustina had this made for her peerless husband.'[6] It is particularly interesting that Vivius Marcianus is shown holding in his left hand what is probably a scroll, presumably reflecting his clerical duties. Besides this, there is the discovery in 1975 of a massive altar at Blackfriars, recording the action of a Governor of Britannia Superior, who, probably between 251 and 259, rebuilt the temple of Isis. It was set up 'In honour of the Imperial House, Marcus Martiannius Pulcher . . . governor appointed by the two emperors, ordered the temple of Isis, which had fallen down through old age, to be restored.'[7] The rebuilding of this temple may reflect both the action of the provincial government in restoring London as the capital, and the proximity of the Governor who may have had a residence in the city at that time.

Altar commemorating the restoration of a temple of Isis in London, by Marcus Martiannius Pulcher. Found in 1975 at Blackfriars.

133

The presence of government officials is again suggested by another large limestone altar, also found at Blackfriars in 1975. Its inscription reads: 'Aquilinus, the emperor's freedman, and Mercator and Audax and Graecus restored this temple which had fallen down through old age, for Jupiter [?] best and greatest.'[8] There is uncertainty as to whether or not this was from a temple of Jupiter, though he is the most likely of several possible deities. Quite apart from this being more evidence of the restoration of London, its mention of an Imperial freedman is of special interest. Aquilinus belonged to an Imperial bureaucracy that made extensive use of slaves, and it was no doubt because he had distinguished himself that he was rewarded with a grant of freedom. As Imperial freedmen were not unusual in provincial capitals, and could be wealthy and influential men, it is possible that his three associates were slaves in the Imperial service.

Another indication that the city had a fairly substantial population is that several major religious monuments were built during the third century, in addition to the restoration of old temples and the construction of new temples. The old temples of Isis and Jupiter(?) were not the only religious buildings to be restored; a marble plinth, possibly of third-century date, was found in 1854 in Budge Row, near the Walbrook, and was dedicated 'To the Mother Goddesses, the district restored [this shrine] at their own expense.'[9] This plinth presumably supported a stone sculpture of the three Mother Goddesses like that found lying near a mosaic pavement close to St Olave's church, in Hart Street, about 1840.[10]

These inscriptions also reflect a population with old and new ideas, and illustrate the transition in religious belief throughout the Empire which was so characteristic of the third century. The ancestral religions were declining in popularity in the face of the growth of various Oriental mystery religions, such as those of Isis, Cybele, Mithras and finally Christianity, all of which were able to flourish in London and elsewhere. The worship of the old gods had little comfort to offer the dying and bereaved, since the souls of the dead were believed to enter a shadowy half-existence in the underworld; in contrast, the mystery cults offered the chance of immortality and happiness in the afterlife. During the early part of the Roman Empire, official resistance to the Oriental religions had been strong; hence the apparent construction of one of their temples or shrines, that of Isis, in London during the late first century, probably reflects the presence of merchants from the eastern Mediterranean where these religions were strongest. By the third century the mystery religions had become so popular that they began to be adopted into the state religion; thus it is not

surprising to find the Governor of Britannia Superior restoring the ruined temple of Isis. Nevertheless, London is unusual among the cities of Roman Britain, in that we can see very clearly the transition to the new mystery religions, and particularly the conflict which eventually culminated in the success of Christianity during the fourth century.

The old deities were still important, however, and are depicted on a remarkable monument whose existence in third-century London was not suspected until 1975. It was an arch built of limestone from Lincolnshire, which had been broken-up during the late fourth century, its pieces having been used in a defensive wall along the river bank. Monumental arches are, of course, well known in the Mediterranean region, but in Britain, apart from the Colchester arch, they have only been found at Verulamium and Richborough, where no more than their foundations survived. The discovery of an arch in London is therefore particularly important: for the first time we know how an arch in Roman Britain was decorated even though we do not know where the arch stood.[11] It is thanks to the reconstruction by Tom Blagg, a specialist in Roman architecture, that so much is now known about its form and decoration. The many deities suggest that the arch may have been associated with a religious precinct, though since it was 7.57 m wide there is no reason why it should not have spanned a main street as a free-standing arch, like those excavated at Verulamium

Sculptured stone from the frieze of the monumental arch, showing Mars (left) and the purse and shoulder of Mercury (right). It had been reused in the late Roman riverside defensive wall of London, at Blackfriars, where it was found in 1975.

Reconstruction of the monumental archway whose fragments were found at Blackfriars in 1975.

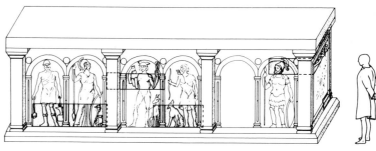

Reconstruction of the screen of gods from fragments found at Blackfriars in 1975.

The London arch was at least 8–9 m high, and has been dated to the third century by its style, since its inscription has not been found. Its main decorative subjects were four full-length classical deities, two of whom were Minerva and Hercules. Above these in the spandrels of the arch were roundels probably with busts of figures representing the seasons. Near the top, on one side was a frieze consisting of busts of divinities, probably depicting the gods of the week (Saturn, Sol, Luna, Mars, Mercury, Jupiter and Venus); on the other side the formal inscription was apparently situated between winged cupids.

The arch was not the only monument discovered at Blackfriars which depicted the traditional classical deities. Parts of a 'Screen of Gods', as it has been called, were also found. It took the form of a free-standing stone wall more than 6.20 m long and 0.57 m thick, which perhaps once stood in a temple precinct.[12] At least three pairs of niches contained sculptured deities; Vulcan and Minerva were in the first pair, Diana and possibly Mercury in the next, Mars and another god in the third. At one end there was a wind god, while at the back of the screen was a series of minor divinities and mythological creatures, including a bull's head, an eagle, and a dancing woman. Monumental screens are unusual in Roman architecture, though one is known to have stood in the precinct of the classical temple of Sulis Minerva at Bath.[13]

The worship of the Oriental cults was in great contrast to the staid formal worship of the ancient deities depicted on the arch and screen. Although many Romans were attracted by the elaborate rituals and intense emotional appeal of the cults, not everyone was convinced of their validity. The contemporary classical writer Minucius Felix wrote of the worship of Isis that the shaven priests, mourning, bewailing, and searching for Isis' lost son, beat their breasts and mimicked the sorrows of the unhappy mother; then when the stripling is found, Isis rejoices, and her priests are full of joy.

And year by year, they cease not to lose what they find or to find what they lose. Is it not absurd either to mourn your object of worship, or to worship your object of mourning? Yet these old Egyptian rites have now found their way to Rome, so that you may play the fool to the swallow and sistrum of Isis.[14]

The worship of Cybele in London is attested by the discovery of various statues, statuettes and other items. Cybele was a manifestation of the Great Mother Goddess who fell in love with a young man called Atys. But he would not respond to her approaches, and when she caught him in an act of infidelity, she drove him mad so that he castrated himself and bled to death. In spite of this, joy was the outcome of religious ceremonies, for, as a god, Atys rose again to give hope in the afterlife to the followers of Cybele. This was a very popular religion in spite of the fact that the priests were eunuchs, and had to castrate themselves as part of their process of initiation.[15] In addition to a stone statue, possibly of Atys, from Bevis Marks in the eastern part of the city and a small statuette said to be of Atys, from the bed of the Thames at London Bridge,[16] undoubtedly the most important find was a pair of bronze forceps also from the river at London Bridge, which may have been used in the castration of priests. Beautifully decorated with the busts of Atys and Cybele, as well as of the deities of the Roman week, this macabre object, now preserved in the British Museum, shows signs of much usage and had been carefully repaired in Roman times.[17]

Minucius Felix, denounced these rites, saying that 'it was a shame to speak' of the worship of Cybele, for 'in deference to this fable her eunuch priests worship her by inflicting the same mutilation on their own bodies. Such practices are not sacred rites but tortures.'[18]

The only temple of a mystery religion so far found in London is one dedicated to Mithras, lord of light. No other discovery of this kind has made a greater impact on present-day Londoners. It was identified in 1954 by Professor W. F. Grimes near the Mansion House. On 18 September publicity overtook the team of archaeologists as they were quietly working on a bombed site that was about to be redeveloped, for on that day the marble head of Mithras, wearing his Phrygian cap, was unearthed, and three days later his neck was found. The discovery of other marble sculptures quickly followed, collectively reflecting the syncretic belief, common in the third century, that all gods are probably different manifestations of the same deity. On 26 September the head of Minerva, goddess of learning, was found. On 4 October the archaeologists found a shallow pit, and in it the marble head of Serapis, Egyptian god of the harvest and the underworld, a marble arm and hand clasping the hilt of a dagger, and the delightful figure of the reclining youth Mercury. On 7 October a marble statue of Bacchus, god

Bronze forceps probably used in the cult of Cybele, from the Thames at London Bridge. Length about 290 mm.

Marble head of Serapis found
in the temple of Mithras,
Walbrook.

of wine, was found together with the figures of Silenus seated on
a donkey, with Pan, a satyr and a maenad (a female attendant)
standing close by. Although it was soon realized that this
temple had been dedicated to Mithras, it was also recognized
that this was where some other remarkable Roman marble
sculptures had been found in 1889, by building labourers.
Housed in the London Museum, they included the figure of a
Genius, perhaps a personification of the prosperity of London,
also the figure of a river god, and a scene showing Mithras
slaying a sacred bull.[19]

The careful excavation of this temple has told us much about
the practice of the Mithraic religion in Londinium during the
third century, though its historical importance, as distinct from
its importance as an archaeological site, should not be
exaggerated. It was only a small building, and held a small but

wealthy congregation, who could express their devotion in erecting a fine temple, and by purchasing the beautifully sculptured heads of deities which had been expertly carved in good quality Italian marble.

The worship of Mithras had been introduced from Asia Minor by the Roman army during the first century A D. As the 'Unconquered' god, Mithras represented courage and was popular with soldiers; his temples have been found primarily in Roman military areas such as northern England and Wales. He also represented honesty, integrity and purity, thus appealing to government officials, merchants and traders, with the result that his temples were also found in many important towns and ports in the Empire, where his followers were taught that Mithras helped men both on earth and after death.

According to legend, Mithras was probably born of life-giving rock, and soon embarked upon a life of hardship, creating good out of the eternal conflict between the forces of Good and Evil. He was commanded by the Sun to pursue and catch a primeval bull, the personification of brute force and

Marble head of Minerva from the temple of Mithras, Walbrook.

139

Mithraic group depicting the bull-slaying, found in 1889, probably in or near the temple of Mithras, Walbrook.

vitality. After a terrible struggle he succeeded, then brought the bull back to his cave where he slew it, and so released its concentrated power for the benefit of mankind. For this reason the bull-slaying scene was the central theme in every temple of Mithras and was represented more than twice in sculptures in the London temple. The marble scene found in the temple in 1889 is typical, and shows the moment when Mithras plunges his dagger into the neck of the bull; as the bull dies new forms of life spring up – from its body useful plants and herbs, from its blood the vine, whilst from its semen all useful animals are created. But there is one sinister shadow on this scene, the scorpion, agent of the Lord of Darkness and Evil, trying to contaminate the creation by attacking the bull's genital organs. On each side of Mithras stand his two attendants, Cautes with an uplifted torch signifying hope, and Cautopates with a down-turned torch representing sorrow. After the death of the bull, Mithras and the Sun celebrated the event with a feast of the bull's flesh and a drink made from a magical herb, and it was the imitation of this feast that was the central act of worship in temples such as that in London. When the feast was over, Mithras mounted the chariot of the Sun and ascended into heaven, from where he guided men, who had the knowledge that Mithras himself had suffered as a man on earth.[20]

The worshippers were divided into seven grades, admission to each of which involved severe tests and rites. The highest was that of *Pater*, the Father, who was responsible for teaching, disciplining and organizing the congregation. But the religion

The temple of Mithras, Walbrook, as excavated in 1954. Beyond the nave and side aisles there lies the apsidal focus of the rites. The large concrete blocks in the nave are recent foundations.

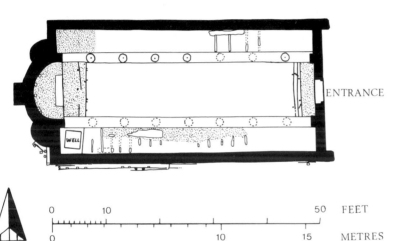

ENTRANCE

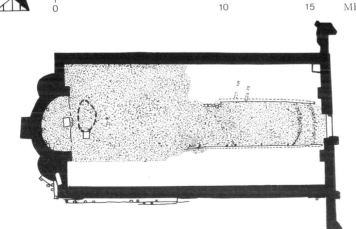

The temple of Mithras, Walbrook. Top: plan of the original building with steps and sunken nave; bottom: a final stage in the temple with raised floors, a pit (outlined) on the site of an earlier pedestal, and, within the apse, a stone support for an altar.

141

Imaginative reconstruction of the interior of the temple of Mithras.

had a serious flaw; unlike its great rival, Christianity, it was restricted to men only, and had no place either for women or for the family. Also it was not totalitarian, and allowed the presence of other deities, which is why the sculptures of so many other gods were found in the temple.

The temple had been built on thick dumps of rubbish beside the Walbrook stream. But as a rectangular building only 7.9 m wide and 17.8 m long, it resembled an early Christian church, particularly as it was aligned east-west, though a semicircular apse at the west end is unlikely to have been found in a church.[21] The congregation entered the temple from the east through a narthex or anteroom 11.1 m wide; having opened the double doors of the temple, they descended four steps to the wooden floor of the nave. At the far end they saw two broad steps which led up to the apse, where there probably once stood an image of Mithras. Sculptures of the two attendants, Cautes and Cautopates, probably stood on either side of the nave, and near the apse were the altars. A low sleeper wall ran along each side of the nave and separated it from the raised wooden floors of the side aisles. It was in the aisles that the congregation sat on benches, the stumps of which were found; the seven columns

Marble head of Mithras from the temple of Mithras, Walbrook.

supporting the roof were a reminder of the seven grades through which the worshippers had to pass.

Quite apart from the layout of the temple, which shows that the rituals took place in the nave, some of the finds proved to be useful clues to the actual nature of the rituals. One such find was the sculpture of the head of Mithras himself, for unlike the others, its surface was in a sugary condition that a marble specialist suggests was the result of its having been burnt. The best explanation for this is that lighted torches had been held against the face during the rituals. The head of Mithras perhaps stood in the apse, where in addition to the use of fire, water was also important in the ritual, and this was drawn from a timber-lined well situated at the west end of the south aisle, close to the apse. Metal candlesticks and fragments of small pottery cups, found on the floor of the temple, suggest that the ritual feast, in commemoration of that held by Mithras, was held in darkened conditions as a reminder of Mithras' cave; chicken bones, also found on the floor, were all that remained of the creatures that had been sacrificed. A magical drink, presumably prepared from a herb, seems to have been drunk during the rites, and was apparently made in a special silver

Decorated silver box and strainer from the temple of Mithras.

box containing a silver infusor. This was one of the most remarkable objects discovered in the temple, because of its extraordinary decoration in relief depicting a variety of animals, including an elephant, snake, lion, hippopotamus, deer and wild boar. There are even mythical griffins which are shown trying to tear open coffin-like boxes, some of which contain men; the meaning of this is far from clear, though there may be a link with Mithras the hunter god.

Of those who worshipped in the temple, Ulpius Silvanus, a veteran of the II Legion Augusta, is the only one who can be identified. An inscription on the aforementioned marble sculpture found in 1889, showing Mithras killing the bull, records that 'Ulpius Silvanus, veteran of the II Legion Augusta, paid his vow; enlisted [or initiated] at Arausio.' Arausio is the modern Orange in southern France, and was a colony for the II Legion.

No trace of sculptured bodies was found to go with the marble heads, and it is believed that they were made of wood or stucco presumably as an economy. This was not the only economy in the temple, since there were also several sculptures in English limestone that were crude compared with the Italian marbles. Among these was the inevitable figure of Cautopates; also one of the Dioscuri (the Heavenly Twins, Castor and Pollux) and a scene showing Mithras killing the sacred bull.

The temple continued in use until at least the middle of the fourth century, various alterations having been made to the building, including raising its floors on various occasions on account of the increasingly wet conditions beside the Walbrook stream, and removing the columns between the nave and aisles. After its initial lavish appearance, the temple gradually declined particularly during the fourth century, presumably reflecting the sinking fortunes of those who worshipped there, until it had become, as Professor Grimes described it, 'a somewhat ramshackle affair'.

It was about this time that a serious threat to the existence of the small Mithraic community led to the hiding of the most precious treasures in the temple. The marble heads were buried in shallow pits beneath the floors in the nave and aisles, while the silver box was hidden behind a stone in the north wall. Exactly when this happened is not clear, but on the evidence of coins it must have been either at the end of the third or during the fourth century. Indeed the head of Mithras may have been broken with an axe before it was buried. Not all the sculptures were saved by burial, however, for the comparatively crude limestone statues were apparently left standing. When the threatened attack on the temple eventually occurred, the visible sculptures were smashed, and pieces scattered for some distance around, the figure of one of the Dioscuri being dumped on the east bank of the Walbrook south of the temple. It is fortunate, therefore, that the people who desecrated the temple were presumably unaware of the buried marbles.[22]

Marble sculptures of Serapis, Mercury and a large hand as found in the temple of Mithras.

Who were these people who desecrated the temple? Although they left no clue other than the broken and scattered images, there can be little doubt that they were Christians. By the third century Christianity had spread throughout the Empire; as it gained converts among even the highest-ranking people in the provinces, we can assume their presence in London. They were feared by the established religions, and were called upon to defend themselves from fantastic charges, such a eating babies, indulging in sexual orgies, and committing incest. In spite of the most terrible persecution, especially by Diocletian at the beginning of the fourth century, Christianity spread into the Senate in Rome, and even into the Emperor's court, and finally among members of the Imperial family. In 312 the Emperor Constantine was himself converted, and at last Christianity was officially recognized. Two years later Restitutus, Bishop of London, together with two other bishops from Britain, attended the important Council of Arles to represent the diocese of London.[23] This recognition of their religion stimulated a vigorous, even vicious, attack on Christianity's chief rival – Mithraism – which they saw as a diabolical travesty of their own beliefs. Outwardly somewhat similar, both religions demanded high ideals, and both conducted secret rites which centred around a sacred meal based upon a sacrifice, in which the worshippers ate flesh or its substitute, and drank a special drink.

The ransacking of the temple in London was not an isolated incident, for in Germany at least four temples of Mithras have been found in a deliberately destroyed state; in Britain, other temples at Rudchester and Carrawburgh in northern England, and at Caernarvon in Wales were also desecrated. Surprisingly, the temple in London was not destroyed, but continued in use until probably after 350; as the sculptures and the silver box were not recovered, however, it is likely that those who went on worshipping at the temple and laid down more floors, were either too scared to recover the hidden treasures, or else did not know of their existence.

These final worshippers left two items: an altar base with a votive deposit of coins of Licinius I (307–24) and Constantine the Great (309–13), and a small mid third-century marble statue of Bacchus with some of his companions – Pan sitting on a vine, the genial fat drunkard Silenus sitting side-saddle on a donkey and clasping a wine cup in his lap, a maenad and a satyr accompanied by a panther. Were the worshippers followers of Mithras or of Bacchus? We are unlikely ever to know, just as it is unlikely that we shall fully understand the significance of the inscription carved on the base of the sculpture: HOMINIBVS BAGIS BITAM (i.e., '[Give] life to the men who wander.')

Stamps of SYAGRIVS and the *chi-rho* monogram on metal ingots from the Thames between Battersea and Wandsworth.

Small pewter bowl bearing an incised Christian *chi-rho* monogram on its base. Found in Copthall Court.

Marble sculpture of Bacchus
and companions from the
temple of Mithras.

Eventually, however, the temple was abandoned, and finally
collapsed.

But what other evidence is there of the Christians of Roman
London? Very little indeed. The fact that just two years after
Christianity had become legitimized there was a bishop of
London, implies that there was a significant, if small, Christian
community there. But all that has been found of them within
the city is a small pewter bowl from Copthall Close, with a
scratched 'Chi-Rho' (the first two Greek letters of the name of
Christ) on the underside of its base. Other than this, several
pewter ingots stamped with the Chi-Rho monogram and the
words 'SPES IN DEO'('Hope in God'), as well as the name
SYAGRIVS, were found in the Thames near Battersea Bridge,
and apparently date from the fourth or fifth century.[24]

London, being the seat of a bishop during the fourth century, presumably had a church, even though it may have been little more than a room or two set aside in a house, as occurred at Lullingstone villa in Kent; or perhaps an individual building somewhat like that found at Silchester.[25] The ancient tradition that the church of St Peter-upon-Cornhill was founded in AD 179 has nothing to support it, particularly since at that time the site was occupied by the Roman basilica, which, as a Roman public building, could not have been used for Christian worship until the fourth century at the earliest. In spite of this, St Peter's church celebrated its eighteenth centenary in January 1979 in the presence of the Bishop of London, and the Lord Mayor and Lady Mayoress. Such an old tradition may in fact preserve a distant and distorted element of truth possibly dating from the end of the Roman period, particularly as the church is centrally placed over the basilica site; perhaps archaeological excavations on this site may one day clarify the background to this curious and persistent tradition.[26]

Although there is ample evidence of the religious beliefs of the people of London during the third century, there is far less evidence of the people themselves. Had the city been densely populated there should be more trace of occupation, but instead the amount of building debris is very small, when compared with that of late-first-century London. Indeed, a careful analysis of occupation rubbish, both in pits and layers, shows that there was a significant decrease in the amount of domestic rubbish in the town after the middle of the second century, and this is taken to reflect a much smaller urban population than that of the late first and early second centuries.[27]

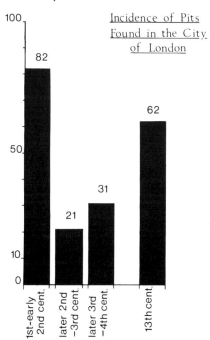

Incidence of Pits Found in the City of London

The relative scarcity of later Roman pits constitutes part of the evidence that a substantial decline occurred in the population of Roman London.

Roman mosaic found in Old Broad Street in 1854.

Traces of houses are few during the third and fourth centuries, though it is clear that a scatter of once fine dwellings used to exist across the city but were destroyed when deep office basements were dug before the last war. Most of these major houses are undated except from the style of the polychrome mosaics which they contained in their principal rooms, though occasionally pottery and coins associated with these buildings do give us a more precise dating. Some were built close to the forum, others along the Walbrook valley, like part of a building that was found in 1869 near the Mansion House, in Queen Victoria Street.

The mosaic from this building is now on display in the Museum of London; it is 6 m long and 4 m wide, with an apsidal north end, and has as attractive and colourful abstract design which overlaid a hypocaust. This must have been in the principal heated living room of a very fine house, though no plan of other parts of the building were found.[28] As art objects the mosaics in these houses are generally of a good provincial quality, and, although colourful, normally have abstract decorations, though a representation of Bacchus formed the central figure in mosaics from Leadenhall Street and Broad Street.

149

Roman mosaic depicting
Bacchus on a tiger, found in
Leadenhall Street in 1803.

Small portions of the plans of several houses have been
recorded and partly dated since the war, and by comparison
with Roman town houses excavated elsewhere in Britain it is
clear that they were large private residences whose rooms were
evidently ranged around a courtyard, and presumably
included an entrance hall, a dining room, bedrooms, kitchens,
and servant quarters. Though mosaics, hypocausts, stone
walls, and fragments of wall paintings are all that have usually
survived, even this incomplete evidence testifies to the wealth
and high standard of living of the occupants. One of those
post-war discoveries was at Lloyds building in Lime Street, just

KEY
- ■ = Foundations of main building
- ▨ = Robbed walls
- ▦ = Ragstone walls unrelated to main building
- ▥ = Red tesselated floor
- ▪ = Pilae
- ▭ = Opus signinum

0   5   10   15 METRES

Moulding

Flavian Pit

4th cent. Pit

Hoard

4th cent. Pit

Late 1st cent Pit

east of the basilica, where part of a Roman building was excavated in 1951. It had stone walls, plain red mosaic pavements and heated rooms, and it had been enlarged in the late third century when a hoard of bronze coins was hidden in a wall. Part of another building, which included a mosaic with a black and white geometric pattern, was found and preserved beneath 11 Ironmonger Lane; and below All Hallows Barking Church, close to the Tower of London, traces of ragstone walls, and a red mosaic pavement overlying pottery not earlier than the late second century, were found in 1928–30 which presumably belonged to another third-century house.[29]

Both these, and other buildings in Southwark, suggest that there was a major change in building technique in London between the first-early second and the third-fourth centuries. The domestic buildings of the earlier period usually had walls of timber and clay, which gave rise to many clay layers on the sites, whereas in the later Roman deposits such clay layers are generally absent, probably because walls were usually built of Kentish ragstone and mortar. It is extremely unusual to find a ragstone wall in anything other than a public building during the earlier period, though foundations of ragstone are not uncommon; and it is exceptionally rare to find traces of clay walls in buildings of the third or fourth century.

The only meaningful plan of a Roman dwelling of the third century so far found is that excavated at Billingsgate from 1968 onwards. In that year the nineteenth-century buildings on the site were cleared away to widen Lower Thames Street, and, as the well-known Roman bath found in 1848 beneath the Coal Exchange became accessible, it was possible to start an archaeological excavation to establish its age and significance. The entire brick-built bath suite, discovered in 1848 and 1859, was soon uncovered, and it was clearly so small that it must

Plan of a third-century building found in Lime Street, 1951–2.

Bird painted on wall plaster found in a Roman well in Queen Victoria Street.

151

Reconstruction model of the small Roman bath building at Billingsgate, with the roof partly cut away to show the interior. The *frigidarium* is on the left, the *caldarium* and its furnace are front right with the *tepidarium* behind.

Opposite above, the arched flue of the furnace which heated the apsidal *caldarium* of the small bath building at Billingsgate. Excavated in 1967.

Opposite below, a seat for two people in the *tepidarium* of the small bath building at Billingsgate. Found in 1848.

have been private. Its square *frigidarium*, where the bather changed and exercised, originally had a red mosaic floor, and it was on this that there stood a small stone-lined water tank that the bather had to use instead of a cold water bath. Entrance to this room was through a doorway from a small vestibule, the well-worn tile doorstep reflecting the constant use of the bath. The vestibule also had an opening into a small apsidal *tepidarium*, the warmth coming from an underfloor hypocaust, and in one wall there was a recessed seat for two people. A third doorway led off the vestibule into the *caldarium*, which was of similar shape and size, and situated next to the furnace supplying the underfloor heating.[30]

Because the bath was far too small to have been a public building, the excavation was extended to the north and east in search of the house to which it was presumably attached. This was soon found, and by 1970 enough of its plan had been uncovered to show that it had at least two, possibly three, wings that partly enclosed the bath, and that it had probably been built during the late second century. The house was built of ragstone and had been deeply set in a terrace at the bottom of the steep hillside, partly in front of a strongly buttressed retaining wall. Each wing was bordered by a corridor, with a plain red mosaic floor, off which there were a number of living rooms, those in the east wing all having been heated, and originally probably floored with mosaic pavements. The bath was a separate building entered through a covered porch from the north

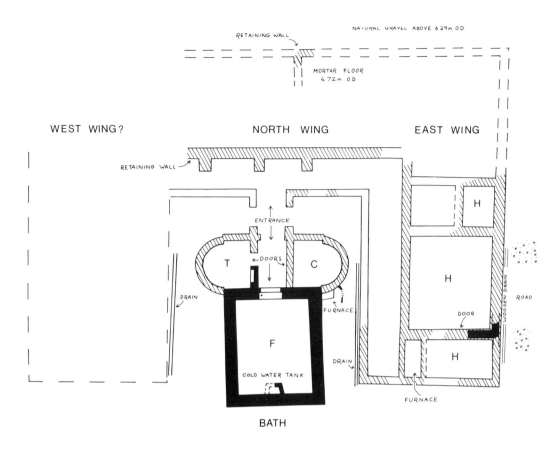

RETAINING WALL

NATURAL GRAVEL ABOVE 6.29m O.D.

MORTAR FLOOR
4.72m O.D.

WEST WING?　　　　NORTH WING　　　EAST WING

RETAINING WALL

ENTRANCE

DOORS

T　　C

H

H

DRAIN

FURNACE

ROAD

DOOR

WOODEN DRAIN

F

COLD WATER TANK

DRAIN

H

FURNACE

BATH

FOUNDATION
WALL

0	10		50		100 Feet

0	5	10		20		30	Metres

Two, possibly three, wings of
a Roman dwelling built
around a small bath house,
found opposite Billingsgate.

Reconstruction of the small
third-century bath and
adjacent dwelling at
Billingsgate.

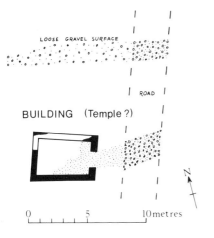

A small temple-like building of the third century found at the south end of St Dunstan's Hill in 1967.

wing of the house, and was placed in such a dominant situation relative to the house as to raise serious doubts about this having been an ordinary dwelling. The doubts are reinforced by the fact that the bath is larger than would be expected in this size of house; also by the fact that the builders evidently had great difficulty in setting the bath and house into the hillside, judging from the high retaining walls and the four major drains that they built. These not only reflected the need for a constant supply of fresh spring water to the bath, but also facilities to carry away excess water.

What purpose other than that of an ordinary dwelling could it have served? Its construction around a bath is most unusual, and, remembering its waterfront location, one possibility is that it might have been a small inn for wealthy travellers visiting the port. Nearby the excavations also disclosed a small stone building with a single room, and a doorway in its east side, that may have been a small temple. It was apparently contemporary with the dwelling at Billingsgate, and fortunately its walls still retained traces of their painted decoration of red lines on a pink background speckled with red splashes.

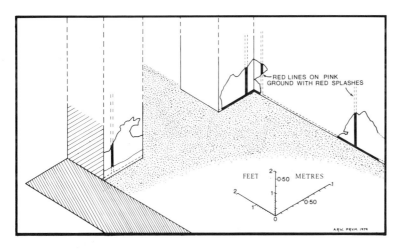

Traces of painted wall decoration near the doorway of the small temple-like building excavated in St Dunstan's Hill in 1967.

155

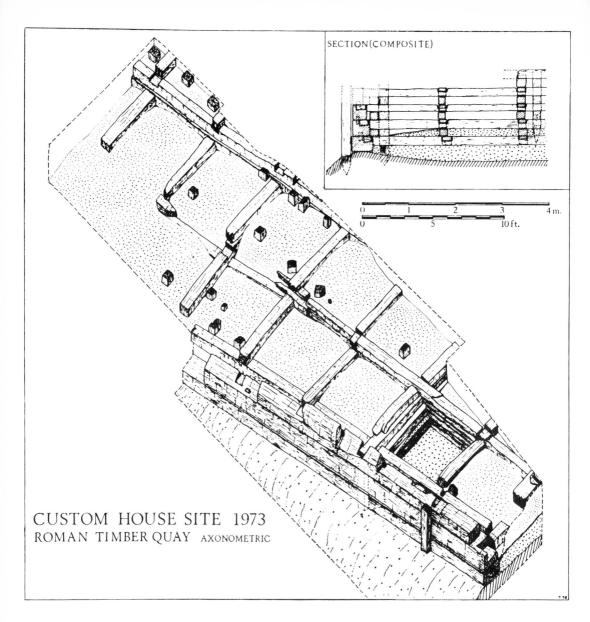

SECTION (COMPOSITE)

CUSTOM HOUSE SITE 1973
ROMAN TIMBER QUAY AXONOMETRIC

Part of the Roman timber quay built in the latter half of the second century.

There is far less evidence of trade in the Roman city during the third century than might be expected, though the recent discovery of a major Roman timber quay between the site of the Tower of London and the mouth of the Walbrook stream is an important indication of at least some trade at that time.[31] This quay was apparently built during the second half of the second century, probably at the end of the century, and although it varies in construction details, perhaps reflecting the work of different carpenters, the final effect was the same – a massive wall of horizontally-laid squared baulks of oak, to which shipping could tie up. The quay was more than half a mile long, and must have been built by civic effort rather than by private enterprise, presumably in yet another attempt to restore the fortunes of the port of Roman London. It was probably designed for use by a variety of ships, such as the beamy flat-bottomed native sea-going sailing vessels of the type that had sunk at Blackfriars, as well as the round-bottomed Mediterranean style of merchant ships, like the third-century vessel that was found in 1910 on the County Hall site beside the river opposite Westminster. But in addition there were river craft which no doubt ranged from dugout canoes to the more substantial native-built river barges like that found in 1959 abandoned in a marshy creek, at Guy's Hospital in Southwark.[32]

It is through the fortunate discovery of part of the quay in 1974 and 1975 at New Fresh Wharf, just downstream of London Bridge, that we are able to reconstruct the use to which these ships were put. It is believed that there was approximately a 2 m depth of water beside the quay, and that this was deep enough for the sea-going trading ships importing goods from Gaul and Germany.[33] They are likely to have been vessels similar to the County Hall ship, whose rounded hull and projecting keel show that, like other ships of Mediterranean design,

Plan and sections of the third-century ship from the County Hall site, Westminster, in 1910.

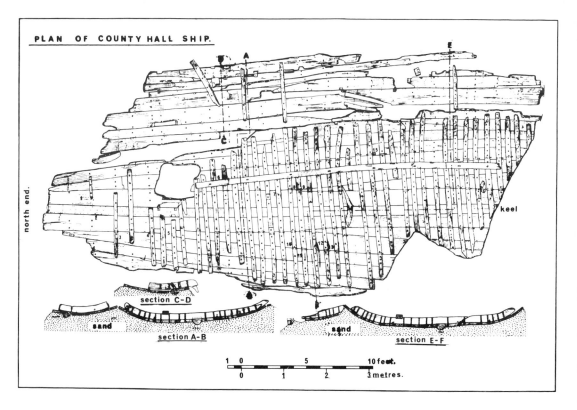

PLAN OF COUNTY HALL SHIP.

north end.

keel

section C-D

sand

section A-B

sand

section E-F

| 1 | 0 | | | 5 | | | 10 feet. |
0   1   2   3 metres.

Part of the Roman ship from the County Hall site, as excavated in 1910.

The north-facing end of the second-century barge found at Guy's Hospital in 1959.

it was designed to work from quays, rather than from tidal beaches.[34] The merchant ship with a cargo of samian ware, that was wrecked in the second century on Pudding Pan Sand, in the Thames estuary, was almost certainly bound for London from a port in Gaul, and was probably a ship of this type.[35]

The quay was particularly well preserved at New Fresh Wharf, and although its timber deck had been destroyed, the upright posts were found which were probably part of a quayside warehouse in which the offloaded goods were stored. Some of the cargo had been damaged during the voyages and while being offloaded, and these breakages were dumped into the river beneath the quay, where they were found by the archaeologists. A major part of the goods were broken pieces of unused samian ware cups, bowls and dishes that had been imported from Gaul; while the remainder was a mass of sherds of Rhenish wares, including a large group of German mortaria mixing bowls, some from the potter Verecundus. Numerous other objects were also found around the quay, including a number of imported figurines of Venus, wooden writing tablets, a wooden bowl, a basket and leather shoes that were perhaps part of the rubbish thrown from the moored ships.[36]

The north-facing end of a shallow-draught river barge, abandoned during the late second century. Found at Guy's Hospital, Southwark, in 1958.

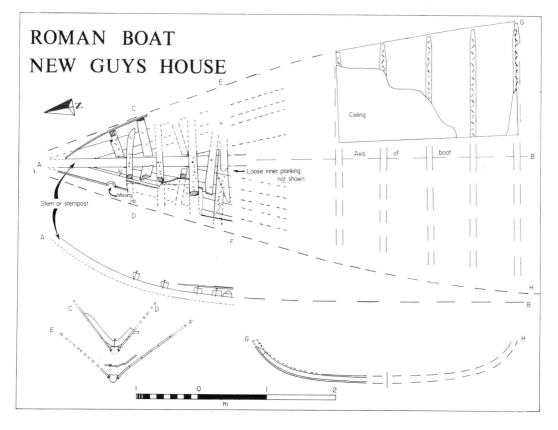

ROMAN BOAT
NEW GUYS HOUSE

159

The ship wrecked at Blackfriars was primarily designed to operate from tidal shores, its broad flat bottom enabling it to load and offload its cargoes on beaches at coastal settlements during low tide, and to set sail at high tide. This ship, built by the Celtic peoples somewhere in north-western Europe, was therefore intended for use in the Atlantic and North Sea; so in the tideless upper reaches of the Thames at London it too needed the use of a quay, such as that at New Fresh Wharf, to offload its cargoes whether they were of millstones or building stone.[37]

The one discovered ship from London that did not require a deep-water quay, however, was the barge from New Guy's House, for although it has a length of roughly 14 m, and a beam of over 4 m, it required less than a metre of water in which to float. Therefore it was evidently designed for carrying goods up and down the Thames between various riverside settlements, and was likely to have been carrying food supplies from the rural areas to London itself. Its total excavation in due course in the grounds of Guy's Hospital should prove particularly rewarding, since traces of its former cargoes may have been trapped under the inner protective lining of planks in its hold.

Despite the probable absence of a large urban population, some of the burials in later Roman London show traces of clear social distinctions in the city. Burial during the third and fourth centuries tended to be by inhumation instead of by cremation, and in spite of the fact that a study of the discovered burials of Roman London is long overdue, it is clear from the expensive lead and stone coffins found how the wealthy were sent into the next world.[38] Occasionally, however, traces of the poor have been found, recognized by their burial in cheap wooden coffins,

Roman stone sarcophagus from the Minories.

A small pot found beside the infant burial in the Minories, 1955.

Fourth-century burial of an infant, about two years old, found in the Minories in 1955.

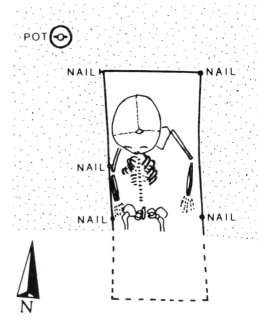

or even, as was found in Warwick Square, merely in a hole in the ground.

Perhaps fairly typical of the poor was the burial of a young child during the late third or fourth century, excavated on a building site in the Minories in 1955.[39] The child was aged between 18 months and two years, and had been buried in a rectangular wooden coffin, constructed of 0.006 m thick wooden boards, held together by iron nails. Even though the wood had decayed, and only the sides of the coffin could be clearly traced in the dark earth, some of the nails were in such a position that they could only have been used to fasten a lid. A recent wall foundation had destroyed the burial from below knee-level, but in spite of this it was possible to reconstruct at least part of the method of burial. No trace of any shroud or dress fittings could be found in the coffin, so it seems that the child's body was naked when it was placed on its back, with the arms close to the sides, the palms of the hands turned downwards.

The next step before the actual burial was to surround the body with lime, and then to nail down the coffin lid. A small pink pottery jug was finally placed beside the coffin, and although chipped through use, its narrow neck suggests that it contained liquid food, perhaps milk, to sustain the infant on its journey to the next world.

The end of Roman London

The end of Roman London during the early fifth century was, until recently, a matter of almost complete comjecture, but important discoveries since 1969 have changed this to a considerable extent. One of the most notable finds was a small Saxon brooch recovered from the collapsed roof debris of the small Roman bath at Billingsgate, for it showed that someone, presumably a Saxon, had been exploring the ruins of Roman London during the fifth century. On this site therefore is preserved important evidence of the change from the Roman culture to the Saxon.

But how this change came about is one of the most earnestly discussed problems relating to the history of London, since it is still far from clear what really happened at the end of the Roman period. The decline of the Roman city had been a slow process, illustrated by the fact that, although it was considered necessary to build a defensive wall about AD 200, fine houses were still being constructed and extended even during the latter half of the third century.[1] But this show of wealth was not restricted to the city, for major buildings were also in use in Southwark, near London Bridge, at a time when the British countryside was enjoying growing prosperity, particularly as reflected in the development of villas, the country farming estates.[2]

This prosperity could not be maintained indefinitely, however, since more fundamental events were eroding the once solid foundation of the Roman Empire. Internal strife and a succession of civil wars cut at the heart of the Empire from within, while from the outside, barbarian raids struck ever deeper to upset the economic, political and military stability of the provinces. In AD 259 Postumus, Governor of one of the German provinces, led a successful revolt against the Emperor Gallienus, and managed to establish an independent Gallic empire in the West, which included Gaul and Britain. It is doubtful if the resulting isolation of the West from the rest of the Empire had much effect on London's economy, since the city's trade at that time seems to have been restricted to the western provinces; nevertheless, this isolation hastened the decline of the Empire. Gaul itself suffered from barbarian invasions, as well as from monetary difficulties leading to the debasement of silver coinage, and the production of wretched little imitation copies of official bronze coins. It is in the second half of the third century that we find clear evidence of troubles, reflected by the burial of coin hoards in Germany, Gaul and Britain, and it is from this period that London itself has six coin hoards. There are two possible explanations for these: the first is that the debasement rendered the coins increasingly valueless, and so they tended to be hidden away until the return of more stable times; and the second is that Saxon raids around the coast and up rivers began to pose so serious a threat to the citizens of major towns such as London, that the inhabitants were forced to hide their money until the danger was past.

Of the late-third-century hoards found in the City, the first was discovered in 1882 in a pot in Lime Street, just east of the Roman forum, and included a gold ring and about five hundred silver and bronze coins, the latest being of Trajan Decius, minted after about 251. Another, smaller hoard was found hidden in a Roman building in Lime Street in 1952, and comprised thirty-two bronze copies of official coins of Gallienus and Tetricus, which, judging from the considerable number of identical coins from the same die, had probably been unofficially minted in London after 270. In 1926 a small hoard of twenty-three coins of similar date had been dug up in Fenchurch Street; and in 1961 nearly six hundred imitations of official bronze coins were found hidden in a small pit dug in a Roman road just south of Newgate Street. The burial must have taken place after 276 because one of the coins was a copy of an official coin of that date. What appears to have been a hoard of slightly later date was found as early as 1786 in Lombard Street, where 'nearly 300 brass' coins of 'Constantinus and Tetricus' were apparently found together. A hoard unearthed in Grove Street, Southwark, in 1864 was particularly interesting because it shows how limited the value of the coins was. It comprised at least 554 small brass 'imitations of the imperial money of the second half of the third century', some of which were of Victorinus (265–67), Tetricus I and II (267–73), and Claudius Gothicus (268–70); it seems that there was no intention of recovering the hoard, since it was buried in an earthenware jar and laid between two skeletons, and to have recovered it would have involved disturbing the burials.[3]

The Saxon threat did not decrease when the Emperor Aurelian recovered the western provinces in 274, for it was partly as a result of Saxon activity that, only twelve years later, Britain was plunged into even further isolation from the rest of the Empire. Marcus Aurelius Mausaeus Carausius, from the Low Countries, was in command of the Roman channel fleet when he suddenly declared himself Emperor of Britain. Although he had been responsible for stopping Frankish and

Saxon pirates from attacking Roman shipping, it was not long before rumours that he had not been returning all the rescued booty to its rightful owners began to circulate. Maximian, junior Emperor in the West, had been in power for only one year when this came to his notice in 286, and, no doubt after investigating the claims, he ordered the execution of Carausius. Unfortunately for Maximian, Carausius was highly regarded in Britain and was able to retain the support of the army and navy there during the next six years. He apparently ruled Britain with considerable ability, and even established a mint in London, which may have been his capital city. Nevertheless, in 293 he was murdered by his minister of finance, Allectus, a less able man, who was eventually defeated in battle in 295 by Constantius Chlorus, junior colleague of Emperor Diocletian.

It was at this stage that London briefly entered the mainstream of Roman history, for, after Constantius' invasion force landed on the coast of Hampshire, a major battle ensued in which Allectus was killed and his army scattered. Part of his army had comprised Frankish mercenaries who, with nothing more to hope for, headed across country for London, perhaps in the hope of finding ships to take them to safety beyond the limits of the Empire. Before long they began to plunder the Roman city, but, just as the citizens of London were about to accept defeat, a group of Roman ships that had become detached from the invasion force hove into view in the Thames in time to save the city. The contemporary writer Eumenius wrote that the ships

had at last reached London, found survivors of the barbarian mercenaries plundering the city, and, when these began to seek flight, landed and slew them in the streets. And not only did they bring safety to your subjects, but, in addition, induced a sentiment of gratitude and pleasure at the sight.[4]

That gratitude was certainly genuine, and is reflected by a discovery in 1922, not in London, but near Arras in France. Among a magnificent hoard of Roman coins and jewellery found during that year, was a gold medallion that had been especially struck in Trier to commemorate the saving of London. On one side it bears the bearded portrait of Constantius Chlorus; on the other is a delightful scene showing a woman, the personification of London, kneeling at a city gate, greeting Constantius, the saviour of the city, who is on horseback, while in the foreground a Roman warship is shown moored in the river Thames. The inscription REDDITOR LUCIS AETERNAE refers to the fact that Constantius was 'the restorer of the eternal light' of Roman civilization.[5]

165

Reverse of the gold medallion
found at Arras, France,
commemorating the arrival of
Constantius Chlorus at
London in AD 296.

After this the dark veil of uncertainty begins to be drawn
across the history of Roman London, for, although there are
several references to the city during the fourth century, none
tells us what it was like, or what status it enjoyed. The fact that
Diocletian continued to mint coins there suggests that it had
formal status, particularly after about 300 when he reorganized
the Empire into twelve dioceses, each of them subdivided into
provinces. The Diocese of Britain comprised four provinces
under the control of a *Vicarius*, but so little is known about the
effect of this division that we are not even sure in which province London was situated – though a thirteenth-century writer
states that London was the capital of the province of Flavia
Caesariensis, and York the capital of Maxima Caesariensis. By
this time York and London were probably the most important
cities in Britain, though as York was in the military zone, it may
have ranked as the senior city, particularly since Constantius
used it as his headquarters while strengthening the northern
defences against the barbarians. He died there on 25 July 306,
and even though it was in York that Constantine I, destined to
become the first Christian Emperor, was proclaimed, London
still continued minting coins until about 326; and, like York, it
was the seat of a bishop in the new established Church.

Clearly, London must have been a major administrative centre at that time, though it must be admitted that passing references to it are insufficient evidence upon which to base the view that it was a large and populous city. The archaeological evidence for the fourth-century occupation of London is very slender – a few pits and walls and the continuing occupation of some Roman buildings.[6] For example, the bath and dwelling at Billingsgate were extensively modified, new floors being built at some time during the fourth century; and the linked flues of the hypocausts in the east wing of the dwelling were blocked between the rooms, and new stoke-holes or furnaces installed so that each room was separately heated. This suggests that the wing may have been divided into separate self-contained living quarters.

From the mid fourth century onwards, there was a sharp decline in the fortunes of London, and we tend to find that a blanket of dark earth was accumulating on certain sites both in the city and in Southwark.[7] In fact the dark earth had already started accumulating as early as the end of the second century on some sites, such as in Milk Street, at the south end of Bow Lane, and on the Post Office site in Newgate Street. But on other sites it began accumulating later. Dark earth is not unique to London for it is found in some other Roman towns such as Canterbury, Winchester and Cirencester. It is not known what the late Roman dark earth represents, though it is thought that this might be soil associated with farming and market gardening inside London – a theory that is perhaps supported by the discovery of fourth-century gullies filled with dark earth, perhaps dug to drain the land for cultivation, in the region around Guildhall on the outskirts of the Roman city.[8]

After the middle of the fourth century the Picts and Scots beyond the frontier strengthened their attacks on Roman Britain, a particularly serious attack occurring in 360. Julian, who was responsible for the Gallic provinces under Emperor Constantine II, sent his general Lupicinus to restore the frontier. Although he was a good soldier, according to the contemporary writer Ammianus Marcellinus, Lupicinus was also 'of haughty demeanour and smacking somewhat of the tragic actor, in whom it was long a matter of doubt whether avarice or cruelty predominated'. He landed at Richborough in Kent, and 'marched to London, that he might there take such decision as the aspect of affairs demanded and might more quickly hasten to the task in hand.' As the centre of communications and presumably a provincial capital, London was the most suitable headquarters for a military campaign.[9]

The success of Lupicinus was short-lived; in 367–68, the Picts and Scots made yet another attack on the northern and

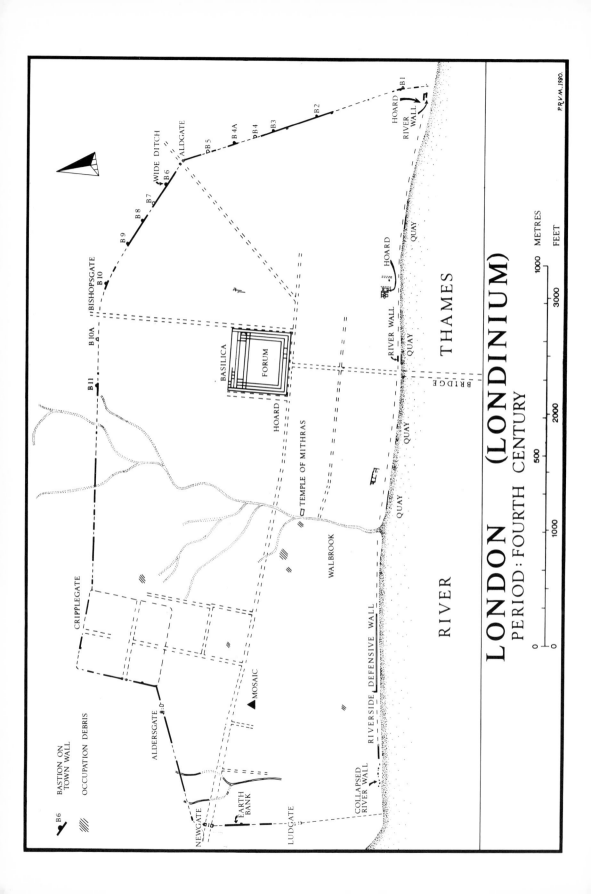

LONDON (LONDINIUM)
PERIOD: FOURTH CENTURY

THAMES

RIVER

BRIDGE

P.R.V.M. 1980.

BASILICA

FORUM

HOARD

HOARD

HOARD

RIVER WALL

QUAY

RIVER WALL

QUAY

QUAY

QUAY

QUAY

TEMPLE OF MITHRAS

WALBROOK

RIVERSIDE DEFENSIVE WALL

COLLAPSED RIVER WALL

EARTH BANK

MOSAIC

ALDERSGATE

NEWGATE

LUDGATE

CRIPPLEGATE

BISHOPSGATE

ALDGATE

WIDE DITCH

B 11

B 10A

B 10

B 9

B 8

B 7

B 6

B 5

B 4A

B 4

B 3

B 2

B 1

B 6   BASTION ON TOWN WALL

OCCUPATION DEBRIS

METRES

FEET

1000   3000

500   2000

1000

0   0

western frontiers, but this time it was in unison with the Saxons from across the North Sea, who attacked the east coast. The result was that Britain was overrun, London was looted, and both the Count of the Saxon Shore, the Roman official in charge of coastal defences, and the Duke of Britain, in charge of Roman land forces, were killed. Emperor Valentinian's reaction was immediate: he quickly sent his general, Theodosius, to clear out the enemy marauders who were devastating the British countryside. Like Lupicinus seven years earlier, he landed at Richborough with a large army and 'marched towards London, an ancient town which has since been renamed Augusta'. When close to London he divided his army into several detachments, and 'attacked the predatory and struggling bands of the enemy who were loaded with the weight of their plunder, and having speedily routed them while driving prisoners in chains and cattle before them, he deprived them of their booty.' The citizens of London were overjoyed as, 'amid scenes of jubilation which recalled a Roman triumph, he made his entry into the city which had just before been overwhelmed by disasters, but now was suddenly re-established almost before it could have hoped for deliverance'.[10]

No certain trace of the plundering has been found in London, though it is just possible that this was the cause of the destruction by fire, after the middle of the fourth century, of the fine house found on the Lloyds site in Lime Street.[11]

Once London was restored, however, Theodosius 'marched with resolution from Augusta, which the ancients used to call Lundinium, with an army which he had collected with great energy and skill.' He rapidly mopped up the marauding bands and 'entirely restored the cities and fortresses which through manifold disasters of the time had been injured or destroyed.'

This was a period of important changes in London, when the defences were strengthened, and approximately the time when, as we have seen, the city was renamed Augusta, presumably as an honour granted for services rendered, though the circumstances are unclear. It was also a time when the city was still the centre of government finance in Britain, for, according to the *Notitia Dignitatum*, a document giving the Roman military and civil establishment in Britain in the late fourth century, Augusta was the headquarters of the 'officer in charge of the Treasury', even though the mint had been closed there *c.* 326.

To Theodosius are attributed important late Roman attempts to strengthen the defences of towns and the coastline of Britain. One of these might be the recently discovered watch-tower, 8 m square, that has been found near the Thames at Shadwell, conveniently placed downstream, but in sight of London. Its stone foundations and surrounding fence have

Opposite, a strengthening of the city defences (bastions, a wide town ditch, and a riverside wall) is the major feature of London during the fourth century. Little evidence of new domestic building has been found within the defences, only traces of decay.

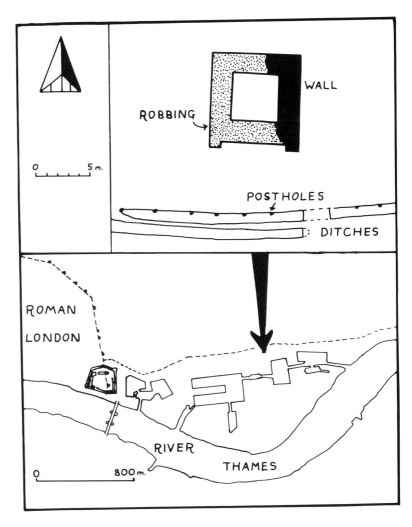

A late Roman signal tower found at Shadwell in 1974.

been dated to the late third or fourth century, and it is considered most likely to have been part of an early-warning system for London, to give notice of Saxon raids.[12] Unfortunately the dating is not sufficiently precise to link the tower with Theodosius, though we do know that he established a system of watch-towers on the Yorkshire coast, and therefore might be expected to have built them elsewhere.

Once the raiders in their long ships reached the city, they probably encountered truly formidable defences in the form of massive bastions, semicircular towers built on to the outside of the city wall to support missile-throwing *ballistae* as well as a new and much wider defensive ditch, and a riverside defensive wall, all of which have been investigated in recent excavations. For the construction of these Theodosius may have been responsible.

The bastions of London have always presented problems of dating and interpretation, particularly as they are of two types: the western group of hollow bastions and the eastern group of solid bastions. Because there were different methods of constructing each group, it has long been assumed that they were built at different periods. But the date of those periods was unknown until fairly recently, though it was suspected that some might be of late Roman date. In 1966, however, a previously unknown hollow bastion, now referred to as 11A, was found just west of Cripplegate; and its curving foundation was found to have been cut through an earlier deposit of rubbish containing thirteenth-century pottery. It is likely, therefore, that all of the other hollow bastions of similar construction are of medieval date.[13]

It was another five years before one of the solid bastions was dated, though, as their masonry construction contained a great amount of stone that had been reused from demolished Roman buildings, particularly tombs in nearby cemeteries, it was

Plan of the late-Roman bastion 10 in Camomile Street, showing sculptures and stone blocks reused from demolished tombs and other buildings. The row of stone blocks at the bottom is the external plinth of the earlier Roman city wall.

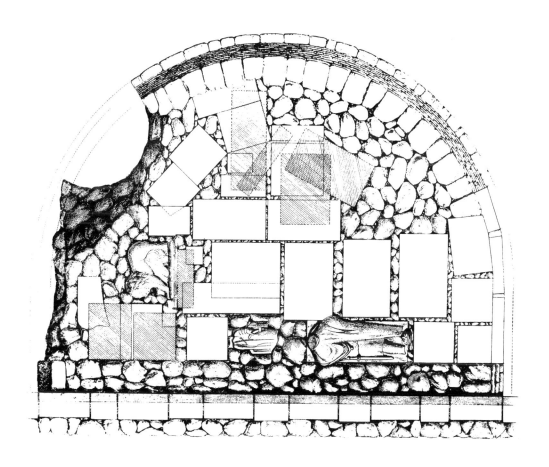

believed that they were of late Roman date. The dating evidence was found in 1971 around bastion 6, just north of Aldgate, where an archaeological excavation was started soon after the office building on the site was demolished. The bastion proved to be still standing more than a metre high, and in its structure there were a number of large sculptured stone blocks which comparison with similar finds in the other bastions in London indicated should be parts of tombs, with sculptured figures and possibly even inscriptions. The only recognizable stone carving, however, was a bolster-shaped piece that may have come from the top of the city wall itself, since similar pieces have been found in most of the solid bastions.

The foundation of the bastion had been dug through an earlier deposit of fourth-century rubbish, showing that the bastion itself could not be of third-century date. Fortunately another, thicker layer of Roman rubbish overlay the foundation and therefore was later in date than its construction, and this included fourth-century pottery and bronze coins dated to the period 364–75. This excavation, therefore, confirmed its Roman date, and suggested that it might have been built during the restoration of Roman town defences by Theodosius after 368. It also showed that London was similar to a number of other Roman towns in Britain, such as Caerwent, Chichester and Great Casterton, all of which had bastions added to their defences apparently at about this time. The excavation also exposed the inner edge of a wide ditch of the fourth century, whose sloping surface was followed by the base of the bastion, proving that ditch and bastion were contemporary. Because no trace of this late Roman ditch had been found elsewhere in London, no doubt because it had been dug away by medieval defensive ditches, it was important to estimate its shape and size. Not much had survived even here, however, so all that could be said was that it was probably much wider than the earlier town ditch, which was itself only about 4.5 m wide. Its inner slope was not so steep, suggesting that it was a normal late-Roman type of wide, flat-bottomed defensive ditch. Another excavation close to the bastion was also important for it revealed part of the earlier Roman town ditch that had evidently been filled in to allow the wider ditch to be dug. In the dumped fill was found a coin of Constans of AD 341–4, indicating that the wide ditch was not dug nor the bastion built until after that date.[14]

A previously unknown late Roman bastion discovered in Vine Street in January 1980 was found to contain reused carved stones, like the other solid bastions, and helped to confirm that, since the solid bastions in London were, as far as can be judged, somewhat similarly constructed above foundation level, it

seems reasonable to assume that all were of the same date; but what the excavation of bastion 6 was unable to explain was why the solid bastions had been built almost exclusively on the eastern half of the city. Perhaps these formed part of an unfinished scheme for the defence of Roman London, though a Roman addition to the bank behind the city wall in Warwick Square suggests that the wide ditch may have been dug all round the defences, the bank being the upcast from the ditch.[15]

Even more difficult to understand than the bastions is the riverside defensive wall. It was originally discovered in 1841 by Charles Roach Smith, who recorded it under Upper Thames Street, between Lambeth Hill and Queenhithe, while a trench for a sewer was being dug. The wall was from 2.5 to 3 m thick, and was built of ragstone, flint and mortar, with courses of bonding tiles, and it somewhat resembled the much earlier landward defensive wall. What was so distinctive about its construction, however, was *a*, that it contained many pieces of sculptured and shaped stone blocks from demolished buildings that had been reused; and *b*, that its foundation comprised a layer of large blocks of sandstone 0.6 m thick, cemented with pink mortar, overlying a layer of chalk supported on oak piles.[16]

Its identification as a late Roman riverside defensive wall remained unchallenged until 1961, when on a building site immediately north of the riverside wall beside modern Lambeth Hill, there was found a curious northward extension of the river wall first recorded by Roach Smith 120 years earlier. But

The external mortared face of bastion 6, as found in Dukes Place, Aldgate, in 1971. It contains many reused sculptured stones.

in this case it lay on an extensive chalk terrace resting on hundreds of timber piles, and seemed in no way defensive. Indeed, at one point a Roman retaining wall led to an upper terrace, while elsewhere a range of steps totalling 2 m in height and built of more reused stones, particularly a massive plinth, supported the hillside slope. It was difficult to understand the purpose of these terraces, though two things seemed clear. The first was that a major monumental stone building or buildings had been demolished to supply building materials, indicating that the terraces and walls were probably of late Roman date like the bastions; and secondly, the river wall recorded by Roach Smith was probably part of a much more extensive series of constructions, which made it unlikely that the wall itself was defensive. Indeed, as none of the other pieces of supposed riverside defensive wall then known had a construction comparable with that found in 1841, and as most of them were not even dated to the Roman period, it seemed that there was no proof that Roman London ever had a riverside defensive wall.[17] It was interesting to note, however, that during the 1170s William Fitzstephen, a medieval historian, wrote after describing the landward city defences, 'On the south, London was once walled and towered in like fashion, but the Thames ... has, in course of time washed away those bulwarks, undermined and cast them down.'[18] The question was raised: was this a genuine memory of a riverside defensive wall, or had Fitzstephen seen the stumps of water-eroded walls of Roman buildings on the foreshore, and believed that these were once parts of a continuous wall? Only new discoveries could provide an answer.

Those new discoveries occurred respectively in 1974–75 at Blackfriars, and in 1977 and 1979 at the Tower of London, to prove positively that there had been a riverside defensive wall. Signs that the wall had existed were first encountered at Blackfriars in 1972 during the excavation of Baynards Castle, a medieval and Tudor royal residence. There was found a short length of the heavily eroded wall overlaid by river gravels, but unfortunately there was no time to investigate it further. The first indication that this was a defensive wall was found nearby in a small excavation across Upper Thames Street in 1974, where a massive collapsed Roman wall was uncovered. Its defensive purpose was only proved in 1975 when a length of about 115 m of the wall was exposed during the rebuilding of the site for a telecommunications centre. There were two styles of wall construction, however, suggesting that it had been built at two different periods. In the eastern part of the site there was a 40 m length of wall seemingly built somewhat in the manner of the wall recorded nearby by Charles Roach Smith, except

The lower part of the late Roman riverside defensive wall found at Blackfriars in 1975. Above its piles and chalk foundation, the outer face of the wall was eroded by the river during the Saxon period.

that its outer face had been eroded by the Thames after the Roman period. Its foundation was of regular rows of oak piles, each approximately 2 m long, that had been rammed into the underlying gravels, while above this was a thick layer of chalk. The wall itself lay on top and was built of ragstone and mortar, and had three courses of bonding tiles built of roof tiles, with a deep offset on the north face at each bonding course. The wall was clearly built with great care and showed no sign of having been hastily constructed; indeed, unlike Roach Smith's wall which may have been partly rebuilt later, it contained no reused stones from earlier buildings. Erosion had reduced its thickness to 1.80 m but it is estimated to have been originally about 2.20 m wide. Another possible sign of its defensive purpose was suggested by a bank of earth and clay that had been dumped against its landward north face. Although it has been identified, the purpose of the bank is still not really clear since there was no trace of a defensive ditch, from which the earth could have been taken, in front of the wall.[19]

In 1977, however, excavation in the Tower of London exposed the eastern end of the riverside defensive wall, over 2.4 m wide, and built on a foundation of timber piles and chalk.

It could not be closely dated on this site, although construction deposits beside the wall did contain pottery of the late third or early fourth century; on applying the radiocarbon test and dating by tree-rings, however, the wall seemed to be of fourth-century date, having been built perhaps after 330, and on this evidence it seems possible that it was built about 370 during the restoration of cities by Theodosius.[20]

In the western part of the Blackfriars site the riverside wall had a different method of construction, which the excavator, Charles Hill, attributed to its having been built on firm clay.[21] He suggested that it was not necessary for the wall to have had an elaborate foundation of piles and chalk there because the ragstone one was sufficiently supported by the clay. The wall was different in other respects too, but it is unlikely that this was likewise caused by differences in the subsoil. For example, it had no courses of roof tiles, and as the wall is believed to have collapsed northwards, away from the river, perhaps it did not have a bank of earth, though this may have been eroded away by the river. A final feature of this wall was that it contained

Altars and other sculptured stones found reused in the partly collapsed late Roman riverside defensive wall, at Blackfriars in 1975.

A fourth-century well found
in 1954 adjacent to the
temple of Mithras.

stone blocks reused from the demolished monumental arch and 'screen of gods'. This wall, therefore, has the appearance of having been constructed at a different time from the wall with the chalk foundation; also, the reused stone suggests that it may have been built with a greater sense of urgency, presumably at a time of crisis. As no dating evidence was recovered from around this wall, it is not known precisely when it was put up, but since additional fortifications were built about 400, according to associated coins at the south-east corner of the city where the Tower of London now stands, it is possible that it was a similar type of defence at the south-west corner.

In spite of the efforts to defend London in the late fourth century, the decline of the city continued, and there are clear traces of neglect. The Walbrook stream, for example, was allowed to silt up between its embankments and began flooding the surrounding areas, despite the fact that occupation rubbish on the ground at that time indicates that there were dwellings near by.[22] Even the river bed in front of the grand timber quay, built a century and a half earlier, was silting up on the New Fresh Wharf site near London Bridge; and yet sherds of amphorae found in the Saxon layers of river gravel indicate that there was some late Roman trade link with the Mediterranean. Trade was, however, apparently at a minimum, and within the city we find few traces of occupation. In fact, very little is known about London after about 370. The houses where people lived, their businesses, and the state of the streets and public buildings, all this remains obscure except that the demolition of the arch and screen, and possibly of some other monumental buildings, suggests that they were unused, unwanted and already in ruins. The general absence of traces of occupation may be indicative of a small scattered population, and an increasing thickness of black earth overlying earlier Roman sites, in both the City and Southwark, suggests that farming within the town defences was increasingly necessary to maintain what was perhaps becoming a subsistence economy.

At Old Ford, only $2\frac{1}{2}$ miles north-east of London, beside the London-Colchester road, a late Roman settlement has been found, which, according to the many Roman coins discovered there, apparently continued in use until at least the beginning of the fifth century.[23] It may well have supplied food to London. Excavations within the city itself show that London was receiving the bulk of its pottery from production centres in Oxfordshire and in the Nene Valley of Cambridgeshire, and from the Alice Holt kilns in the New Forest near Farnham in Surrey. In fact, a few sherds of North African red-slip ware have also been found, but in such small quantities from the period after 360 that they are unlikely to reflect trade with North Africa, being instead perhaps the personal possessions of officials who had moved from the Continent to London.[24]

Among the unsuccessful bids for the throne which continued to weaken the Empire in the late fourth century, that of Magnus Maximus in Britain must have had a serious effect. In 383 he declared himself Emperor, and stripped the country of troops when he crossed to the European mainland in a bid to support his claim. He failed, but before his defeat in 388, it seems that he intended to use London as his headquarters in Britain, since he probably started minting coins there, each stamped with the mint mark A V G, referring to its official name of Augusta.

During the last years of the fourth century, Britain was repeatedly under attack from barbarians beyond the frontier, and about 396 general Stilicho ordered an expedition to sail to Britain to restore its defences yet again. By 399 the security of Britain had been achieved, even though little is known about these barbarian attacks. Until recently there was no hint that London might have been involved, but in 1977 excavations at the Tower of London revealed a massive Roman wall that was perhaps built during the 390s as part of Stilicho's campaign.[25] This wall is 3.2 m thick and is believed to be later than the riverside defensive wall with the chalk foundation which lies immediately to the south. Perhaps originally built to replace the latter, the later wall is still standing 2.2 m high, and is displayed in the Tower of London where the visitor can see stones from demolished earlier Roman buildings reused in its construction. It is the dating evidence that is so crucial in

understanding its significance, for soon after the wall had been
completed, and before the mortar rendering could become
weathered, dumps of earth were piled up against the landward
face of the wall, and it was in these that many coins were found,
the latest being of Valentinian II (375–92). This shows that the
wall was probably built after 375, and so its construction, as a
strengthening of the defences in the south-east corner of the
city, presumably relates to barbarian attacks after the great
raid of 369.

It is even possible that the wall at the Tower of London was
built during the ten years after 399 when Britain was once again
in difficulties, for it was Stilicho himself who left the towns of
Roman Britain defenceless when he withdrew the troops to
tackle the barbarian forces, led by Alaric, who in 401 attacked
Italy itself. Cities in Britain were on their own then, and
London was among the towns that had to defend themselves
against the inevitable attacks. Buried hoards of coins are an
important indicator of troubled times, and three hoards of the
beginning of the fifth century have been found in and around
London. Although they may have been hidden as a result of
Saxon attacks, it was also possibly owing to the declining value

A paint brush is used to
uncover the late Roman coin
hoard scattered in the
furnace of the Roman
building at Billingsgate.

179

of money, their owners hoping for more stable times later. One of these hoards was found in Chilton Grove, Bermondsey, in what was once the countryside near London, the hoard of more than 250 copper coins dating from about 380–400, having been buried in a pot.[26] The remaining hoards were found inside the Roman city. One of these was found in 1777, close to the recently discovered late Roman wall at the Tower of London, and comprised a silver ingot, inscribed in Latin 'from the workshop of Flavius Honorinus', and gold coins of Arcadius and Honorius which prove that the hoard was buried after 395.[27] The second hoard was found in the dwelling at Billingsgate, and comprised over 273 copper coins that seem to have been hidden in a wall of its east wing. Eventually, while the building was either a decaying ruin, or was being demolished during the fifth century, the hoard fell on to the floors of a furnace and an adjoining corridor. Once again the latest coins were of Arcadius and Honorius, and therefore the hoard must have been hidden after 395. The fact that the hoards were never recovered need not carry the sinister implication that their owners were unable to recover them, for, after about 407, new coins were not going into circulation in Britain. Barter was increasingly used, and the hoarded coins therefore became worthless, and their recovery pointless.

How much later than 400 the coins fell to the floor in the Billingsgate dwelling is not known, but clearly it was before the roof collapsed, for they lay beneath the layer of roof debris; but also it was probably after the coins had ceased to have any value, otherwise somebody would have picked them up. The hoard shows that Romans were still living in the building after 395, a date which is also suggested by another find from the site. A furnace for heating part of the east wing still contained the wood-ash from the last time that the hypocaust was used for central heating the apartment; and it was under this ash that a coin of Theodora (337–41) was found, together with fragments of a Palestinian amphora probably made in Gaza to transport wine during the fourth or early fifth-century.[28] It is therefore likely that Romans were living in the building during the first decade of the fifth century, when the final break with Rome occurred.

Bronze brooch from Tower Street. 68 mm long.

Already defenceless without the Roman army, the towns in the western provinces during that decade were in a desperate plight, as barbarian raids led to a complete breakdown of the Roman administration. Indeed, in an attempt to rectify the situation three usurpers took control of Britain between 406 and 411. When the last of these, Constantine III, withdrew the remaining troops from Britain, first to restore the western provinces, and then to make an unsuccessful bid for the throne,

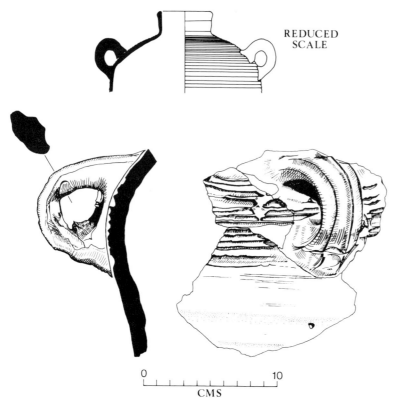

REDUCED
SCALE

0 _____ 10

CMS

Fragments of a late Roman
amphora from Palestine,
found in the furnace of the
east wing of the Roman
building at Billingsgate. A
partial reconstruction of the
amphora type is shown
above.

the towns in Britain apparently rebelled and took control of
their own defences. In spite of this, Emperor Honorius sent
letters in 410 to the towns in Britain, telling them to guard
themselves, and it seems that at this stage some of the towns
were employing Germanic mercenaries to defend them, and in
payment were probably giving them land to farm in the
countryside. It is thought that this may have happened in and
around London, even though here the mercenaries are so far
represented merely by a bronze brooch from Tower Street and
by two buckles and a brooch of Germanic style; one of these
buckles came from Smithfield where a Roman cemetery lay and
the other from Lothbury, while the brooch was found at Billingsgate.[29] Some doubts have been expressed, however, as to what
extent such objects as these represent the mercenaries, though
Saxon settlement areas around London dating from the fifth
century have been found at Mucking in Essex, Mitcham and
Guildown in Surrey, and at Hanwell in Middlesex, perhaps on
land given to the soldier-farmers in return for defending
London. It is extremely difficult to judge what was happening,
since the most important means of dating sites, Roman coins,
ceased to be brought into Britain in any quantity soon after 400.

Bronze buckle from West
Smithfield. 83 mm wide.

181

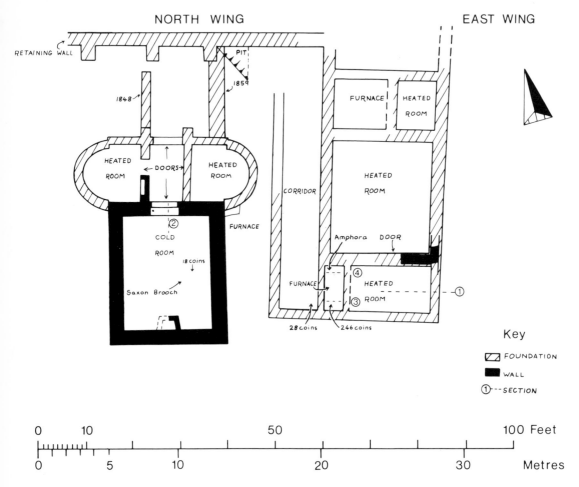

RETAINING WALL

PIT

1859

1848

FURNACE   HEATED ROOM

HEATED ROOM   ←DOORS→   HEATED ROOM

CORRIDOR   HEATED ROOM

② COLD ROOM

18 coins

FURNACE

Saxon Brooch

Amphora   DOOR

④ FURNACE   HEATED ③ ROOM   --①

28 coins   266 coins

Key

▨ FOUNDATION
■ WALL
①--SECTION

0   10   50   100 Feet

0   5   10   20   30   Metres

Plan of the Roman building at Billingsgate during the late fourth and early fifth centuries. Section numbers refer to the drawing opposite.

Opposite, sections of strata recorded in the Roman building at Billingsgate. Section 1 includes the hill-wash deposits (layers 6–9) above the east wing of the dwelling. Section 2 illustrates the location of the Saxon saucer brooch in the collapsed roof debris of the bath. The coin hoard (Section 3) and the Palestinian amphora (Section 4) were found in the furnace of the east wing.

When the Roman administration in Britain collapsed during the early years of the fifth century, the organization of Roman town life seems to have declined peacefully into a haphazard kind of existence. In the house at Billingsgate this seems to have occurred between about 400, when the hoard was hidden in the house and the hypocaust was still in use, and perhaps about 450 when a Saxon brooch was lost in the ruins of the bath building.

The departure of the Roman inhabitants of the Billingsgate building took place quietly, and presumably without any violent trouble from a Saxon raid. It is as if one day the people simply packed up their possessions and left to find a new and more peaceful life elsewhere, away from the Saxon raiders. The pattern here, as in so many other Roman towns, seems to be that Roman town life gradually faded away, perhaps helped by particularly virulent epidemics that occurred from time to time. The house and bath at Billingsgate remained deserted and slid into slow decay, merely to be used for a time by squatters who

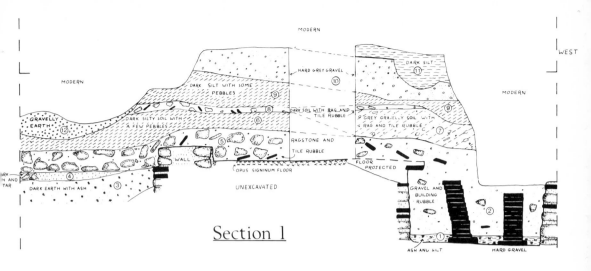

Section 1

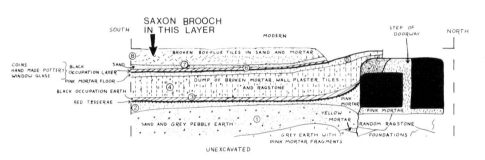

Section 2

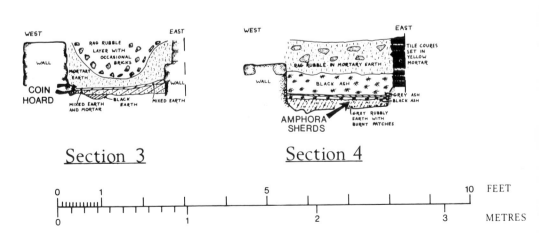

Section 3　　　Section 4

A rough hearth of tiles overlying silt and a mortar floor, suggesting early-fifth-century squatter occupation in a room of the former Roman palace in Bush Lane. Scale shows feet.

left their own rubbish on the floors – rubbish that included some hand-made pottery of Roman style.[30]

In addition to the hoard scattered on the floors of the east wing, eighteen more coins of similar date were found on the pink mortar floor of the *frigidarium* of the baths, together with a scatter of smashed green window glass – a sure sign of an abandoned building.

Homeless squatters living in the abandoned rooms of once fine buildings are an important symptom of a decaying city, and fortunately one other London site has yielded traces of them. It was a room at the south end of the former Governor's palace, close to Suffolk Lane, where an excavation in 1964–65 exposed a rough hearth made from tile fragments set into an earth floor overlaid by late Roman rubbish.[31] The squatters had burnt fires against the painted wall plaster of the room with an obvious disregard for the building. But their activities had followed a long period of decay, during which silt had gradually accumulated over the mortar floor of the room, and pieces of plaster from the walls had fallen into the silt. Ultimately, presumably in the fifth century, large quantities of rubbish had been dumped into the room, perhaps in a last attempt to drive out the squatters and tackle the increasing social problem and the consequent health hazard. These dumps also included a few hand-made sherds.

Collapsed roof tiles from the
east wing of the Roman
building at Billingsgate.
Probably early fifth century.

At Billingsgate it was perhaps the decay of the house and
bath that finally drove out the squatters, the first clear sign of
advanced decay being the tumbled roof tiles lying cracked and
broken where they had fallen beside the east wing.

The shells of garden snails of the Roman period were found
under some of the tiles. The north wing of the house seems to
have been slowly engulfed in silt and rubbish sliding down the
hillside; and it was this silt that spread over the doorstep of the
bath entrance, into the vestibule, then gradually and finally
over the doorstep of the *frigidarium* to fan out over the floor. In
time, perhaps around the middle of the fifth century, the
vaulted tile roof of the *frigidarium* collapsed on to the pink
mortar floor, and a tree may have started growing in the
north-east corner of the room, its root forcing down the buried
red mosaic floor. It was about then that the Saxon woman may
be presumed to have stepped through the open doorway of the
frigidarium, and, walking on the collapsed roof debris, dropped
her brooch near the middle of the room. At that time the thick
brick walls of the bath were probably standing to their full
height, though the windows were merely openings in the walls.
The date of the Saxon saucer brooch is difficult to place with
any precision in the fifth century, though an apparently identical brooch undoubtedly from the same workshop, was found in

Fragments of fifth-century
hand-made pottery. From St
Dunstan's Hill (top), and
from the bath and dwelling at
Billingsgate. All of soft lumpy
grey ware except the lowest,
which is of a soft pink fabric.

185

Two apparently identical Saxon saucer brooches of the fifth century from the Roman bath at Billingsgate (left), and from a Saxon grave at Mitcham, Surrey. Diameter of inner circle 26 mm.

1918 or 1919 in a Saxon grave at Mitcham, in Surrey, associated with a fifth-century glass cone beaker.[32]

The story of the Billingsgate site does not end there, for after the roof tiles had slid to the ground around the east wing of the house, a general absence of building rubble suggests that someone demolished its ragstone walls to ground level, and took away almost all the stone, presumably to construct a new building elsewhere. More time passed, represented by several dark layers, probably of silt and hillwash, containing only late Roman pottery, which deeply buried the east wing of the house, until eventually the dark layers were covered by a deposit of hard-rammed gravel containing fragments of twelfth-century pottery.

It is dangerous to reconstruct too much of the nebulous history of London during the fifth and sixth centuries from so few sites – but that is almost all the evidence that exists at present. It is as if by 410 a veil was fully drawn across the scene, leaving a darkness of knowledge into which theories stab like torch beams seeking any clues to what happened between about 400 and 600.

Maybe London during the late fifth and sixth centuries had a small semi-rural farming population, and in that time changed imperceptibly from a Roman to a Saxon culture. The Roman character and administration would gradually have died away during the fifth century, and this semi-rural population, living within the convenient city defences, remained until a Saxon administration was established in the early seventh century.[33]

Stages in the recovery of Roman London

Considering that it was as recently as 1973 that a permanent archaeological research unit was set up to study the origin and history of the City of London, with a staff of about sixty, it is a wonder that any research on a site so vast and complex as the City could have been carried out before that time. At best the investigation of buried London depended upon the enthusiasm of a succession of individuals, both amateur and professional. Nevertheless a great deal was achieved before 1973, above all in mapping parts of the Roman city, though it had long been clear that any individual efforts were hopelessly inadequate in the face of the large-scale destruction of the ancient sites in the course of rebuilding.

1666–1940

Sir Christopher Wren was the first to try to understand the layout of Roman London, following several discoveries of Roman remains made during the rebuilding of the City after the Great Fire of 1666. Charles II had appointed him 'Surveyor-General and Principal Architect for rebuilding the whole City' while he was still in his thirties', and it was then that he and his contemporaries recorded Roman burials and potters' kilns under St Paul's cathedral, a Roman road beneath the tower of St Mary-le-Bow in Cheapside, and various other features of the Roman city, including an ancient stream.[1] Wren correctly reasoned from these finds that, contrary to popular belief in a prehistoric origin, London had been created by the Romans, though he was wrong in his assessment of its internal layout. He had been Professor of Astronomy at Gresham College in Bishopsgate Street before the Great Fire, and it was behind its red brick walls that he came to know the first person to publish an archaeological record of a London site. Dr John Woodward was a geologist in addition to being Professor of Physic, but he was particularly well known for being bad-tempered and cantankerous. On one occasion he was thrown out of the Council of the Royal Society for grossly insulting Sir Hans Sloane, and on another he was involved in a sword fight with a colleague, first in Bishopsgate Street and then in the College quadrangle. His fellow professors had made fun of his interest in Roman London, and so he published his views to

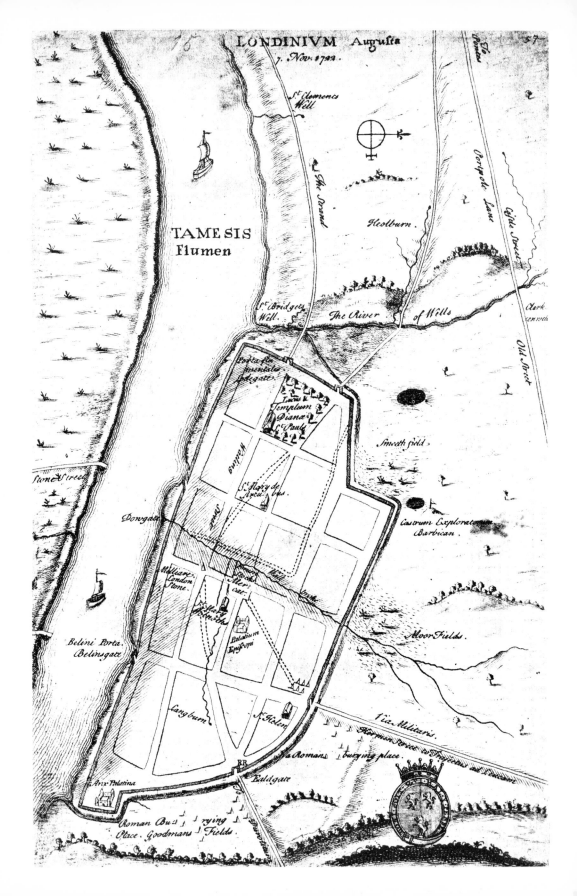

LONDINIVM Augusta
7. Nov. 1722.

TAMESIS
Flumen

St Clements Well

The Strand

Heolburn

Portpole Lane

Fyke Street

Old Street

Clark enwell

St Bridgets Well.

The River of Wills

Porta Ex trinitate Aldgate

Lucus & Templum Dianæ St Pauls

Smeoth field

Candwy

St Mary de Arcubus

Castrum Exploratorum Barbican

Dongate

Stone Street

Milliare London Stone.

Bech Mercat

Wall

Porch

St Mary Colnith

Palladium Episcopi

MoorFields

Belini Porta. Belinsgate

Langburn

St Helen

Via Militaris

Roman Street to

burying place.

RR

Ealdgate

Arx Palatina

Roman Bur: Place. Goodmans Fields.

rying

justify himself, in particular applying his interest in geological strata to archaeological layers.[2] As well as describing the construction of the Roman and medieval city wall, he investigated the remains of a Roman building which overlay an earlier Roman cemetery found on a building site at Bishopsgate.

Even though Wren and Woodward had begun to study Roman London, there was general ignorance about the buried city. This is particularly well illustrated by the remarkably imaginative plan published by William Stukeley in 1722, which included a temple of Diana on the site of St Paul's cathedral![3]

Opposite, suggested plan of Roman London by Stukeley in 1722.

Plan of Roman London published by C. Knight in 1841.

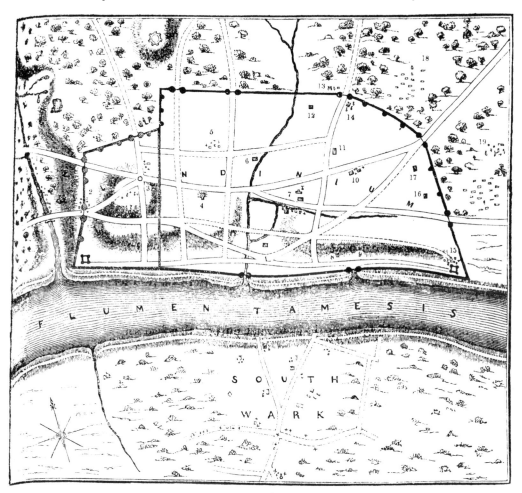

[PLAN OF ROMAN LONDON.]

1. Vases, Coins, and Implements found in Fleet Ditch, after the Great Fire.
2. Sepulchral Monument at Ludgate, ditto.
3. Urns, Sepulchral Remains, and Pavement at St. Paul's, ditto.
4. Causeway at Bow Church, ditto.
5. Tiles and Pottery at Guildhall, 1822.
6. Tesselated Pavement in Lothbury, 1805.
7. Buildings, Coins, &c., in Lombard Street and Birchin Lane, 1730, 1774, and 1785.
8. Roman Coins and Tiles at St. Mary-at-Hill, 1787.
9. Pavements and Urns by St. Dunstan's in the East, 1824.
10. Pavement in Long Lane.
11. Tesselated Pavement in Crosby Square.
12. Pavement in Old Broad Street.
13. Cemetery outside Bishopsgate, 1723.
14. Sepulchral Remains inside Bishopsgate, 1707.
15. Coins, Sepulchral Monument, &c., in the Tower, 1777.
16. Tesselated Pavement in Crutched Friars, 1787.
17. Pavement in Northumberland Alley, Fenchurch Street.
18. Cemetery at Spitalfields, 1576.
19. Cemetery and Monument in Goodman's Fields, 1787.

It was not until the nineteenth century that a major effort was made to understand Roman London; but this was in response to the fact that much of the buried city was being uncovered and destroyed on building sites. A writer in 1841 declared that, during the previous twenty-five years, 'there has probably been crowded as much demolition, reconstruction and transformation of all kinds, within the limits of old London, as has taken place in all the preceding interval.'[4] Most of the traces of the medieval city were destroyed without prior notification, and little of the Roman city was recorded, as is shown by the plan of Roman London that was published by Charles Knight in 1841, on which only nineteen discoveries were listed.[5]

The great stimulus to recording the remains of Roman London was provided by Charles Roach Smith, a chemist, who, from 1834 to 1855, devoted much of his spare time to the study of Roman and medieval London. He did not have an easy time in his self-appointed task of trying to get the Corporation of London to collect its antiquities and to do more with the collection it had begun in 1826, to create a city museum. Indeed, because the Corporation refused, he began a museum of his own above his shop in Lothbury, and opened it to scholars. Roach Smith became such a highly vocal public critic of the Corporation that in 1840, according to his own evidence, they reacted by devising a pointless road-widening scheme that would evict him from his lucrative premises. He replied by suing the Corporation, who preferred to settle out of court, but he was forced to move to No. 5 Liverpool Street. This merely strengthened his resolve to make the Corporation accept its responsibilities, but that body had other priorities, and in due course had him arrested for receiving stolen property – the antiquities that they did not want! He was acquitted, but the dispute came to a head in 1841 when Corporation officials threatened to banish him from the site of the new Royal Exchange, and when he in turn threatened to defend himself with a shotgun if necessary!

Although some of these events involved Sir William Tite, the architect of the Royal Exchange, particularly after he became vice-president of the Royal Institute of British Architects, the main cause of the dispute lay with an alderman of the Corporation of London – Richard Lambert Jones, a man so ruthless, unpleasant and powerful that he was generally known as 'the City Dictator'. As Chairman of the Improvements, Library, London Bridge rebuilding, Royal Exchange rebuilding and other committees of the Corporation, his word was law, and he objected to the criticisms of a mere chemist.[6] When the details of the Royal Exchange affair were made public in 1845,[7] the Corporation found itself in an embarrassing situation, particu-

Charles Roach Smith, the father of London's archaeology.

Opposite, Charles Roach Smith's museum at No. 5 Liverpool Street, about 1850.

F.W.FAIRHOLT.   H.HIMBAULT. SC.

GENERAL VIEW OF THE REMAINS OF THE ROMAN VILLA, ON THE SITE OF THE NEW COAL EXCHANGE.

The *tepidarium* and *frigidarium* of the small Roman bath discovered at Billingsgate in 1848.

larly as they had still not created a museum around the many antiquities recovered from the site. Even though it was the following year when they donated the antiquities to the Guildhall Library, the Corporation delayed the opening of a public museum in Basinghall Street until 1868.[8]

Charles Roach Smith published his researches in various articles, but primarily in his great work, *Illustrations of Roman London*. One of his last functions before retiring from London in 1855 was to be on the steering committee which established the London and Middlesex Archaeological Society, whose journals have ever since remained the main publishing medium for the archaeological researches in London.

These efforts in the early and middle parts of the nineteenth century encouraged others to investigate Roman London, with the result that there followed a series of major archaeological discoveries, starting with the finding and preservation of a Roman bath in 1848 on a site opposite Billingsgate.[9] John Price, an energetic young official of the London and Middlesex Archaeological Society, was one of the early researchers, and in 1869 recorded a magnificent Roman mosaic that was found in

Queen Victoria Street. This find created such great public
interest – more than 50,000 people having visited the site in
only three days – that the Corporation decided to preserve it in
their new museum.[10] In 1876 Price dismantled a late Roman
bastion on the city wall in Camomile Street, in which he found
re-used a series of fine Roman funeral sculptures, and these too
went to the museum.[11] His assistant was an architectural artist
called Henry Hodge, who about 1880 distinguished himself by
recording a series of Roman and medieval discoveries which
included parts of the city wall, a Roman cemetery, and a major
part of the second basilica or town hall – the most important
building in Roman London. Information was accumulating,
and when between 1903 and 1912 two more amateur archaeologists, Philip Norman and Francis Reader, recorded and
published many other discoveries on building sites, particularly those connected with the ancient city defences, a picture of
what Roman London was once like was beginning to emerge.[12]

It was time to take stock of the situation, and in 1909 the first
detailed study of the Roman city was published in the *Victoria
County History* volume on London, which included nearly three

Crowds visiting the Roman
mosaic pavement found near
the Mansion House in 1869.

hundred discoveries in contrast to the mere nineteen published some seventy years earlier. The Guildhall Library and Museum had made very little effort to recover antiquities, however, and were glad to leave the site work to keen amateurs. Their apathy was severely shaken just after this, however, when the London Museum was created, and its staff was eager to fill its empty showcases with the remains of Roman London. The Guildhall Museum clerk was instructed to step up his work on the City building sites, acquiring objects from the workmen, and after 1914 a new museum clerk, Frank Lambert, managed to find time to undertake some on-site recording instead of merely finding objects.

The London Museum, in Lancaster House, viewed this new interest in Roman London with some reservations, and to avoid a clash with the Guildhall Library added a semi-official member, George 'Stony Jack' Lawrence, an antique dealer in Wandsworth, to its staff. Born in 1862 and the son of a pawn-broker, Lawrence was alive to the value of antiquities, and managed to develop a direct business link with the workmen on City building sites. He was well known for the constant flow of labourers who visited his shop, but as the objects were always the property of the site owners it was not in the interests of either the finder or Lawrence to note exactly where they had been found. Although most of the Roman collection of the London Museum was knowingly acquired illegally, Dr (as he then was) Mortimer Wheeler, the director of the museum in the late 1920s wrote that, 'but for the efforts of Mr G. F. Lawrence ... most of the objects ... would have been irretrievably lost.'[13] In spite of this, when Wheeler became director in 1926, Lawrence ceased to be a member of the museum staff.

For nearly thirty years after this, Wheeler maintained a particular concern for the archaeology of London, and his main endeavour was to try to establish professional research. He knew that it was already too late for many sites, since the constant rebuilding of offices had by now relentlessly destroyed a great deal of the Roman city. When Lambert left the Guild-hall Museum in 1924 he was replaced by Quentin Waddington, who was able to undertake only a little site work in addition to running the museum. It was Wheeler who took the lead in organizing the next assessment of Roman London, as Volume 1 of the London report by the Royal Commission on Historical Monuments. When this was published in 1928 it summarized the knowledge of Roman London, and Wheeler, who was the main author, described its character with an intuitive and informed insight that remains largely correct half a century later.[14] As soon as the report was published, Wheeler and Lord Crawford, chairman of the Royal Commission, pressed the

Corporation to appoint an archaeological assistant at the
Guildhall Museum; but the Library Committee of the Corporation, as the body responsible for the Museum, merely agreed to
the museum clerk having a volunteer helper. Once again the
Corporation of London had abrogated its responsibility. Disgusted at its lack of interest in his initiative, Wheeler
approached the Council of the Society of Antiquaries. Even
though the Society had only limited funds, it immediately
agreed to finance the post of an archaeological investigator. In
1929 Eric Birley, later to become Professor of Romano–British
History and Archaeology in the University of Durham, was the
first to take up the post, but he left after investigating only one
site, and was replaced in the same year by Gerald Dunning,
who attempted to solve some of the outstanding problems of
Roman London. One of these was to discover the plan of the
Roman basilica or town hall, but equally important was his
study of the two great fires of Roman London that had occurred
in AD 60 and about 130 respectively. Dunning left in 1934 to
become an Inspector of Ancient Monuments and a leading
authority on medieval pottery, and was replaced by Frank
Cottrill.

Cottrill, later to become curator of Winchester Museum,
made one of the most outstanding individual contributions to
our records of Roman London during his three years of visiting
City building sites. It is a pity that the lack of finance and
facilities made it impossible to publish his records back in the
'thirties, but they are stored in the archives of the Museum of
London and with his collaboration are being prepared for
publication. Cottrill was responsible for investigating many
sites, including the Roman city defences, the first basilica and
forum (which was not then identified), several roads, a classical
temple, as well as discovering a vital part of the inscribed tomb
of Julius Classicianus, the Roman Procurator.

When Cottrill left in 1937 he was not replaced, though in
1939 Quentin Waddington was at last given an archaeological
assistant, Adrian Oswald. This occurred on the eve of the
Second World War, when all thoughts of Roman London were
soon to be put aside. In the short time available, Oswald
discovered the Roman gate at Aldersgate and an important
part of the Roman forum, a fascinating promise of the wealth of
history yet to be recovered from beneath London's streets.

1945–1959

One-third of the historic City of London having by 1945 been
destroyed by German bombing, this provided a unique opportunity to discover the history and plan of Roman London. From

the beginning, it was clear that there would be a struggle to achieve the full-time professional team essential for excavating the sites.[15] The Society of Antiquaries took the lead and appointed a committee, which included the Chief Inspector of Ancient Monuments, to consider how to organize and finance the programme of excavations. The result was the establishment of the Roman and Medieval London Excavation Council, and William Grimes, the Director of the London Museum in succession to Wheeler, agreed to direct the excavations in an honorary capacity.

During the fifteen years that followed, the Excavation Council kept a small permanent archaeological team working in the City, and in spite of the small scale of the operation Professor Grimes (as he later became as Director of the Institute of Archaeology in London) was able to achieve a great deal.[16] In particular he tackled the date of the Roman city wall, and showed that it had been built not long after 190. He discovered that the defences in the Cripplegate area differed from the rest of the Roman city wall, and in a series of careful excavations surprised everyone by finding the military fort. Many other details were recovered, not least of these being confirmation that London was of Roman origin, and that the Walbrook stream that divided the city into two equal halves was very much smaller than had previously been thought. His most spectacular discovery, however, was the famous temple of Mithras. It was in this that he found the clearest detailed evidence yet of pagan worship in London, as well as probable traces of the early Christian community in that city.

The discovery of the temple also brought to public notice another important fact, namely that the scale of the archaeological work was hopelessly inadequate, and in his book about his excavations Professor Grimes squarely places the principal blame on the Corporation of London.[17] During those fifteen years, when the Corporation's own Guildhall Museum was receiving the important antiquities from City sites, including the Mithraic sculptures, the Corporation donated only £550. Even the church of St Bride in Fleet Street gave double this sum, though the main grant of over £26,000 was donated by the Ministry of Works. Once again Sir Mortimer Wheeler stepped in, and having visited the temple site, he, as President of the Society of Antiquaries, wrote to *The Times* in 1954 and said of the work of the Excavation Council that while its 'skill is unimpeachable, its scale is pathetically inadequate'. A much greater effort was required to discover the Roman and medieval history of London, but he stressed that 'to attempt this, as at present, with four or five pairs of hands is like attacking a battleship with a pea-shooter'.

The discovery of the temple raised yet another problem, that of the need to preserve outstanding monuments from the past for future generations. The temple itself was exceptionally well preserved, with traces of many timber structures, such as floor and bench supports, which had survived only because of the waterlogged conditions of the site. When the marble head of Mithras himself was found in 1954, the god became an instant celebrity, and the site was besieged by the public. On one day alone it was estimated that 35,000 people had walked around the temple, the queue being nearly a mile long. Scholars, press and public pleaded for the temple to be preserved, though the developer, a subsidiary of the Legal and General Property Company, wrote to *The Times* that this was 'impossible'. This view was supported by Sir David Eccles, Minister of Works, who had visited the site. He reported the problem to the Prime Minister, Sir Winston Churchill, and a little later announced how much its preservation would cost: £100,000 was needed to bridge the temple, while delays and lost rent would cost another £400,000. At that time only the Ministry of Works considered the possibility of funding such sums.

Sir Mortimer Wheeler raised these points when he wrote to *The Times*:

The archaeological advice cited on behalf of the Minister of Works in respect of the very remarkable temple must not be taken as representative of archaeological opinion. There can be no doubt that the proper solution of the matter is to preserve the building under its modern successor. To do so would involve a readjustment of plans and a certain expenditure, but is not, of course, impossible.

Other scholars rallied in support, but someone wrote that it seemed that the temple was to be 'sacrificed on the altar of expediency'. Had the cost been borne jointly by the government, the developer and the Corporation of London, and compensating rentable space built into the enormous Bucklersbury House–Temple House complex, this very small temple could have been saved. Although one feels every sympathy for the Legal and General Property Company who considered that they had done enough for archaeology, it is clear that this would represent a small loss in proportion to the on-going profits from what is still one of the largest office blocks in the City. A compromise suggested by the developer, that the temple be re-erected on an adjacent site, helped to solve the problem as far as the public was concerned; but in fact the so-called 'temple of Mithras' that was created out of the rubble of its demolished walls, on a site above a car park in Queen Victoria Street, soon became a travesty of what was actually found, and, as it stands, has little value to anyone.[18] However, it could even now be used as the basis for a full-sized reconstruction of the temple that would make it a unique reminder of London's Roman origin.

Soon after the war, the Corporation considered closing the Guildhall Museum, and transferring its entire collection to the London Museum.[19] Fortunately this was not done, and in 1949 they employed Ivor Noël Hume to visit building sites and to recover objects for the museum collection. They enlarged its staff as a department under the Guildhall Library, and in 1950 Norman Cook became its Keeper. The policy of the museum remained essentially what it had been in the past – primarily to recover interesting groups of objects from the building sites. In effect, this policy, together with a total lack of funds, severely restricted archaeological work, but in spite of this Noël Hume was able to make an extraordinary contribution to the record of Roman London during the seven years he was at the museum.

One of his most important finds was the public baths, recorded under the most difficult building-site circumstances imaginable, on the Sun Life Association site in Cheapside, almost opposite the church of St Mary-le-Bow. But he found much more – traces of the destruction by Boudica in AD 60, parts of several Roman streets, and the remains of various houses, particularly in Watling Street and in Lime Street. He also derived a large amount of information about the Walbrook stream from the site of Bucklersbury House, and recovered many of the Roman religious offerings and examples of industrial waste that had been thrown into the stream. His most unusual discovery, however, was the contents of a Roman well that included the leather trunks of a young dancing girl or acrobat, a wooden ladder more than 4 m long, an almost complete decorated Gaulish bowl, and an adult human skull with a wooden post driven through the side. It is unfortunate that the policy of the Guildhall Museum at that time made it impossible for Noël Hume to publish his site work; as a result, when he left in 1957 to become the chief archaeologist at Colonial Williamsburg, Virginia, USA, the extent of his achievement was not realized. Fortunately, as with Frank Cottrill, those site records are now being prepared for publication at the Museum of London in collaboration with Noël Hume, and the information will be available in due course.[20]

1960–1980

Of necessity this final stage must be a personal account of the most recent archaeological exploration of Roman London, for soon after joining the staff of the Guildhall Museum in 1959, I started archaeological recording on building sites, even though

it was not until 1961 that I officially became the next 'excavations assistant', such was the pressure of work. The investigations in the latter part of 1959 included finding traces of the
Boudican destruction close to the Roman forum, and Roman
structures in the bed of the Thames off Dowgate; but in a sense
this was continuing my amateur efforts which, since 1954, had
been carried out on a number of City building sites, particularly
in the region of Lombard Street, close to the Roman forum, and
in Southwark. The important fact at this stage, not generally
realized, is that the Guildhall Museum did not consider itself
responsible for City archaeology during the 1950s and 1960s
since the Roman and Mediaeval London Excavation Council
was already carrying out excavations. This explains why the
job of the 'excavations assistant' was primarily supposed to be
one of salvaging antiquities from building sites, and why for
more than two decades after the war the Corporation did not
vote any money for its own museum to undertake archaeological research. Indeed, it explains why the job carried that curious title, together with just enough tools to enable the finds to
be recovered.

The lack of resources at Guildhall Museum meant that the
archaeological situation in London became exceptionally
serious in 1962 when Professor Grimes and the Excavation
Council stopped their programme of research, which had
begun in 1946. This imposed upon my own unsupported efforts
the sole responsibility for any archaeological field work, an
unenviable situation that, but for two exceptions, was to continue for a decade. As early as 1960 my museum colleague
Ralph Merrifield had started writing the monumental study of
Roman London that was eventually published in 1965, but this
not only served to highlight the desperate need for much more
site investigation, but also gave archaeology a much-needed
sense of direction. An archaeological policy, however unofficial,
was needed and as early as 1960 it was clear that this must
combine both salvage work on building sites and some formal
excavation. The basic problem of lack of funding by the
Corporation meant that reliance had to be placed upon volunteers, and that various unofficial means of financing the
archaeological work had to be found.

It was also clear that certain sites were of outstanding
importance, as they had the potential of enabling us to discover
much more information about the history, status and layout of
Roman London than had the average site. These included the
city defences, the forum, the Roman streets, and an area
beneath and just east of Cannon Street station that was probably formerly occupied by a public building. In order to
help achieve the best results, the method of excavation was

gradually changed from digging narrow trenches to under-taking more extensive excavations that would expose wider areas of buried buildings.

The first formal excavation using volunteers was carried out in 1960 just east of Cannon Street station, where later research proved the existence of a palatial Roman residence, probably that of the Governor of Britain. In 1962–63 volunteers helped on other formal excavations which uncovered Roman roads in King Street, and a Norman church in Nicholas Lane, off Lombard Street; and volunteers also helped in rescue excavations on a Roman shipwreck in the Thames at Blackfriars, and on the city defences in Cooper's Row.

With time and money so restricted, the excavations had to be specifically aimed at recovering certain essential data from the sites, yet flexible enough to follow up unexpected discoveries. The first aim was to record the character of the natural subsoil and its height above Ordnance Datum, to provide information for a geological map of the ancient site of London; the second was to recover pottery to date the first occupation deposits on every site, in order to show how and when Roman London grew from the embryo settlement just north of London Bridge. The third was to recover as much of the plan of any Roman buildings as possible, since this was the only way to determine their purpose. Fourth, any pottery and coins in layers contemporary with the construction, modification and destruction of the buildings were essential to date their history; and fifth, objects were sought that might reflect the use of a site, whether domestic or industrial.

The formal excavations, rescue and salvage work, carried out on thirty-five sites from 1959 to the end of 1963, gave us a great deal of new information about many aspects of the Roman city – its defences, streets, buildings, industries, cemeteries, geology, and even about its origin. The only problem was that there was no opportunity to process and publish that information other than as summaries in the *Transactions* of the London and Middlesex Archaeological Society.[21] However, Ralph Merrifield included as much as possible in his book *The Roman City of London*, published in 1965.

Two very important discoveries in 1964, however, led to further advances: the first was the unearthing of part of a major Roman building in Corbet Court, Gracechurch Street; this at last, together with the mapping of this forum area by Ralph Merrifield, made it possible to link various fragmentary discoveries and show that they belonged to a single Roman building, which in due course proved to be an early basilica and forum. The second was the discovery of an enormous Roman public bath building in Huggin Hill, opposite Queenhithe.

This was found on one hot day in July 1964 as the site was being levelled by a bulldozer in preparation for rebuilding. It was immediately clear that here lay a major Roman building whose curving wall suggested that it may have been a bath. Although permission was obtained to carry out an emergency excavation during the long August Bank holiday week-end, there was an urgent need to find many volunteers and tools. In addition to making contact with the existing group of volunteers, help was also requested from two other archaeological groups: the Wandsworth Historical Society led by Nicholas Farrant, and the West Kent Border Archaeological Group led by Brian Philp. Both appreciated the urgency of the problem and very kindly stopped their own planned excavations to dig in London. The success of that week-end was primarily due to their enthusiastic and exhausting efforts, and among the many discoveries, much of the west end of this very large public bath building was unearthed, including its hot steam room, the *caldarium*, and the cold water bath.

Out of this week-end was born the City of London Excavation Group, later the City of London Archaeological Society, which formalized week-end volunteer excavations on a regular basis throughout the year. Nicholas Farrant kindly agreed to act as my week-end site supervisor, while during the week, and with a smaller team of volunteers, I carried out further excavation and, of course, the main site recording. The result, therefore, was that with the help of volunteers, it was now possible to establish excavations on every day of the week for a duration of months, in addition to salvage work on building sites. In 1965 Mrs Irene Wade became a second week-end site supervisor, and in 1968 Roger Inman became a third. The debt to these three, and to the very many volunteers, is incalculable, for in those difficult years they helped to keep archaeology alive in the City of London.

After some initial week-end excavations on the Huggin Hill baths to clarify uncertainties of its plan, I transferred the now considerable volunteer effort to a site in Bush Lane, where we uncovered the east wing of the Roman palace in eight weeks of emergency excavation, immediately prior to the start of rebuilding. After this, work began on alternate week-ends on three new sites on the west and north sides of Guildhall, during which the eastern defences of the Cripplegate Roman fort were uncovered.

While the Group was excavating yet another part of the Roman palace in 1966, just east of the forecourt of Cannon Street station, a major new site was opened up adjacent to the Central Criminal Court, in Warwick Square. The Central Criminal Court Extension Committee, through the City

Architects' Department, had agreed to spend up to £3,000 to clear modern obstructions, an offer that resulted in the uncovering of medieval houses, including the town house of Warwick the Kingmaker, and crucial dating evidence for the Roman city defences. The grant, however, was not to be administered by the Museum, and, without a comparable grant from the Library Committee to pay for the archaeological work, reliance had to be placed wholly upon the weekday volunteers. The City Engineer's Department also helped, when in the following year they voted £1,300 to clear obstructions on the site of the Roman and medieval gate at Aldgate, and at Billingsgate, where they cleared an area adjacent to the Roman bath that had become available with the demolition of the Coal Exchange.

The volunteer commitment to City archaeology was by now very considerable, and had, in my opinion, proved its worth. It would have been of enormous help to have had an archaeological assistant, and a modest budget to administer, particularly on site clearance, on the finds and on the site records. But this was not to be for some years to come. Meanwhile, in 1968, while uncovering the first clear traces of fifth-century occupation in London, preserved in layers overlying the Roman bath at Billingsgate, another equally important site had become available in the Roman forum area. That it was possible to excavate this new site at the corner of Fenchurch Street and Gracechurch Street was primarily due to Ralph Merrifield, but as I was too heavily committed at Billingsgate on a site that was soon to be protected as an ancient monument and preserved in the basement of an office block, I was unable to direct yet another major excavation at this stage. Fortunately Brian Philp and his team from Kent agreed to deal with the new site, and, with grants from the Department of the Environment and also the Corporation of London, they unearthed vital information about the early development of London, and recovered a major portion of the plan of the Roman forum.[22] In fact, for some months it was possible to visit the site and see the remains of the origin of London, including parts of a building destroyed by the fire of AD 60: and at Billingsgate, ten minutes later, to be gazing down at the destruction rubble representing the end of Roman London, with the early fifth-century rubbish left by squatters who had been living in the ruins of the Roman bath.

There was no decline during 1969 in the number of sites being rebuilt and available for archaeological excavation. Three sites were selected upon which to expend the main effort: the eastern half of the Roman public baths at Huggin Hill, which was excavated by the weekday volunteers; the Billingsgate bath site where the Excavation Group were uncovering the adjacent Roman dwelling, together with more evidence of

fifth-century occupation: and finally an exceptionally well pre-served fifteenth-century shipwreck at Blackfriars that was excavated and recorded as an emergency. All of this was in addition to the archaeological salvage work on many building sites. In 1968 the Museum was separated from the Guildhall Library to become a department in its own right, but even though £1,000 had been voted for archaeological work in 1969, only £107 was actually made available in spite of the heavy archaeological commitment. In consequence the estimate for 1970 was reduced to £500.[23]

In 1971 Max Hebditch became Director of the Guildhall Museum, and was 'frankly amazed that such low sums were being spent on the archaeology of the most important urban site in Britain'.[24] An archaeologist himself, he set about establishing research on a realistic basis in the City, and for the first time since 1961 others were brought in to share the burden of directing site excavations. While I uncovered Baynards Castle, my

General view of the archaeological excavation at the Central Criminal Court, Warwick Square, in 1966. Medieval and modern foundations cut across Roman features in the foreground; in the background lies the Roman city wall.

museum colleague Hugh Chapman excavated just inside Aldgate and discovered an early Roman fort, and Tony Johnson
was temporarily employed to direct an excavation in the basement of Bush Lane House, on the site of the Roman palace.

Both the museum and the archaeological organization called
'Rescue', led by Martin Biddle, pressed the Corporation of
London to establish a research unit to investigate future City
sites, the attendant publicity and questions in Parliament
creating a reminder of the Mithras situation eighteen years
earlier.[25] But this time the Corporation was not apathetic, for in
June 1973 the Court of Common Council agreed to set up the
Department of Urban Archaeology, and in the following
October Brian Hobley was appointed Chief Urban Archaeologist. It is perhaps fitting that, in the end, it was the Corporation and the Guildhall Museum that created the research unit
which generations of archaeologists had known was essential to
the discovery of Roman London. Indeed, this was the last
major act of the Guildhall Museum before it was merged with
the London Museum to form the Museum of London.

Since 1973 Brian Hobley has built up a staff of about 60,
which with an annual budget of over a quarter of a million
pounds, mostly granted by the Department of the Environment
and property developers, has been bringing to the study of
Roman London a level of effort and expertise that is dramati-
cally enlarging our view of the Roman city. Riverside quays,
city defences, streets, houses and religious monuments, as well
as objects, have all come under very close scrutiny, and this is
supported by a full departmental academic publications programme mainly through the Museum of London and the
London and Middlesex Archaeological Society. It was before
this, however, that a similar, but considerably smaller
archaeological unit was established in Southwark under the
direction of Harvey Sheldon of the Museum of London, and
this too has transformed our knowledge of the Roman and
medieval suburb at the south end of London Bridge.

But what of the work carried out during the half-century
before the creation of the Department of Urban Archaeology?
Much of this is still unpublished, though, except for the work of
Professor Grimes, its publication is now the responsibility of the
Department. For my own part, I am deeply indebted to many
people for kindness and help far beyond ordinary bounds, not
only to my site supervisors and volunteers, but also to various
officers of the Corporation of London, particularly my Museum
colleagues, and to members of the City Architect's and City
Engineer's Departments. There are two people to whom I am
especially indebted, however: Ralph Merrifield and Professor
William Grimes, both of whom were always available with

friendship and advice. During my own period of stewardship, which now spans a quarter of a century, it is significant that the major discoveries normally involved many other people. Some finds, such as the Roman ship at Blackfriars and the Huggin Hill baths, began as chance discoveries, but others were the result of an organized hunt for the truth; of these the Roman palace, the forum, and compiling a geological map of the City were perhaps the most satisfying for the Roman period investigations.

The contoured geological map has taken the longest to compile, but as early as 1959 it was clear that such a map was fundamental to any research on the Roman city, the geology and natural land forms doubtless having determined the areas of human settlement, land use and environment. No such map existed then, but, although twenty years later the map is still far from complete, there is now sufficient information for the geology to be reconstructed, and this is to be included in the next published edition of the regional Geological Survey map.[26] Until 1959 Ordnance Survey levels had rarely been used on City archaeological sites, but it was clear that they too were necessary, so that now it is possible to relate widely separated sites and understand such things as drainage patterns and the physical geography of the sites of major areas of development and defence in the Roman city. The map of the Cripplegate fort, for example, and the modern land forms in the area suggest that the ground was fairly flat during the Roman period. In fact this was not so, for the area inside the south gate was at least 3 m higher than the north-east corner of the fort.

The years up to 1972 now seem like a bad dream, with missed opportunities and the ruthless destruction of large parts of Roman London. For example, to see an elaborately decorated Roman mosaic pavement destroyed without being able to uncover and record it, is a tragic experience. In fact it will never be known how much potential knowledge was lost for ever. For a very long time the buried city of Roman London was in desperate need for scholars to discover its history, but there was little official help.[27] As Professor Grimes wrote in 1968, 'the challenges so presented had to be taken up, but always with an awareness that the rules to be followed were not those of archaeology.'[28] At least an attempt was made, but the extent to which in our various ways we managed to achieve a measure of success is for our successors to judge, for it will be their duty to test our conclusions and, where possible, to check our evidence.

Sources of Illustrations

Notes and bibliographical references

Introduction

1 Calendar 1973, Plea 631.

2 Merrifield 1965; 1969; Grimes 1968.

3 Final excavation reports are being published in the *Transactions* of the London and Middlesex Archaeological Society, and in monographs published jointly by that society and the Museum of London. Interim reports are published in *The London Archaeologist*.

4 Marsden 1961; 1963; 1965; 1967A; 1967B; 1968A; 1968B; 1969A; 1969B; 1970; 1971A; 1971B; 1972.

Chapter I

1 Prehistoric flint flakes are occasionally found in the City, for example in Aldermanbury (*Excavation Notebook*, X, p. 51) and in Cannon Street (*Excavation Notebook* X, p. 67). A Bronze Age collared urn dating from 1500–1200 BC was found in 1974–5 in brickearth on the Post Office site in Newgate Street (I. Longworth in *Antiquaries Journal* LVII, pt. 1, 1977, pp. 51–52, 61–62, pl. XII). Recently an Iron Age inhumation burial was found in the Tower of London (unpublished). The continuing absence of substantial traces of prehistoric settlement both in the formal excavations of Professor W. F. Grimes, myself and the Department of Urban Archaeology, and on the City building sites, rules out the possibility of a prehistoric origin of London (Grimes 1968, p. 3).

2 Merrifield 1969, pp. 28–32; Merrifield 1975, pp. 48–49; Philp 1977, pp. 7–9, 33–35. Merrifield however states that there is no direct evidence that the first occupation of London was military (Merrifield 1969, p. 30).

3 On the Public Cleansing Depot site in Upper Thames Street the river gravels containing pottery of the first and second centuries included large pebbles indicating a fast flow of the river at that time. The later Roman river gravels had smaller pebbles in a grey silty sand suggesting a slower river flow. A possible interpretation is that the tidal limit had reached London during the latter part of the Roman period, though the possibility that this change was caused by a local variation in the river flow cannot be ruled out.

(Excavation Register groups 546, 565, 567, 568; *Excavation Notebook* VI, p. 27, 35, 37, 39, 45, 51).

4 Sheldon 1978, pp. 19–20.

5 Cassius Dio, *Roman History*, LX, 20; *RCHM* 1928, p. 9: Webster and Dudley 1973, p. 53.

6 *BM Guide* 1951, fig. 36, no. 5. (sword), plate XXV, no. 5. (helmet); *Archaeologia* vol. LXIX, pp. 25–26, fig. 25 (sword). The excellent state of preservation of the helmet suggests that it was from a waterlogged site.

7 Merrifield 1969, pp. 22–24.

8 See Sheldon and Schaaf 1978, pp. 59–88; and Vulliamy 1930, pp. 296–300.

9 See pp. 28–29.

10 *Archaeological Journal* vol. XLII, p. 274; *RCHM* 1928, p. 148.

11 Chapman and Johnson 1973, pp. 60–62; for comment see Marsden 1978, pp. 89–91.

12 At 30–32 Lombard Street (Marsden 1965, pp. 138–39), and at the corner of Gracechurch Street and Fenchurch Street (Philp 1977, pp. 7–9).

Chapter II

1 Marsden 1972, pp. 840–45.

2 Marsden 1963, pp. 72–75 (ditch at Barclays Bank, Lombard Street); Norman and Reader 1912, pp. 318–19, fig. 26 (stream).

3 The ditch, found at the west corner of Lime Street and Fenchurch Street, will be published in a forthcoming report by A. Boddington.

4 Marsden 1965, pp. 138–39. At least two other east-west roads probably existed from the beginning of London: a road beneath part of Cannon Street and Eastcheap, which in 1961 was found overlying the natural surface (*Excavation Notebook* VIII, p. 30). This road was also recorded in 1833 as overlying the natural brickearth, but as the section drawing shows the unlikely construction of the adjacent Roman walls as having no foundations, this drawing must be used with caution (Merrifield 1965, p. 115). Another road was found in 1966 immediately south of Corbet Court, off Gracechurch Street, also immediately overlying the natural brickearth.

5 These discoveries by B. Philp indicate a radical change of plan between the two pre-Boudican phases, but, apart from the formal planning of streets and timber buildings, there is no evidence that the first phase was military. No military objects were found, and clearly this phase requires a more detailed examination on neighbouring sites to determine the exact nature of the primary occupation (Philp 1977, pp. 7–9). Before the recent investigations on the origin of London, Merrifield was the main proposer of the theory of its possible military origin (Merrifield 1965, pp. 32–35: 1969, pp. 28–31; 1975, pp. 48–49). This was because so many towns had originated around Roman military centres, though he recognized that 'there is no direct evidence . . . either from structures or small finds, that the first occupation of London was military' (Merrifield 1969, p. 30). Initially the discovery of the Aldgate fort by Chapman seemed to support the theory (Chapman and Johnson 1972, pp. 71–73), but for a reappraisal see Marsden 1978 pp. 89–92. The location of the fort apparently across the road to Colchester would seem to be possible evidence of its early date, perhaps before the construction of the road.

6 Philp 1977, p. 9.

7 The sequence of Roman structures in the forum area is described by Philp (1977) and Marsden (1978). Had a military phase existed in London, then the earliest layers should contain military objects. Their absence means that London contrasts with other sites which apparently had a military beginning (e.g., Richborough, Colchester, Chichester and Gloucester). The absence of a basilica at this primary phase is not significant, for initially even the Claudian *colonia* of Aequum in Dalmatia merely had an open area to serve as a forum, and behind it were the civic offices and the curia (Wilkes 1969, p. 369). The existence of a gravelled market-place in London preceding the forum building, may mirror the usual development of urban fora in Britain. For example, at Leicester an open space was laid out in the late first century, but it was not until the 120s that the forum-building was constructed (Wacher 1974, p. 338; Hebditch and Mellor 1973, pp. 36–37). Also at Chichester a gravelled open space seems to have preceded the forum (Wacher 1974, p. 245; Down 1978, p. 180).

8 Philp 1977, p. 9.

9 For the timber-framed building in Fenchurch Street see Philp 1977, pp. 10–16; also Boddington forthcoming. A metre-thick deposit of charred grain was found in the easternmost room by Boddington, and an analysis by P. Boyd indicates that, as at least

some of it was imported from the Mediterranean, it is likely to have been seed-grain (Boyd forthcoming). The portico linked the various rooms to unite the building, though the somewhat formal plan as reconstructed by Philp is but one of several possibilities which need not be so regular. Based on Philp's reconstruction Frere has suggested that it might have been an official building (Frere 1979, p. 101).

10 Frere 1972, pp. 13–23.

11 Marsden 1965, pp. 138–39.

12 Marsden 1968B, pp. 32–35.

13 *RCHM* 1928, p. 155. See also map in Haverfield 1911.

14 The cemetery was found at 112–14 Fenchurch Street and 17–18 Billiter Street (*Excavation Notebook 1924*, p. 95). For the Claudian use of Purbeck marble see Dunning 1949, pp. 14–15, and Hawkes and Hull 1947, p. 349. For the outer cemeteries of Roman London see *RCHM* 1928, pp. 153–63. It is curious that the Billiter Street–Fenchurch Street cemetery was not included in the *RCHM* 1928, for Waddington was a member of the Royal Commission Committee (*RCHM* 1928, p. xii).

15 Marsden 1967, pp. 211–12.

16 Johnson 1973, pp. 58–64.

17 *Annals*, XIV, 33, quoted in *RCHM* 1928, pp. 1–2.

18 Lawrence 1940.

19 Lewis and Reinhold 1966, pp. 337–38.

20 Haverfield 1911, pp. 169–70.

21 Mócsy 1974, p. 126.

22 Alföldy 1974, p. 84.

23 Sheldon 1978, pp. 57–65.

24 *RCHM* 1928, pp. 192–94; Dawson 1969–70; 1971; Merrifield 1970; Merrifield and Sheldon 1974.

25 Hammerson 1978, pp. 588–92. Of the total number of Claudian coins from the following early Claudian sites, copies comprise: Colchester 56%, Richborough 36%, Verulamium 26%, Hod Hill 33%. From the later Claudian sites they comprise: Sea Mill, Glos. 90%, Cirencester 82%, Silchester 81%, Exeter 93%. But Wroxeter, a later Claudian site, has only 26% copies. For the copy Claudian coin from period 1 in Fenchurch Street see Philp 1977, pp. 7, 44.

26 Bird and Marsh 1978, p. 529. Strictly, the coins and pottery date the roadside occupation which is believed to be contemporary with the construction of the roads in Southwark (Sheldon 1978, pp. 20–30). The pottery from the earliest stratified deposits in the City broadly supports a late Claudian date for the founding of London. For example the following samian ware stamps were recovered from the bottom of the first rubbish deposit above the natural brick-earth on a site in Plough Court, off Lombard Street, in the Roman city centre just south of the forum (Marsden 1968B, pp. 32–35, bottom of layer 3): MODESTUS of La Graufesenque generally dated *c.* AD 40–65, BASSVS of La Graufesenque generally dated *c.* AD 50–70, and SILVANVS of La Graufesenque generally dated *c.* AD 50–65. (Report kindly supplied by Mr B. Hartley and Miss B. Dickinson in 1979.)

Chapter III

1 *Annals* XIV, 33, quoted in *RCHM* 1928, p. 2, historical details of the Boudican rebellion are described in Webster 1978, and in Frere 1974, pp. 103–111.

2 For the destruction deposits in Colchester see: Crummy 1974; Webster 1978, pp. 113–20; Hull 1958, pp. 153–58, 198–202.

3 Lambert 1922, pp. 57–58.

4 Dunning 1945.

5 An updated record of probable Boudican fire deposits, shown on page 30, is as follows:
59–60 Gracechurch Street (*Excavation Notebook* VI, p. 25).
St Swithin's House, Walbrook (Hume 1954).
30–32 Lombard Street (Marsden 1965, pp. 138–39).
West Corner of Lime Street and Fenchurch Street (Boddington forthcoming).
East corner of Gracechurch Street and Fenchurch Street (Philp 1977, pp. 9–17).
10 St Swithin's Lane (Hobley and Schofield 1977, p. 57).
19–21 Birchin Lane (Dunning 1945, p. 51).
55 Gracechurch Street (*Excavation Notebook* IV, pp. 86–87).
Aldgate (Chapman 1973, p. 7).
All Hallows, Lombard Street (MS notes by A. Oswald in the Museum of London).
18–20 Southwark Street (Marsden 1971B, p. 21).
It is unlikely that the fire recorded at St Michael's Church, Crooked Lane, occurred in AD 60 (Kempe 1832, pp. 192–94).

6 Philp 1977, p. 19; Chapman 1973, p. 7; Marsden 1971B, p. 21.

7 Dunning 1945, pp. 76–77.

8 Marsden 1971B, p. 21.

9 Boddington forthcoming.

10 *Excavation Notebook* VI, p. 25.

11 Lambert 1922, p. 57; Wheeler 1946, p. 189.

12 Wheeler 1946, p. 191, no. 20.

13 Hume 1954.

14 Chapman 1973, pp. 5–6.

15 Philp 1977, p. 19.

16 Marsden 1963, p. 75, walls 'c'.

17 *RIB*, 12.

Chapter IV

1 Lethaby 1923, pp. 33–42; Marsden 1975, p. 3; Smith 1860, p. 32.

2 Lambert 1915, pp. 225–35.

3 It was first realized that an earlier building underlay the large forum about 1928 (*RCHM* 1928, p. 42). The possibility that it was a temple was mentioned in Merrifield 1965, p. 143; and that it might have been a government building, in Wacher 1974, pp. 88–91.

4 Some of the difficulties of plotting Roman walls in the forum area were described by Merrifield 1965, p. 135. Before the first forum was recognized as such, it was described as a 'proto-forum' (Philp 1977, pp. 17–21). After careful re-plotting it was eventually recognized as a normal basilica-forum (Marsden 1978, pp. 96–98). Subsequently and independently Frere also recognized it as a basilica-forum (Frere 1979, p. 101). Special thanks are due to Mrs Sara Pafitt who undertook the laborious job of accurately plotting the Roman structures on the maps. For the piers see Philp 1977, pp. 40–43.

5 Wacher 1975, p. 207.

6 Tacitus, *Agricola* 21.

7 Merrifield 1965, pl. 125; Marsden 1969B; Marsh and Tyers 1976; Macartney 1914, p. 225.

8 *RIB*, 9.

9 Dating is based on the fact that the temple underlies the second forum, and that it had unusual foundations similar to those of the first forum.

10 Turner and Skutsch 1960.

11 *RIB*, 8.

12 Philp 1977, pp. 23–24.

13 *Journal of Roman Studies*, vol. XXV, 1935, p. 215.

14 Philp 1977, pp. 22–24.

15 Marsden 1978, pp. 96–102.

16 For the ditch at Crutched Friars (Merrifield 1965, site 336); for the ditch in Dukes Place (Maloney 1979, pp. 293–94); a similar ditch was disclosed at the Bastion 6 site in Dukes Place (Marsden forthcoming).

17 Roskams 1978, pp. 204–05.

18 Frere 1979.

19 Excavated by D. Perrin for the Department of Urban Archaeology of the Museum of London (*Britannia* vol. X, 1979, p. 313).

20 *RCHM* 1928, p. 177, no. 103; Wheeler 1946, p. 51.

21 Ferguson 1974, pp. 23–26.

22 Wright, Hassall and Tomlin 1976, pp. 378–79.

23 Wheeler 1946, p. 108. There is no certainty, however, that these rattles from London were used in the worship of Isis. See also Harris 1965, pp. 80–81.

24 *Journal of Roman Studies*, vol. 26, pp. 254–55.

25 Sticotti 1913, pp. 67–98.

26 *Excavation Notebook* VII, p. 35; Marsden 1963, p. 74, fig. 3, the gravelled area at the north-east end of the site.

27 Marsden 1976, pp. 3–26.

28 Seneca, *Moral Epistles* vi. 1–2, quoted in Lewis and Reinhold 1966, p. 228.

29 Grimes 1968, pp. 136–41; Marsden 1976, pp. 30–46.

30 Marsden 1978.

31 *Guildhall Museum Catalogue* 1908, p. 57, no. 270, pl. XIX, i.

Chapter V

1 *RIB*, 7.

2 Chapman 1974, p. 176,

3 *RIB*, 15; *RCHM* 1928, p. 176, no. 64.

4 Merrifield 1965, site 222.

5 Marsden, Dyson and Rhodes 1975, pp. 175–81.

6 *Ibid*, pp. 199–201.

7 Merrifield 1965, sites 50, 283.

8 Merrifield 1960.

9 *RCHM* 1928, p. 176, no. 58.

10 Chapman 1974, pp. 174–75.

11 *RIB*, 21.

12 *RIB*, 15.

13 Willcox 1977. The large population of London in the late first century must mean that there was an agricultural policy for the region. Nowadays it takes more than an acre of cropped land, plus the products of the forests, to support one 'average' human being. The actual amount of land required to support a person during the Roman period is not known, but would vary according to differing standards of living, types of diet, farming methods, and so on; but this modern 'average' figure is a useful yardstick. (Dudley Stamp 1961, pp. 23, 117).

14 Marsden 1969, p. 7.

15 Willcox 1978.

16 Report by J. Watson in Chapman 1973, pp. 51–53.

17 Report by D. Rixson in Sheldon (ed.) 1978, pp. 173–74, 603–05.

18 Report by A. Jones in Sheldon (ed.) 1978, p. 601.

19 *Excavation Group* 197.

20 Report by J. Bird and G. Marsh in Sheldon (ed.), 1978, pp. 527–32.

21 Peacock 1977; *Excavation Groups* 1117, 1160, 1162.

22 *RCHM* 1928, p. 177, nos 101, 102; Merrifield 1965, pl. 111.

23 Merrifield 1977, pp. 390–94; *RCHM* 1928, pl. 68.

24 Chapman 1974, pp. 175–76.

25 *RCHM* 1928, p. 176, no. 61. pl. 63.

26 Philp 1977, pp. 22–23.

27 Excavation by S. Roskams. *Britannia* vol. X, 1979, p. 313.

28 *Excavation Notebook III*, p. 20.

29 *RCHM* 1928, pp. 118–19. The excavators considered that as the void under the floor lay below the contemporary ground level, it was perhaps a hypocaust. It is difficult to find a parallel, however, and also to see how the heating could work.

30 *Excavation Notebook III*, pp. 1–2.

31 *RIB*, 6.

32 *RCHM* 1928, p. 154.

33 Marsden 1969, pp. 4–6.

Chapter VI

1 Jones 1949; Hassall 1973; Davies 1976; Mann and Jarrett 1967; Frere 1974, p. 226.

2 *RIB*, 19.

3 Chapman 1973, p. 48, no. 9.

4 *RCHM* 1928, pl. 60 no. 15; pl. 7.

5 Davies 1976, p. 141.

6 Grimes 1968, p. 38; Merrifield 1965, p. 100; 1969, p. 111.

7 Marsden 1976, pp. 34–37.

8 Webster 1958, p. 86, no. 157; Merrifield 1965, pl. 98; for a dagger and its scabbard from Copthall Court see Spencer 1961.

9 Marsden 1975.

10 Marsden 1975, p. 52.

11 Marsden 1963, pp. 72–73.

12 Marsden 1975, pp. 63–64.

13 *RIB*, 5.

14 *RIB*, 21.

15 Marsden 1975, pp. 54–59.

16 *RIB*, 8.

17 Marsden 1975, pp. 70–71; for mortaria bearing the stamp P.PR. B ( ) and P.P. BR ( ), and for the two stamped tiles from Brockley Hill see G. Marsh and P. Tyers in Sheldon (ed.) 1978, p. 534.

18 Merrifield 1969, pp. 72–73.

19 Marsden 1975, pp. 12–100.

20 *RCHM* 1928, p. 44.

21 Wacher 1974, p. 338.

22 Lethaby 1923, pp. 33–42.

23 Martin 1926, p. 321.

24 *Current Archaeology* vol. 5 (1977), pp. 370–71.

25 Wheeler 1946, pp. 38–39, pl. XI.

26 Marsden 1978, p. 100–02.

27 Carcopino 1956, p. 258.

28 Marsden 1976, p. 61, no. 60.

29 Marsden 1975, pp. 70–71.

30 Merrifield 1965, p. 146.

Chapter VII

1 Dunning 1945, pp. 52–61.

2 Dunning 1945, p. 57.

3 Dunning 1945, p. 60.

4 Sheldon 1975, p. 278; 1978, pp. 36–39.

5 *Excavation Notebook 1924–39*, p. 32.

6 The dumping of rubbish in the river was recorded on the Public Cleansing Depot.

7 Roskams 1978, p. 204; *Britannia* vol. 10, 1979, pp. 313, 317.

8 Merrifield 1962; A. Graham in Sheldon (ed.) 1978. pp. 510–16.

9 *RCHM* 1928, p. 189.

10 Sheldon 1975, p. 283; Marsh and Tyers in Sheldon 1978, pp. 534–37.

11 Merrifield 1962.

12 Wright, Hassall and Tomlin 1976.

13 *RIB*, 2.

14 Marsden 1976, pp. 22–23, 38.

15 Maloney 1979, p. 293.

16 Marsden 1968, p. 9, levels C and D. There is some slight evidence to suggest that the fort might have continued in use into the later Roman period. The west gate of the fort shows considerable wear from usage, the sill of the doorway to the north tower having been renewed at least once, probably as an adjustment to the raising of the road level; and the road through the gate itself had been made up at least twice. But since the blocking of the gate did not have a foundation of clay and flints, as did the city wall, it seems likely that it was done later, and that the gate continued in use after the town defences were built. This could account for the wear. Similarly the re-metallings of the intervallum road found in Windsor Court, and the presumably continuing use of the main Roman street positions in the fort into recent times need not necessarily reflect a military use of the fort. More important, however, are the alterations to the barrack buildings found on the site of St Alban's church, Wood Street, where a slight verandah or corridor wall had been removed and replaced by shallow gullies defining the road. This could imply the continuing use of the fort beyond the twenty or thirty years suggested here. (Grimes 1968, pp. 30–39).

17 Marsden 1975, pp. 73–78.

18 Marsden 1975, p. 77.

Chapter VIII

1 Sheldon 1978, pp. 36–38; Merrifield 1965, end plan.

2 Grimes 1968, pp. 47–56, fig. 20; Marsden 1965, p. 135, fig. 1; 1970, pp. 2–7; Norman and Reader 1912, p. 276; Maloney 1979, pp. 294–95.

3 *RCHM* 1928, pp. 83–92; Bird 1978, p. 127; Maloney 1979, pp. 294–95.

4 Merrifield 1965, sites W.3, W.5, W.10; Marsden 1970, pp. 2–6; 1965, pp. 135–36.

5 Marsden 1969, pp. 20–23. (Aldgate); 1970, pp. 8–9. (Ludgate).

6 Crummy 1977, pp. 92–100; *RCHM* 1928, pp. 98–99.

7 Merrifield 1965, G8.

8 Grimes 1968, pp. 29–32.

9 Grimes 1968, pp. 50–51.

10 Marsden 1965, p. 135; 1970, pp. 2–4.

11 Marsden 1970, pp. 2–6

12 *RCHM* 1928, p. 35.

13 Marsden 1967C.

14 Marsden 1965B.

15 Taylor and Cleere 1978.

16 Marsden 1976B.

17 Frere 1974, pp. 285–89.

Chapter IX

1 Marsden 1976, pp. 22–23.

2 Marsden 1976, pp. 51–52.

3 Marsden 1968, pp. 8–9.

4 *RCHM* 1928, pp. 137–38.

5 *RIB*, 17.

6 *RIB*, 11.

7 Wright, Hassall and Tomlin 1976, p. 378, no. 2; *Current Archaeology* no. 57, p. 316.

8 Wright, Hassall and Tomlin 1976, p. 378, no. 1; *Current Archaeology* no. 57, p. 316.

9 *RIB*, 2.

10 *RCHM* 1928, plate 6.

11 Blagg 1977, pp. 311–15.

12 Blagg 1977, p. 315.

13 Cunliffe 1969, pp. 28–33.

14 Minucius Felix, *Octavius* vi, xxiii. 1–4, quoted in Lewis and Reinhold 1966, p. 574.

15 Ferguson 1974, pp. 26–28.

16 *RCHM* 1928, pl. 14; Merrifield 1969, p. 183; Harris 1965, p. 102.

17 Merrifield 1969, pp. 183–84; Harris 1965, pp. 109–12.

18 Minucius Felix, *Octavius* vi, xxiii. 1–4, quoted in Lewis and Reinhold 1966, p. 574.

19 Wheeler 1946, pp. 45–46.

20 Daniels 1962.

21 Grimes 1968, pp. 98–117.

22 Merrifield 1977.

23 *RCHM* 1928, pp. 4–5

24 Wheeler 1946, p. 25; *Proceedings of the Society of Antiquaries*, second series, vol. II (1861–4), pp. 87–88, 253–58; Phillips 1859; Hughes 1977. The name Syagrius on the ingots has been presumed to refer to the ruler in Gaul who was defeated by the Franks in AD 486, and therefore that they are evidence of trade between London and Gaul during the latter half of the fifth century (Biddle, Hudson and Heighway 1973, pp. 18–19). There is no justification for this exceptionally late attribution since several people with this name held important office during the fourth century (e.g. the *notarius* to the Emperor Valentinian mentioned in AD 369). I am grateful to Kenneth Painter of the British Museum for his comments on the alternative names.

25 Frere 1976.

26 Whittington 1875, p. 301; Wheeler 1934A; rejoinder by Myres 1834; reply by Wheeler 1934B.

27 Apart from the lack of later Roman deposits, a noticeably small number of Roman rubbish pits has been found in London dating from after the mid-second century. The total of pits recorded by the Guildhall Museum since the war is 82 from the mid first to mid second century, and 46 from the late second to the end of the fourth century. Therefore on average 64 per cent of discovered pits date from the first third of the Roman period. On specific archaeological excavations, which unfortunately have all been situated near the outer limits of the Roman city, the following dated pit totals were recorded:-

Site	mid 1st century — mid 2nd century	mid 2nd century — late 4th century
Aldgate (Chapman 1973)	17	3
Foster Lane (Lambert 1915, p. 245)	37	4
Warwick Sq. (Marsden 1969, pp. 3–7)	1	2
Guildhall (Marsden 1968, pp. 5–10)	7	7

To check against the possibility of the smaller number of later Roman pits being due to their having been dug from considerably higher archaeological levels which were later removed, a count was made of the 11th to 13th century pits also recorded by the Guildhall Museum since the war. Since 85 had been recorded the smaller number of later Roman pits seems likely to reflect a decline in occupation.

It is possible, however, that the later Roman occupation deposits may have been extensively destroyed during the Middle Ages, thus accounting for at least part of their general absence. Had this been the case it is likely to have been reflected by a high percentage of later, instead of earlier, Roman residual pottery in medieval deposits. The Roman residual pottery in 30 medieval pits was studied, and of 466 closely datable sherds 240 were found to be of the mid first to mid second century, 226 of later Roman date. This means that about 50 per cent of the sherds belong to the first third of the Roman period, at least on the sites where the medieval pits were investigated, once again suggesting that in the last two-thirds of the Roman period there was a real decline in the amount of rubbish, and that in turn this presumably reflects a significantly smaller urban population compared with the earlier Roman period.

28 Price 1870.

29 Merrifield 1965, sites 151, 358, 359.

30 Tucker 1848; Chaffers 1849; note by T. Gunston in the *Journal of the British Archaeological Association*, I. vol. 24, 1868, pp. 295–97.

31 Tatton-Brown 1974, pp. 122–28; Schofield and Miller 1976.

32 Marsden 1965B.

33 Marsden forthcoming.

34 Marsden 1974B.

35 Smith 1907.

36 Schofield and Miller 1976, 395; K. Hartley in Hobley and Schofield 1977, p. 62.

37 Marsden 1967C.

38 *RCHM* 1928, pls 57, 58.

39 Marsden 1968B. pp. 38–40.

Chapter X

1 Merrifield 1965, site 331.

2 Frere 1974, pp. 317–18; Sheldon 1978, pp. 39–43.

3 *RCHM* 1928, pp. 189–90.

4 *RCHM* 1928, pp. 3–4.

5 *RCHM* 1928, p. 33, pl. 67.

6 See Chapter IX, note 27.

7 Dark earth has been found overlying occupation deposits of the second century; Roskams and Schofield 1978, pp. 227–30, *Britannia* vol. X, 1979, pp. 313, 317.

8 Marsden 1968A, pp. 6–7.

9 *RCHM* 1928, pp. 5–6.

10 *RCHM* 1928, pp. 5–6.

11 *Excavation Notebook 1949–55*, p. 55.

12 Johnson 1975.

13 Grimes 1968, pp. 71–78.

14 Maloney 1979.

15 Marsden 1970, p. 3, layer 10.

16 Roach Smith 1842, pp. 150–51.

17 Marsden 1967B.

18 Fitzstephen in Stow 1970 (ed.), p. 502.

19 Hill, Millett and Blagg 1980.

20 *Britannia* vol. IX, 1978, pp. 453.

21 Hill, Millett and Blagg 1980.

22 Blurton 1977, pp. 20–21.

23 Sheldon 1971; 1972.

24 Fulford 1977.

25 *Britannia* vol. IX, 1978, p. 453.

26 Hoard in the Museum of London.

27 Painter 1972, p. 87, pl. XXVI.

28 Kindly identified by analysis and dated by David Peacock of Southampton University. See also Riley 1975, pp. 27–31. Before the analysis by Dr Peacock this was incorrectly believed to have been a B-ware amphora of the latter part of the fifth century.

29 Smith 1909, pp. 148–49. Perhaps there should be added part of a glass stemmed beaker found in Lime Street (Guildhall Museum cat. no. 5492), which is thought to have been imported from the Rhineland. It is of a type which is believed not to have outlasted the 5th century (Harden 1956, pp. 137–39).

30 Hand-made pottery in Roman styles has been found on a number of sites in and around London, and where its stratigraphical and coin associations are clear it seems to be of early 5th century date. In the City this pottery had been identified at Billingsgate (*Excavation Register* groups 1280, 1321, 1322, 1323, 1325, 1326, 1327). St Dunstan's Hill (*Excavation Register* groups 1251, 1257), Bastion 6 site (*Excavation Register* groups 1332, 1337, 1338), and at the Roman palace site in Cannon Street (*Excavation Register* group 976). Outside the City it has been recognized at Old Ford (Sheldon 1971, p. 58, no. 6; p. 61, no. 9) associated with coins of Magnus Maximus and Honorius. It has also been found at Fulham (Arthur and Whitehouse 1978, pp. 63–71).

31 Marsden 1975, pp. 77–78.

32 Wheeler 1935, pp. 116–18; Bidder and Morris 1959, pp. 73, 79; Welch 1975; Evison 1972; 1978.

33 In spite of the varying theories extant about the fate of Roman London, the continuing apparent absence of any significant trace of occupation in the city during the latter half of the 5th and the 6th century, must lead to the conclusion that, on the present evidence, the city was probably largely unoccupied (see Grimes 1968, pp. 153–54). Since the exceptionally late dating claimed for the supposed B-ware amphorae from Billingsgate (see Chapter X, note 28), and the Syagrius pewter ingots from Battersea (see chapter IX, note 24), is so uncertain, the burden of proof that London continued to be occupied, particularly as a trading centre, at such a late period must lie with those who propose such a theory (Justinian, *Digest*, xxii, iii, 2). This proof has yet to be found.

Chapter XI

1 Wren 1750, part II, section 1, pp. 264–67.

2 Woodward 1713.

3 Stukeley 1724, pp. 112–13.

4 Craik, 1841, p. 162.

5 Craik, 1841, p. 157.

6 This is not the place to do justice to the work of Charles Roach Smith, whose prime publication on Roman London was *Illustrations of Roman London*, published in 1859. A biography of this remarkable man is much needed, especially as various manuscript papers have recently been acquired by the Museum of London. His papers are to be found in many museums and archives in Britain and abroad, especially France. (Kidd 1977; 1978; Hobley 1975). For R. Lambert Jones see Jones 1863.

7 *The Builder* 1845, pp. 558, 582, 583, 585, 595, 596, 612, 621.

8 Welch 1893, pp. 22, 23.

9 See Chapter IX, note 30.

10 Price 1870.

11 Price 1880.

12 Norman and Reader 1906; 1912.

13 Wheeler 1946, p. 4.

14 *RCHM* 1928.

15 Wheeler 1944.

16 Grimes 1968.

17 Grimes 1968, p. 219.

18 Grimes 1968, p. 235.

19 Hume 1978, pp. 11–12.

20 The Cheapside baths are now published in collaboration with Noël Hume (Marsden 1976).

21 See Introduction, footnote 4; Grimes 1968, p. 220.

22 Philp 1977.

23 Hebditch 1978, p. 25.

24 Hebditch 1978, p. 25.

25 Biddle, Hudson and Heighway 1973.

26 Marsden 1972.

27 A view expressed by generations of archaeologists (see Haverfield 1911, pp. 141–43).

28 Grimes 1968, p. 238.

Bibliography

ALCOCK L., 1975, *By South Cadbury is that Camelot . . . .* London.

ALFÖLDY G., 1974, *Noricum.* London.

BIDDER H., MORRIS J., 1959, 'The Anglo-Saxon cemetery at Mitcham'. *Surrey Archaeological Collections* 56: 51–131.

BIDDLE M., HUDSON D., HEIGHWAY C., 1973, *The future of London's past.* Published by 'Rescue'.

BIRD J., MARSH G., 'The samian ware', in Sheldon (ed.), *Southwark Excavations 1972–74*: 527–32. London and Middlesex Archaeological Society and Surrey Archaeological Society joint publication.

BIRD J., 1978, 'The first drawing of the Classicianus inscription'. *Collectanea Londiniensia, LMAS* Special paper No. 2: 124–27.

BLAGG T., 1977, 'The London Arch'. *Current Archaeology* no. 57: 311–15.

BLURTON T. R., 1977, 'Excavations at Angel Court, Walbrook, 1974'. *Trans. LMAS* 28: 14–100.

BODDINGTON A., 1979, 'Excavations at 48–50 Cannon Street, City of London, 1975'. *Trans. LMAS* 30.

BRITISH MUSEUM, 1951, *Guide to the Antiquities of Roman Britain.*

CALENDAR A., 1973. *London Assize of Nuisance 1301–1431.* London Record Society.

CARCOPINO J., 1956, *Daily Life in Ancient Rome* (Penguin edn).

CHAFFERS W., 1849, 'On a Roman building discovered in Lower Thames Street, in the City of London'. *Journal of the British Archaeological Association* IV: 38–45.

CHAPMAN H., JOHNSON T., 1973, 'Excavations at Aldgate and Bush Lane House in the City of London 1972'. *Trans. LMAS* 24: 71–73.

CHAPMAN H., 1973, 'Excavations at Aldgate, 1972'. *Trans. LMAS* 24: 1–56.

——, 1974, 'Letters from Roman London'. *The London Archaeologist* 2: 173–76.

COTTRILL F., 1936, 'A bastion of the Town Wall of London, and the sepulchral Monument of the Procurator Julius Classicianus'. *The Antiquaries Journal* XVI, No. 1: 1–7.

CRAIK G., 1841, 'Roman London', in Knight C., (ed.), *London* I London: 145–68.

CRUMMY P., 1974, *Colchester, Recent Excavations and Research.* Colchester Excavation Committee.

——, 1977, 'Colchester, the Roman fortress and the development of the Colonia'. *Britannia* VIII: 65–105.

CUNLIFFE B., 1969. *Roman Bath.* Report No. XXIV of the Research Committee of the Society of Antiquaries of London.

——, 1968, *Fifth Report on the excavations of the Roman fort at Richborough, Kent.* Report No. XXIII of the Research Committee of the Society of Antiquaries of London.

DANIELS C., 1962, *Mithras and his temples on the Wall.* Museum of Antiquities of the University of Durham.

DAVIES R., 1976, 'Singulares and Roman Britain'. *Britannia* VIII:134–44.

DAWSON G., 1969–70 'Roman London Bridge'. *The London Archaeologist* 1: 114–17, 156–60.

——, 1971, London Bridge – a rejoinder'. *The London Archaeologist*: 224.

DOWN A., 1978, *Chichester Excavations* III. (Phillimore) Chichester.

DUNNING G. C., 1945, 'Two fires of Roman London'. *Antiquaries Journal* XXV: 48–77.

——, 1949, 'The Purbeck marble industry in the Roman period'. *Archaeological Newsletter*, March: 14–15.

EVISON V., 1972, 'Glass cone beakers of the "Kempston" type'. *Journal of Glass Studies* XIV: 48–66.

——, 1978, 'Early Anglo-Saxon applied disc brooches'. *Antiquaries Journal* LVIII, pt I: 88–102; pt II: 260–78.

Excavation Notebooks: Manuscript notebooks of the Museum of London, recording daily site observations and the context of *Excavation Register* groups.

Excavation Register group: the accession number, in the Excavation Register of the Museum of London, of a group of objects usually from a single deposit.

FERGUSON J., 1974, *The Religions of the Roman Empire.* London.

FRERE S., 1972, *Verulamium Excavations* I. Report No. XXVIII of the Research Committee of the Society of Antiquaries of London.

——, 1974, *Britannia.* London, (Cardinal edn).

——, 1976, 'The Silchester church: the excavation by Sir Ian Richmond in 1961'. *Archaeologia* CV: 277–302.

——, 1979, 'Town planning in the western provinces', in *Festschrift zum 75 jährigen Bestehen der Römisch-Germanischen Kommission*: 87–103.

FULFORD M., 1977, 'Pottery and Britain's foreign trade in the later Roman period', in D. Peacock (ed.). *Pottery and early commerce*, London: 35–84.

GRIMES W. F., 1968, *The Excavation of Roman and Medieval London.* London.

Guildhall Museum Catalogue 1908. Published by the Corporation of the City of London.

HAMMERSON M., 1978, 'The Coins', in Sheldon (ed.), *Southwark Excavations 1972–4*, 2. London and Middlesex Archaeological Society and Surrey Archaeological Society joint publication: 587–600.

HARDEN D. B., 1956, 'Glass vessels in Britain and Ireland. A.D. 400–1000', in Harden D. (ed.), *Dark Age Britain, Studies presented to E. T. Leeds*. London.

——, 1978, 'Glass "sports cup" from Toppings and Sun Wharves: 1970–72', in Sheldon (ed.), *Southwark Excavations 1972–74*, London and Middlesex Archaeological Society and Surrey Archaeological Society joint publication: 605–07.

HARRIS E. and J., 1965, *The Oriental Cults in Roman Britain*. Leiden.

HASSALL M., 1973, 'Roman soldiers in Roman London', in Strong D. (ed.), *Archaeological theory and practice*. London: 231–37.

HAVERFIELD F., 1911, 'Roman London'. *Journal of Roman Studies* 1: 141–72.

HAWKES C., HULL M., 1947. *Camulodunum*. Research Report No. XIV of the Society of Antiquaries of London.

HEBDITCH M., 1978, 'Towards the future of London's past'. *Collectanea Londiniensia, LMAS* special paper No. 2: 23–31.

HEBDITCH M., MELLOR J., 1973. 'The Forum and Basilica of Roman Leicester'. *Britannia* IV: 1–83.

HILL C., MILLETT M., BLAGG, T., 1980. 'The Roman riverside wall and monumental arch in London'. *LMAS* special paper No. 3.

HILL W. THOMSON, 1955. *Buried London*. London.

HOBLEY B., 1975, 'Charles Roach Smith (1807–1890), Pioneer Rescue Archaeologist'. *The London Archaeologist* 2: 328–33.

HOBLEY B., SCHOFIELD J., 1977, 'Excavations in the City of London: first interim report, 1974–75'. *Antiquaries Journal* LVII, pt 1: 31–66.

HUGHES M., 1977, 'The analysis of Roman tin and pewter ingots', in W. A. Oddy (ed.). *Aspects of early metallurgy*. Published by Historical Metallurgy Society and British Museum Research Laboratory: 41–50.

HULL M. R., 1958, *Roman Colchester*. Report No. XX of the Research Committee of the Society of Antiquaries of London.

HUME I. N., 1978, 'Into the jaws of death ... walked one'. *Collectanea Londiniensia, LMAS* Special Paper No. 2: 7–22.

HUME I. N. and A., 1954, 'A mid-first century pit near Walbrook'. *Trans. LMAS* XI (NS), pt III: 249–58.

JOHNSON T., 1973, 'Excavations at Bush Lane House, 1972'. *Trans. LMAS* 24: 56–70.

——, 1975, 'A Roman signal tower at Shadwell, E.1'. *Trans. LMAS* 26: 278–80.

JONES A., 1949, 'The Roman Civil Service (Clerical and sub-Clerical grades)'. *Journal of Roman Studies* XXXIX: 38–55.

JONES, R. LAMBERT, 1863, *Reminiscences of the Public Life of Richard Lambert Jones Esq.*, London. (Copy in Guildhall Library.)

KEMPE A. G., 1832. 'An account of antiquities discovered on the site of the Church of St. Michael, Crooked Lane ...' *Archaeologia* 24: 190–201.

KIDD D., 1977, 'Charles Roach Smith and his museum of London antiquaries'. *British Museum Yearbook* II: 105–35.

——, 1978, 'Charles Roach Smith and the Abbé Cochet', in Centenaire de l'Abbé Cochet – 1975. *Actes du Colloque International d'Archéologie*. Rouen 1978: 63–77.

LAMBERT F., 1915, 'Recent discoveries in London'. *Archaeologia* 66: 225–74.

——, 1922, 'Some Recent Excavations in London'. *Archaeologia* 71: 56–112.

LAWRENCE L. A., 1940, 'A hoard of plated Roman denarii'. *Numismatic Chronical*, Series 5, 20: 185–89.

LETHABY W. R., 1923, *Londinium: Architecture and the Crafts*. London.

LEWIS N., REINHOLD M., (eds) 1966, *Roman Civilization Sourcebook II: The Empire*. London.

LIVERSIDGE J., 1975, 'Painted wall-plaster'. *Trans. LMAS* 26: 199–201.

MACARTNEY M., note about Roman finds at St Paul's cathedral, and drawings by John Conyers. *Proceedings of the Society of Antiquaries*, series 2. 1914, 26: 218–28.

MALONEY J., 1979, 'Excavations at Dukes Place: The Roman defences'. *The London Archaeologist*, 3: 292–97.

MANN J., JARRETT M., 1967, 'The division of Britain'. *Journal of Roman Studies* LVII: 61–64.

MARSDEN P., 1961, 'Archaeological finds in the City of London, 1960'. *Trans. LMAS* 20, pt 4: 220–23.

——, 1963, 'Archaeological finds in the City of London, 1961'. *Trans. LMAS* 21, pt 1: 70–77.

——, 1965A, 'Archaeological finds in the City of London, 1962'. *Trans. LMAS* 21, pt 2: 135–39.

——, 1965B, 'A boat of the Roman period discovered on the site of New Guy's House, Bermondsey, 1958'. *Trans. LMAS* 21, pt 2: 118–31.

——, 1967A, 'Archaeological finds in the City of London, 1963–4'. *Trans. LMAS* 21, pt 3: 189–221.

——, 1967B, 'The riverside defensive wall of Roman London'. *Trans. LMAS* 21, pt 3: 149–56.

——, 1967C, *A Roman ship from Blackfriars, London*, Guildhall Museum monograph.

——, 1968A, 'Archaeological finds in the City of London 1965–6'. *Trans. LMAS* 22, pt 1: 1–17.

——, 1968B, Some discoveries in the City of London, 1954–9'. *Trans. LMAS* 22, pt 1: 32–42.

——, 1969A, 'Archaeological finds in the City of London, 1966–8'. *Trans. LMAS* 22, pt 2: 1–26.

——, 1969B, 'The Roman pottery industry of London'. *Trans. LMAS* 22, pt 2: 39–44.

——, 1970, 'Archaeological finds in the City of London, 1966–9'. *Trans. LMAS* 22, pt 3: 1–9.

——, 1971A, 'Archaeological finds in the City of London, 1967–70'. *Trans. LMAS* 23, pt 1: 1–14.

——, 1971B, 'Report on Recent Excavations in Southwark: part II'. *Trans. LMAS* 23, pt 1: 19–41.

——, 1972, 'Mapping the birth of Londinium'. *The Geographical Magazine*, September: 840–45.

——, 1974A, 'Two pit groups in the City of London'. *Trans. LMAS* 25: 282–84.

——, 1974B, 'The County Hall ship, London', *International Journal of Nautical Archaeology* 3: 55–65.

——, 1975, 'Excavation of a Roman palace site in London, 1961–72'. *Trans. LMAS* 26: 1–102.

——, 1976A, 'Two Roman public baths in London'. *Trans. LMAS* 27: 1–70.

——, 1976B, 'A boat of the Roman period found at Bruges, Belgium, in 1899, and related types', *International Journal of Nautical Archaeology* 5: 23–55.

——, 1978. 'The discovery of the civic centre of Roman London'. *Collectanea Londiniensia*, London and Middlesex Archaeological Society, Special paper No. 2: 89–103.

MARSDEN P., DYSON T., RHODES M., 1975, 'Excavations on the site of St Mildred's church, Bread Street, London, 1972–4'. *Trans. LMAS* 26: 171–208.

MARSH G., TYERS P., 1976, 'Roman pottery from the City of London'. *Trans. LMAS* vol. 27: 228–44.

MARTIN W., 1926, 'Roman remains: Lombard Street – Gracechurch Street'. *Trans. LMAS* (NS). V, pt III: 317–23.

MERRIFIELD R., 1960, 'A first-century coin hoard from Budge Row, London'. *Numismatic Chronicle* (Sixth Series) XX: 279–83.

——, 1965, *The Roman City of London*. London.

——, 1969, *Roman London*. London.

——, 1970, 'Roman London Bridge: further observations on its site'. *The London Archaeologist* 1: 186–87.

——, 1975, *The Archaeology of London*. London.

——, 1977, 'Art and religion in Roman London', in Munby J., Henig M., (eds), *Roman Life and Art in Britain*, British Archaeological Reports No. 41, pt 1: 375–406.

MERRIFIELD R., SHELDON H., 1974, 'Roman London Bridge: – a view from both banks'. *The London Archaeologist* 2: 183–91.

MÓCSY A., 1974, *Pannonia and Upper Moesia*. London.

MYRES J. N. C., 1934, 'Some thoughts on the topography of Saxon London'. *Antiquity* VIII: 437–42.

NORMAN P., READER F., 1906, 'Recent discoveries in connexion with Roman London'. *Archaeologia* LX: 169–250.

——, 1912, 'Futher discoveries relating to Roman London, 1906–12'. *Archaeologia* LXIII: 257–344.

PAINTER K., 1972, 'A late-Roman silver ingot from Kent'. *Antiquaries Journal*, LII: 84–92.

PEACOCK D., 1977, 'Pompeian Red Ware', in Peacock D. (ed.), *Pottery and early commerce*. London: 147–62.

PHILLIPS J., 1859, 'Thoughts on ancient metallurgy and mining . . .'. *The Archaeological Journal* XVI: 37–38.

PHILP B. J., 1977, 'The forum of Roman London'. *Britannia* VIII: 1–64.

PRICE J. E., 1870, *A description of the Roman tesellated Pavement found in Bucklersbury; with observations on analogous discoveries*. London.

——, 1880, *On a Bastion of London Wall, or Excavations in Camomile Street, Bishopsgate*. London.

RIB: COLLINGSWOOD R. G., WRIGHT R. P., 1965, *The Roman Inscriptions of Britain*. Oxford.

RILEY J., 1975, 'The pottery from the first season of excavation in the Caesarea Hippodrome: *Bulletin of the American Schools of Oriental Research*, No. 218.

ROACH SMITH C., 1842, 'Observations on Roman remains recently found in London'. *Archaeologia* 29: 145–66.

——, 1859, *Illustrations of Roman London*. London.

——, 1860, 'On some late discoveries in Roman London'. *Trans. LMAS* 1: 31–34.

ROSKAMS S., 1978, 'The Milk Street Excavation'. *The London Archaeologist* 3: 199–205.

ROSKAMS S., SCHOFIELD J., 1978, 'The Milk Street Excavation: part 2'. *The London Archaeologist* 3: 227–34.

RCHM 1928: Royal Commission on Historical Monuments, vol. III, *Roman London*, HMSO.

SCHOFIELD J., MILLER L., 1976, 'New Fresh Wharf: 1, the Roman Waterfront'. *London Archaeologist* 2: 390–95.

SHELDON H., 1971, 'Excavations at Lefevre Road, Old Ford, E.3'. *Trans. LMAS* 23, pt 1: 42–77.

——, 1972, 'Excavations at Parnell Road and Appian Road, Old Ford, E.3'. *Trans. LMAS* 23, pt 2: 101–47.

——, 1975, 'A decline in the London Settlement A.D. 150–250?'. *The London Archaeologist* 2: 278–84.

——, (ed.) 1978, *Southwark Excavations 1972–4* I and II. Joint publication of the London and Middlesex Archaeological Society and the Surrey Archaeological Society.

SHELDON H., SCHAAF L., 1978, 'A survey of Roman sites in Greater London'. *Collectanea Londiniensia.* London and Middlesex Archaeological Society: 59–88.

SMITH R. A., 1907, *Proceedings of the Society of Antiquaries of London*, (2nd series) 21: 268–92.

——, 1909, 'Anglo-Saxon remains'. *VCH. London.* London: 147–70.

SPENCER B., 1961, 'Two additions to the London Museum'. *Trans. LMAS* 20, pt 4: 214–15.

SPURRELL F. C. J., 1885, 'Early sites and embankments on the margins of the Thames Estuary'. *Archaeological Journal* XLII.

STAMP L. DUDLEY, 1961, *Applied Geography*, (Pelican edn).

STICOTTI P., 1913, *Die Römische Stadt Doclea in Montenegro*, Schriften der Balkankommission, Antiquarische Abteilung VI.

STOW J., 1970 edn, *The Survey of London*, Everyman edition of book published in 1958.

STUKELEY W., 1724, *An account of the antiquities and Remarkable curiositys in Nature or art*. London.

TATTON-BROWN T., 1974, 'Excavations at the Custom House site, City of London 1973'. *Trans. LMAS* 25: 117–219.

TAYLOR J. DU P., CLEERE H., 1978 *Roman shipping and trade: Britain and the Rhine provinces*. Council for British Archaeology research report No. 24.

THOMAS C., 1959, 'Imported pottery in Dark Age western Britain', *Medieval Archaeology* 3: 89–111.

Trans. LMAS: Transactions of the London and Middlesex Archaeological Society.

TUCKER C., 1848, 'Notice of the Roman remains lately discovered in Lower Thames Street'. *Archaeological Journal* V: 25–33.

TURNER E., SKUTSCH O., 1960, 'A Roman writing tablet from London'. *Journal of Roman Studies* 50: 108–11.

VCH: Victoria County History of London 1, 1909.

VULLIAMY C. E., 1930, *The archaeology of Middlesex and London*. London.

WACHER J., 1974, *The towns of Roman Britain*. London.

WEBSTER G., 1958, 'The Roman military advance under Ostorius Scapula', *Archaeological Journal* CXV: 49–98.

——, 1970, 'The military situations in Britain between AD 43 and 71'. *Britannia* I: 179–97.

——, 1978. *Boudica*, London.

WEBSTER G., DUDLEY D., 1973, *The Roman conquest of Britain*. London.

WELCH C., 1893, *The Guildhall Library and its work*. Corporation of London.

WELCH M., 1975, 'Mitcham Grave 205'. *Antiquaries Journal* LV, pt 1: 86–95.

WHEELER R. E. M., 1934A, 'The topography of Saxon London', *Antiquity* VIII: 290–302.

——, 1934B, 'Mr. Myres on Saxon London: a reply'. *Antiquity* VIII: 443–47.

——, 1935, *London and the Saxons*, London Museum.

——, 1944, 'The rebuilding of London'. *Antiquity* XVIII: 151–52.

——, 1946, *London in Roman Times*, London Museum Catalogue No. 3.

WHITTINGTON R., 1875, 'St. Peter's Church, Cornhill'. *Trans. LMAS* IV: 301–12.

WILLCOX G., 1977, 'Exotic plants from Roman waterlogged sites in London'. *Journal of Archaeological Science* 4: 269–82.

——, 1978, 'Seeds from the late 2nd century pit F 28 (B III – Za)', in Sheldon H., (ed.), *Southwark Excavations 1972–1974*: 411–13.

WILKES J., 1969, *Dalmatia*. London.

WOODWARD J., 1713, *An account of some Roman urns and other antiquities lately digg'd up near Bishopsgate Street …*, London.

WREN C., 1750, *Parentalia, or memoirs of the family of the Wrens*.

WRIGHT R. P., HASSALL M. W. C., TOMLIN R. S. O., 1976, 'Inscriptions'. *Britannia* VII: 378–79.

Index